ENGLISH Made Simple

The Made Simple series
has been created
primarily for self-education
but can equally well
be used as
an aid to group study.
However complex the subject,
the reader is taken
step by step,
clearly and methodically
through the course. Each volume
has been prepared by
experts,
using throughout the
Made Simple technique of teaching.
Consequently the gaining
of knowledge now becomes
an experience to be enjoyed.

Accounting	Export
Acting and Stagecraft	French
Additional Mathematics	Geology
Advertising	German
Anthropology	Human Anatomy
Applied Economics	Italian
Applied Mathematics	Journalism
Applied Mechanics	Latin
Art Appreciation	Law
Art of Speaking	Management
Art of Writing	Marketing
Biology	Mathematics
Book-keeping	Modern Electronics
British Constitution	Modern European History
Calculus	New Mathematics
Chemistry	Office Practice
Childcare	Organic Chemistry
Commerce	Philosophy
Commercial Law	Photography
Company Administration	Physical Geography
Computer Programming	Physics
Cookery	Pottery
Cost and Management Accounting	Psychology
Data Processing	Rapid Reading
Dressmaking	Retailing
Economic History	Russian
Economic and Social Geography	Salesmanship
Economics	Secretarial Practice
Electricity	Soft Furnishing
Electronic Computers	Spanish
Electronics	Statistics
English	Transport and Distribution
English Literature	Typing
	Woodwork

ENGLISH   Made Simple

Arthur Waldhorn, Ph.D. and
Arthur Zeiger, Ph.D.

Advisory editors
Ronald South, M.A., Ph.D. and
Joan South

Made Simple Books
W. H. ALLEN   London
A Howard & Wyndham Company

Made and printed in Great Britain
by Richard Clay (The Chaucer Press), Ltd., Bungay, Suffolk
for the publishers W. H. Allen & Company Ltd.,
44 Hill Street, London W1X 8LB

First edition, April 1967
Reprinted, December 1967
Reprinted, August 1969
Reprinted, January 1971
Reprinted, September 1972
Reprinted, May 1974
Reprinted (with revisions), January 1976
Reprinted, April 1977

ISBN 0 491 01920 3 Paperbound

Preface

This book has been designed for the adult reader who wishes to improve his English, studying either alone or with a teacher. A poor ability to write or speak effectively is today probably the greatest single bar to advancement in any job, and socially it can lead to misunderstanding or loneliness. It is often much easier to make use of the first well-worn phrase that comes to mind than to search for the precise thought, with the *exact* words to describe it.

Anyone who sets out to acquire a greater control over the language he speaks and writes will find it immeasurably rewarding; he will achieve positive and immediate communication with others which brings with it greater efficiency at work and a genuine self-confidence in all personal relations. Moreover, because words are so vital to thought, the thoughts themselves will inevitably become clearer and more incisive as skill with words increases. It will be easier to go unerringly to the essential point in any statement, however woolly its wrappings, and in turn transmit ideas to other people, with increasing authority and grace.

Of course, learning to express oneself precisely and vividly is not possible without work and self-discipline, but *English Made Simple* will ease the path for anyone prepared to make the effort. Its scope is wide. It can be read with benefit, for instance, by the professional man or woman whose English is rusty; by the student working at A- or O-level G.C.E. or similar examinations; by the advanced foreign student; by the aspiring writer who wants to increase his command over words—or by the interested reader who simply wants to write clear and lively letters. Almost anyone just browsing casually will be fascinated by the examples and exercises to be found on any page of the book.

For the student working alone it might be best to start by looking down the Table of Contents to select those topics where help is most needed. If it is not certain where strengths and weaknesses lie, Test Number 1 can be used as a means of self-diagnosis, and the initial choice of topics should be based on any errors revealed by that test. The comprehensive series of exercises, with answers for self-testing, will indicate at each stage whether the contents of that section are mastered.

Finally, the book can serve as an excellent work of reference. The logical and orderly arrangement of material, the Index and the unusually full Table of Contents, make it the sort of thorough and authoritative guide to our language which should find a place on every bookshelf.

RONALD SOUTH
JOAN SOUTH

Table of Contents

SECTION 2—SENTENCE ERRORS

SECTION 3—PARAGRAPHS AND PARAGRAPHING

SECTION 4—PUNCTUATION

SECTION 5—SPELLING

SECTION 6—BUILDING A VOCABULARY

SECTION 7—STYLE

SECTION 8—FAULTY DICTION:

SECTION 9—LETTER WRITING

THE SENTENCE AND ITS PARTS

TEST NO. 1

Note: Do this test before proceeding to the first section. Check your answers with those provided at the end of the book. Note your major weaknesses, and give particular attention to the sections which try to remedy these weaknesses.

SENTENCE ERRORS

Part I: Choose the correct form for each of the following:

EXAMPLE. Jack and Jill (*is, are*) over the hill. *are*

1 Ken is one of those singers who (*is, are*) always off key.
2 There (*go, goes*) Julia and her favourite parakeet.
3 Each of the contestants (*has, have*) a chance to win a trip to the North Pole.
4 The healthiest specimen among the monkeys (*was, were*) chosen to imitate the television actor.
5 I gave a pound to the cashier (*who, whom*) I think works on Saturdays only.
6 Between you and (*I, me*) and the barman, I find Sazaracs potent cocktails.
7 Leave all arrangements to (*her, she*) and (*me, I*).
8 I expected the caller to be (*he, him*).
9 If one tries to whistle while laughing, (*he, they*) must be highly optimistic.
10 Each of these bananas has a split in (*its, their*) side.
11 Jean's scent smells (*sweet, sweetly*).
12 The police (*seeked, sought*) in vain to find the murderer.
13 Years ago, I (*saw, have seen*) Scaramouche in silent films.
14 If he had entered the building, I (*saw, had seen, would have seen*) him.

Part II: Rewrite the following sentences to assure **clarity** and **correctness**.

1 If we all strive towards peace, one may hope that the world will be a better place to live in.
2 Wash your hair with *Squeaky Lotion* and then you should use *Eeky Hair Tonic*.
3 I expect Bill to arrive early and bringing his cousin Ann.
4 Put the lemonade in the refrigerator that is warm.
5 His ankle broken, his owner had the racing colt destroyed.

1

SPELLING

Correct any misspelt word. If the word is correct, let it remain as it is.

embarrased	plagiarize	reciept
forcable	adjustable	picknicing
proceed	hieght	manageable
boundries	supersede	benefitted
marraige	dynamoes	valleys

PUNCTUATION

Insert punctuation wherever needed. If no punctuation is needed, let the sentence remain as it is.

1 Jane answer the telephone.
2 The athlete who performs well pleases the crowd.
3 If I draw a thousand pounds from the bank I shall be only nine hundred pounds overdrawn.
4 Millie who has several suitors loves none of them.
5 Gretchen he begged won't you for goodness' sake share a sandwich with me.

VOCABULARY

Part I: Give the opposite of the following words:

EXAMPLE: good   *bad*
1 symmetrical
2 malevolent
3 polygamy
4 benign
5 loquacious

Part II: Give a synonym for each of the following:

EXAMPLE: happy   *delighted*
1 gourmet
2 fortuitous
3 plethora
4 remuneration
5 histrionic

THE SENTENCE

A group of words that express a complete meaning makes a sentence. In order to have a meaning, two elements are necessary: **a subject,** a person or thing to speak about, and **a predicate,** something to say about the person or thing.

SUBJECT AND PREDICATE. No sentence can exist without both subject and predicate. Suppose, for example, that somebody speaks the name *Pagliacci.* He has not spoken a sentence; for though he has named a person whom he can speak about, he has supplied no **predicate.**

Now, suppose that somebody else utters the word *laughs.* He has not a sentence either, because he has named no **person or thing** to say his word about—he has named no **subject.**

If the two words are joined, however, a sentence emerges: *Pagliacci laughs.* It is a 'complete thought', a 'full meaning'. The sentence may be extended by enlarging the subject:*

Pagliacci, the funniest clown in Europe, laughs.

Or by enlarging the predicate:

Pagliacci laughs mockingly, bitterly, ironically.

Or by enlarging both subject and predicate:

Pagliacci, the funniest clown in all Europe, laughs mockingly, bitterly, ironically.

Consider the following group of words:

The beautiful girl of the fairy tale, a drudge by day and a princess by night.

Here, a person is named and described in some detail, but the group of words appears somehow incomplete: something else is needed. By adding *has vanished*, the need is supplied:

The beautiful girl of the fairy tale, a drudge by day and a princess by night, has vanished.

The long group of words underlined simply enlarges the subject, which essentially consists of the word *girl;* a predicate was required and *has vanished* fulfills the requirement.

Now consider this group of words:

Have been stolen by a highly organized and exceedingly clever gang of international thieves operating from a dozen ports throughout the Near East.

Here, again, something is lacking: much has been said—but about what? The subject is lacking.

The jewels have been stolen by a highly organized and exceedingly clever gang of international thieves operating from a dozen ports throughout the Near East.

RECOGNIZING SUBJECT AND PREDICATE. In order to decide which word or words make up the subject, simply ask: **Whom or what are we speaking about?**

Barking dogs never bite.

Plainly, dogs are here spoken about; *dogs*, therefore, is the subject. *Barking* simply describes the subject further.

A rare instance of charity by a miser is news.

Since an instance is being spoken about, *instance* is the subject.

In order to decide which word or words make up the predicate, simply ask: **What is said about the subject?**

A fool and his money are soon parted.

What is said about the subject (*a fool and his money*)? The answer, [*they*] *are soon parted*, makes up the predicate.

The inclusion of proper names in a dictionary might be defended on the ground that it would be convenient to have them there.

Here, the subject is *inclusion* (the full subject is *The inclusion of proper names in a dictionary*); and the predicate, the statement about the subject, is: *might be defended on the ground that it would be convenient to have them there.*

* The subject here is indicated by a single line drawn beneath it, the predicate by a double line.

KINDS OF SENTENCES. Sentences have three purposes: to state, to ask, and to command.

1 **Sentences that state.** A sentence that makes a statement (or denies it) is called a **declarative sentence.**

The boy stood on the burning deck.

2 **Sentences that ask.** A sentence that asks a question is called an **interrogative sentence.**

Did the boy stand on the burning deck?

3 **Sentences that command.** A sentence that expresses a command is called an **imperative sentence.**

Boy, stand on the burning deck!

Exercise No. 1

Six of the word-groups below are sentences. Pick them out, underlining each subject once and each predicate twice.

1 Death spares none.
2 Death, which antiquates antiquities and strikes down the innocent.
3 Death, the final adventure, armed with no terrors.
4 Let no man be called fortunate until he is dead.
5 O eloquent, just, and mighty Death!
6 As if every one had meant to put his whole wit in a jest and resolved to live a fool the rest of his dull life.
7 Life is made up of marble and mud.
8 It is life near the bone where it is sweetest.
9 Variety's the very spice of life.
10 Life is just one darned thing after another.

THE PARTS OF SPEECH

The term **part of speech** refers to the job that a word does in a sentence—to its **function** or use. Since there are eight separate jobs, words are divided into eight classes or **eight parts of speech: noun, pronoun, verb, adjective, adverb, preposition, conjunction, interjection.**

JOB, FUNCTION, USE	PART OF SPEECH	EXAMPLES
1 To name a person, place, thing, quality, state, or action.	Noun	Adam, London, pen, wit, joy, laughter.
2 To substitute for a noun.	Pronoun	he, she, it.
3 To express action—or non-action (state of being).	Verb	run, talk; think. is, was, will be.
4 To modify (describe or limit) the noun and pronoun.	Adjective	*strong* man, *ugly* city, *limited* quantity, *few* hours.
5 To modify any verb, adjective, or adverb.	Adverb	think *quickly*, *unusually* ugly, *very* quickly.
6 To show the relationship between a noun or pronoun and some other word.	Preposition	cart *before* horse, dog *in* manger, bombs *over* Berlin.
7 To join two words or two groups of words.	Conjunction	Jack *and* Jill; candy is dandy *but* liquor is quicker.
8 To display emotion.	Interjection	Good God! Heigh-ho! Hurrah!

A word is a noun, verb, adjective, or other part of speech, depending on its use—and on its use only. That is to say, a word is a noun if it is used like a noun, if it names; it is a preposition if it is used like a preposition, if it shows the relationship between nouns; and so on. In the following passage note that the word **round** is used in **five** different ways:

As I round the corner of the building, I reflect that our round world spins *round* and *round* on its axis, at the same time making a circle *round* the sun that results in the *round* of the seasons.

(*a*) I *round*—verb, expresses action.

(*b*) *round* world—adjective, because it modifies the noun *world*.

(*c*) spins *round* and *round*—adverb, modifies verb *spins*.

(*d*) circle *round* the sun—preposition, shows relationship between two nouns, *circle* and *sun*.

(*e*) *round* of the seasons—noun, names something.

Exercise. Indicate the part of speech of the italicized words:

> *Jack and Jill went up* the *hill*
> To fetch a *pail of water.*
> *Jack fell down* and *broke his crown*
> *And Jill came* tumbling *after.*

WORD	PART OF SPEECH	REASON
Jack	noun	names a person
and	conjunction	joins two nouns (*Jack, Jill*)
Jill	noun	names a person
went	verb	expresses action
up	preposition	shows relationship of *went* to *hill*
hill	noun	names a thing
pail	noun	names a thing
of	preposition	shows relationship of *water* to *pail*
water	noun	names a thing
fell	verb	expresses action
down	adverb *	modifies verb *fell*
broke	verb	expresses action
his	pronoun **	substitutes for noun *Jack's*
crown	noun	names a thing
came	verb	expresses action
after	preposition	shows relationship of *Jill* to *Jack*—she came *after* (him).

Exercise No. 2

Indicate the part of speech of the italicized words:

1
> *Mary had* a *little lamb*
> Its *fleece was white* as *snow,*
> *And everywhere* that Mary *went*
> The lamb was sure to go.
> *He followed her to school one day,*
> That *was against* the *rule;*
> It *made* the *children* laugh and play
> To see a lamb *in* school.

2 This is my *only* copy, a fact I realized *only* now.

* Alternative description: If *the hill* were understood as following *down*, it would be a preposition showing the relationship of *Jack* to *hill* (understood).
** Alternative description: When the possessive case of the third person personal pronoun (*his*) is followed by a noun (*crown*) it may also be described as a possessive adjective limiting *crown*. (See page 34).

3 I *single* out each *single* woman.
4 He seems a *stone* image—with a heart of *stone*.
5 They *run* wildly to escape the common *run* of people.
6 We all *love* people in *love*.
7 The *quick brown fox jumps over* a *lazy dog*.
8 *He stood hesitantly on* the *board, gazed longingly at* the *water, but never dived into it.*
9 *Ouch!*
10 *But me no buts.*

THE NOUN

The noun names some person, place, thing, quality, state, or action.

COMMON AND PROPER NOUNS. A **common** noun is a **general** name, **common** to all persons and a **proper** noun is a **particular** name, denoting a person or thing **different from** every other.

COMMON NOUN	PROPER NOUN
man	Henry James
city	Edinburgh
hill	Tower Hill
smith	Captain John Smith
book	*Tom Sawyer*
poem	'The Waste Land'

Note: Proper nouns are always given a capital letter. Common nouns are given capitals only when they begin sentences.

Exercise No. 3

Give capitals to the proper nouns in the following passages:

1 The hudson, a river 306 miles long, flows south to new york bay. It was discovered by a dutch explorer named henry hudson.
2 The students—who came from china and japan—preferred science to history, esperanto to english, mechanics to music. All, however, were required to take a course entitled introduction to british institutions.
3 Both mammon and mercury were gods once. Today, *mammon* means 'riches' and *mercury* signifies 'a heavy silver-white metallic element'.

CONCRETE AND ABSTRACT NOUNS. A **concrete** noun is the name of anything **physical**, anything that can be touched, seen, heard, smelt or otherwise perceived by the senses.

An **abstract** noun is the name of a quality, state, or action. It is an **idea,** and so may not be touched, seen, heard, smelt or otherwise perceived by the senses.

CONCRETE NOUN: coward, democrat, beggar.
ABSTRACT NOUN: fear, democracy, poverty.

Exercise No. 4

Pick out the concrete and the abstract nouns in the following passages.

1 In proportion as the manners, customs, and amusements of a nation are cruel and barbarous, the regulations of their penal code will be severe.
2 In proportion as men delight in battles, bull-fights, and combats of gladiators, will they punish by hanging, burning, and the rack.

COLLECTIVE NOUNS. A **collective noun** names a **group** of individuals **as** if they were **one** individual. Singular in form, it is plural in meaning.

jury	flock	committee
family	mob	regiment

The collective noun is considered either as a singular or as a plural, depending on the purpose it serves.

The committee was unanimous.

(That is, the committee acted as a unit, as a single entity.)

The committee were arguing among themselves.

(That is, the committee were obviously acting as individuals, not as a unit.)

Exercise No. 5

Underline the collective nouns in the following list:

board, journey, classics, class, ministry, churchmen, nation, people, group, Chinese, books, assembly.

INFLECTION. Inflection denotes the change in spelling that a word undergoes to show a change in meaning. Noun inflection, which is called **declension,** shows changes in **number** (*man, men*), **gender** (*man, woman*) and **case** (*man, man's*).

NUMBER. Number is the form of a noun that shows whether it is singular or plural—whether it refers to one or more than one.

SINGULAR: *girl, country, joy.*
PLURAL: *girls, countries, joys.*

The Plural Number. (*a*) Regularly, the plural of nouns is formed by adding -*s* to the singular: *lands, lovers, books, battles.*

(*b*) Singular nouns ending in -*s*, -*x*, -*z*, -*sh*, or -*ch* form the plural by adding -*es*: *kisses, misses; taxes, waxes; mazes, blazes; dishes, wishes; churches, birches.*

Note: The ending -*s* is added when the plural has no more syllables than the singular; the ending -*es* is added when the plural has one more syllable than the singular. Thus the singular *book* and the plural *books* alike have one syllable; therefore -*s* only is to be added in forming the plural. But singular *kiss* has one syllable and plural *kisses* has two syllables; therefore -*es* is to be added in forming the plural. As a guide to spelling, pronounce the singular and plural of the noun.

(*c*) Singular nouns ending in -*y* preceded by a consonant form the plural by changing the -*y* to -*i* and adding -*es*: *fly—flies; vanity—vanities; soliloquy—soliloquies.**

Note: Singular nouns ending in -*y* preceded by a vowel form the plural by adding -*s*: *day—days; chimney—chimneys; monkey—monkeys.*

(*d*) Singular nouns ending in -*o* preceded by a consonant generally form the plural by adding -*es*: *hero—heroes; Negro—Negroes; potato—potatoes.* (But there are many exceptions to the generalization: *solo—solos; halo—halos; piano—pianos.*)

(*e*) Singular nouns ending in -*o* preceded by a vowel form the plural by adding -*s*: *seraglio—seraglios; curio—curios; cuckoo—cuckoos.*

* The *u* of soliloquy has the sound of the consonant *w* and so does not violate the principle.

(*f*) Singular nouns ending in -*f* or -*fe* generally form the plural by changing the *f* to *v* and adding -*es*: *thief—thieves; calf—calves; self—selves; wife— wives; life—lives; knife—knives.* (But there are many exceptions to the generalization: *grief—griefs; turf—turfs; cliff—cliffs; fife—fifes; safe—safes; strife—strifes.*)

(*g*) **Eight** nouns form their plural by **mutation**—by changing an inside vowel: *man—men; woman—women; tooth—teeth; foot—feet; mouse—mice; dormouse—dormice; louse—lice; goose—geese.*

(*h*) **Four** nouns form their plurals by adding -*en* or *ne*: *ox—oxen; cow-kine;** *child—children; brother—brethren.**

(*i*) Compound nouns form their plurals by adding -*s* to the most important word of the compound: *mother-in-law—mothers-in-law; court-martial—courts-martial; will-o'-the wisp—will-o'-the wisps; good-bye—good-byes.*

Note: Compounds written without hyphens regularly add -*s* to form the plural: *pickpocket—pickpockets; spoonful—spoonfuls; stepmother—step-mothers.*

(*j*) Foreign nouns, unless they have been thoroughly naturalized, form their plurals according to their native declension. There are several thousand foreign nouns in occasional English use.

SINGULAR		PLURAL
	Latin	
addendum		addenda
alumnus		alumni
datum		data
erratum		errata
	Greek	
analysis		analyses
basis		bases
crisis		crises
phenomenon		phenomena
thesis		theses
	French	
bandeau		bandeaux
Monsieur		Messieurs

(*k*) Foreign nouns in frequent use generally have two plural forms—their native plural and their English -*s* (-*es*) plural.

SINGULAR	ENGLISH PLURAL	FOREIGN PLURAL
	Latin	
apparatus	apparatuses	apparatus
aquarium	aquariums	aquaria
formula	formulas	formulae
millenium	milleniums	millenia
ultimatum	ultimatums	ultimata
	Greek	
automaton	automatons	automata
gymnasium	gymnasiums	gymnasia
hippopotamus	hippopotamuses	hippopotami
lexicon	lexicons	lexica

* The more frequent plurals are, of course, *cows* and *brothers;* however, they have different connotations.

SINGULAR	ENGLISH PLURAL	FOREIGN PLURAL
	French	
adieu	adieus	adieux
flambeau	flambeaus	flambeaux
portmanteau	portmanteaus	portmanteaux
trousseau	trousseaus	trousseaux
	Italian	
bandit	bandits	banditti
concerto	concertos	concerti
Fascist	Fascists	Fascisti
libretto	librettos	libretti

(*l*) Some nouns have two plural forms, each form with its own meaning. Thus:

SINGULAR	PLURAL
index	Books have *indexes*
	Numbers have *indices*
die	Machinists use *dies*
	Gamblers use *dice*
genius	*Geniuses* have high intelligence quotients
	Genii act as guardian or demonic spirits

(*m*) Some nouns are used only in the plural.

alms	blues	dregs
athletics	billiards	economics
bellows	commons	forceps

(*n*) The plurals of letters, signs, numbers, and of words regarded as words form the plural by adding 's.

> Cross your *t*'s and dot your *i*'s.
> Omit +'s and −'s.
> Excise all the *this*'s and *that*'s.
> They were at 6's and 7's.

Exercise No. 6

In the list below, convert all singular nouns into the plural number and convert all plural nouns into the singular number. (Consult your dictionary when in doubt—as occasionally you are sure to be.)

duty	swine	appendices
flies	spoonful	series
monkey	lice	*p* and *q*
brethren	courts-martial	strata
goose	passer-by	oasis
mongooses	hanger-on	madam
sheep	dice	beaux
Negro	gin-and-tonic	seraphim
domino	genius	mathematics
half	apparatus	dilettanti

GENDER. In English nouns, **gender** indicates sex or the absence of sex. Four genders are distinguished:

1 **Masculine Gender:** male human beings or animals.
boy, father, Joseph; bull, cock, stallion

2 **Feminine Gender:** female human beings or animals.
   girl, mother, Josephine; cow, hen, mare
3 **Neuter Gender:** objects without sex.
   flower, fire, furnace
4 **Common Gender:** human beings or animals that may belong to either sex.
   cousin, parent, child, fish, bird

Denoting Gender. In nouns, gender may be indicated in any of three ways: **by a different word, by a changed termination, and by an added word.**

By a different word.

MASCULINE	FEMININE
buck	doe
bull	cow
cock	hen
colt	filly
lord	lady

By a changed termination.

MASCULINE	FEMININE
actor	actress
baron	baroness
god	goddess
hero	heroine
widower	widow

By an added word.

MASCULINE	FEMININE
billy goat	nanny goat
bridegroom	bride
landlord	landlady

Exercise No. 7

Supply the words that fit the following definitions:

1 An old maid.
2 A female dog.
3 A female foal.
4 The wife of a baron.
5 A female guard in a prison.
6 A male cat.
7 A man who owns and leases land.
8 A man who cares for sheep.
9 The female counterparts of *Master*, *Mr.*, and *M.*
10 The male analogue of *widow*.

PERSONIFICATION. Sometimes objects or forces, normally of neuter gender, are **personified**—regarded as persons; consequently, they are endowed with masculine or feminine gender.

Crops fail at times, but Death always reaps his harvest.

Then Ire came in, his hand upon his knife.

She has her sister-ships.

Fame smiled, displaying her false teeth.

Note: Personifications are often given capitals.

CASE. In English nouns, **case** refers to the change in form that shows the grammatical relationship of nouns to other words in the sentence.

Whether a noun initiates an action or receives it, the form remains constant (that is, the spelling of the noun does not change):

John threw the *bull.*

The *bull* threw *John.*

The noun changes its form (or spelling) only when it is used to show possession: *John's* cape eluded the *bull's* horns.

Therefore, some grammarians insist that English nouns have two cases only: the **common case** and the **possessive case.** However, though the principle is valid, it creates as many difficulties as it solves, since it complicates nomenclature. Throughout this book, consequently, the traditional **three cases of nouns** are recognized.

The Nominative Case. A noun is said to be in the **nominative (or subjective)** case when it acts as the **subject of a verb,** as a **predicate nominative,** as a **word in direct address (vocative),** or as an **appositive** of another word in the nominative case.

Subject of a Verb. To determine the word or words acting as its subject ask **who?** or **what?** before the verb. The answer yields the subject.

Jonah was in the belly of the whale for three days and three nights.

Who was in the belly of the whale? The answer, *Jonah,* is the subject of the verb *was.*

Shadrach, Meshach, and *Abed-nego* fell down bound into the midst of the burning fiery furnace.

Who fell down? The triple subject is *Shadrach, Meshach, Abed-nego.*

The *nations* are as a drop of a bucket.

What are as a drop of a bucket? The *nations*-subject.

How beautiful upon the mountains are his *feet.*

Here the subject does not precede the verb, as normally it does. Nevertheless, the method of finding the subject remains the same. **What** are beautiful: *feet*-subject.

A bruised *reed* shall he not break, and the smoking *flax* shall he not quench.

There are two verbs in the preceding sentence: *shall break* and *shall quench; he,* the subject of each, is located by asking **who?** before the relevant verb.

Predicate Nominative. After a **linking verb** (a verb that expresses a state of being rather than an action and acts as a kind of equal sign linking subject and predicate) the **nominative case is used.** The most common of the linking verbs is **be** (*is, was, will be, have been, had been,* etc.); but *become, seem, appear, prove, look,* and about fifty other verbs may be used as linking verbs.

Note in the following examples how the predicate nominative (italicized) serves to define or explain the subject.

God is *one.*

The Bible is a little-known *book.*

The Bible has become a little-known *book.*

We shall have been *friends.*

We remain *enemies.*

The poet turned *traitor.*

Direct Address. The word used to address a person directly is termed **the nominative of direct address.**

Villain, unhand her!

Oh *Judgement*, thou art fled to brutish beasts!

Will you roam, *Romans?*

Your enemies, *my friends*, are my enemies.

Appositive. A noun is said to be an **appositive** of another noun, or in **apposition** with another noun, when it **identifies the same person or object under another name.** A noun is in the nominative case if it is in apposition with another noun in the nominative case.

Tom, the piper's son, stole pigs.

A bugler, Little Boy Blue, went into hiding.

Mary, a gardener, planted cockle-shells.

Possessive Case. A noun is in the **possessive** (also called **genitive**) case when it adds *'s (apostrophe s)*, or simply the apostrophe, **to indicate ownership, source or origin, manufacture or authorship, association or connexion,** and similar relationships.

Uses of the Possessive.

Ownership: Marco's millions, Edward's eye teeth.

Source or origin: Adam's sin, God's country, the pope's encyclical, mother's son.

Manufacture or authorship: Johnson's baby lotion, Johnson's *Lives of the Poets.*

Association, connexion, attribute, or duration: a woman's work, a month's delay, at swords' point.

Formation of the Possessive. To form the possessive singular, add **apostrophe s** to the simple (nominative) form of the noun.

child's play	Keats's odes
woman's work	Thomas's doubts
Harold's hope	Dickens's novels

Note: Only the apostrophe is added if another *s* would cause sibilants (*s*-sounds) to pile up: rather than *Aristophanes's comedies, Dr. Seuss's cartoons,* **prefer** *Aristophanes' comedies, Dr. Seuss' cartoons.*

To form the possessive plural, add **only the apostrophe** when the simple (nominative) plural form of the noun ends in *s,* but add **apostrophe s** when the simple plural does not end in *s.*

PLURAL ENDING IN S	PLURAL NOT ENDING IN S
horses' tails	children's play
Thomases' doubts	people's voices
devils' delights	freshmen's folly
ladies' day	oxen's burdens
Negroes' advance	brethren's resolve

To form the plural of a group of words containing a single idea (**group genitive**) add **apostrophe s** to the last word.

brother-in-law's virtues

brothers-in-law's virtues

The Y.M.C.A.'s programme

Gilbert and Sullivan's *Iolanthe.*

In formal usage, inanimate objects do not take the possessive case, except for some constructions that have long been in the language.

pages of a book (rather than *a book's pages*)

principles of grammar (rather than *grammar's principles*)
process of evolution (rather than *evolution's process*)
leaves of a tree (rather than *a tree's leaves*)
BUT:

goodness' sake	day's march
conscience' call	hair's breadth
razor's edge	earth's surface

Objective Case. A noun is said to be in the objective case when it acts as **the direct object of a verb, the indirect object of a verb, the object of a preposition,** or as an **appositive** of another word in the objective case.* (**Object** implies the person or thing receiving an action: *John hit Mary. Mary,* the object, receives the action that *John,* the subject, initiates.)

Direct Object of a Verb. To determine the word or words acting as object of the verb ask **whom?** or **what?** after the verb. The answer yields the object.

Well hast thou fought the better *fight.*

Well hast thou fought **what?** The answer, [the better] *fight,* is the object of the verb *hast fought.*

She approved my *reason.*

She approved **what?** The object of approved is *reason.*

God, sitting on his throne, sees *Satan.*

God sees **whom?** *Satan* is the object of the verb sees.

Spirits, when they please, can either *sex* assume.

Spirits can assume **what?** The answer, *sex,* is the object of the verb *can assume,* even though it comes before *assume.*

Death his *dart* shook.

Death shook **what?** His *dart.* Here, again, the object precedes the verb.

Indirect Object of a Verb. Besides naming the **direct object,** the person or thing receiving an action, a verb may also have an **indirect object,** the person for whom or to whom, or the thing for which or to which an action is performed. To determine the indirect object (which usually comes before the direct object) ask **to whom? to what?** or **for whom? for what?** after the verb.

The professor taught his *students* grammar.

The professor taught **to whom?** The answer, [his] *students,* yields the indirect object.

The actress showed *producers* her talents.

Showed **to whom?** *Producers* is the indirect object.

She wrote the *soldier* a love-letter.

Wrote **to whom?** The answer, *soldier,* is the indirect object.

He bought his *wife* a floor-mop.

He bought **for whom?** *Wife* is the indirect object.

He gave the museum a shrunken head.

Gave **to what?** *Museum* is the indirect object.

Object of Preposition. The preposition shows the relationship between its object and some other word or words in the sentence.

shade of a *tree*
water in the *bucket*
rain on the *roof*
lady into *fox*
Navy versus *Army*

* The noun is in the objective case when it acts as the *subject of the infinitive.* (See *infinitive.*)

Appositive. A noun is in the objective case if it is in apposition with another noun in the objective case.

He arrested Tom, *the piper's son.*

They found the bugler, *Little Boy Blue.*

The wedding guest listened to the mariner, an old *loon.*

Exercise No. 8

In the following sentences, state *what case* each of the italicized words is in and explain briefly the reasons for your statement.

Example: *Truth*, crushed to earth, shall rise again.

Truth is in the nominative case because it is the subject of the verb *shall rise.*

1 *Cleo* refused *Tony* his request.
2 It was *David*, the *king*, *priest*, and *prophet* of the Jewish *people.*
3 *Man* is the *architect* of his own *character.*
4 O *Judgement*, thou art fled to brutish *beasts.*
5 Well, Brando, you have played *Brutus; Brutus* has lost.
6 The *Queen of England's palace* is a quarter of an *hour's drive* from the centre of *London.*
7 The *plural* of the possessive *forms* baffled the *ingenuity* of *grammarians* for a considerable *time.*
8 Try *Guiness's Stout* for *goodness' sake.*
9 Did you see *Shelley* clearly?
10 The happy *man's* without a *shirt.*

THE PRONOUN

The pronoun substitutes for the noun (as its derivation from Latin **pro** meaning 'for' and **nomen** meaning 'name' indicates). Like the noun, it designates a person, place, or thing; but, unlike the noun, it designates without supplying the name. The following sentence exemplifies the difference.

He butters parsnips.

The pronoun *he* designates someone but does not supply his name; the noun *parsnips* designates and names as well.

Usually the pronoun refers to a word that names the person, place, or thing being discussed. Such a word is called an antecedent:

Jukes has no problems because *he* has no mind.

Here the pronoun *he* has for its antecedent the noun *Jukes:* the noun establishes the identity of the person whom the pronoun merely designates.

KINDS OF PRONOUNS. If it were not for the substitutions that the pronouns make possible, repetitious and awkward sentences, rife with distorted meanings, would be inevitable. Consider the following sentences, the first of which employs and the second of which avoids pronouns:

When Abdul looked at his wives and listened to their cackling, he wondered about polygamy.

When Abdul looked at the wives of Abdul and listened to the cackling of the wives of Abdul, Abdul wondered about polygamy.

Depending on the kinds of substitutions they effect, pronouns are generally divided into eight classes: **personal, demonstrative, indefinite, relative, interrogative, numerical, reflective, reciprocal.**

THE PERSONAL PRONOUN—indicates **the speaker (first person), the person spoken to (second person), or the person, place, or thing spoken about (third person).**

The declension of the personal pronoun (the forms it takes to show different relations) follows:

FIRST PERSON (MASCULINE AND FEMININE)

	SINGULAR	PLURAL
NOMINATIVE	I	we
POSSESSIVE	my *or* mine	our *or* ours
OBJECTIVE	me	us

SECOND PERSON (MASCULINE AND FEMININE)

	SINGULAR	PLURAL
NOMINATIVE	you	you
POSSESSIVE	your *or* yours	your *or* yours
OBJECTIVE	you	you

THIRD PERSON

	SINGULAR			PLURAL
	MASCULINE	FEMININE	NEUTER	
NOMINATIVE	he	she	it	they
POSSESSIVE	his	her *or* hers	its	their *or* theirs
OBJECTIVE	him	her	it	them

THE DEMONSTRATIVE PRONOUN—*this, that, these,* and *those*—points out a person or thing specifically:
This (*that*) is the forest primeval.
These (*those*) were the happy days.
Note: When the demonstrative is followed by a noun which it limits or restricts, it is classified as an adjective:
This forest is primeval.
Those days were happy.

THE INDEFINITE PRONOUN—refers to persons or things generally rather than specifically. Often the antecedents are understood but not stated.
I know *something.*
Somebody loves me.
One must do his duty.
The following list includes the indefinite pronouns most commonly employed.

all	everybody	nobody
another	everyone	nothing
any	everything	nought
anybody	few	one
anyone	least	one another
anything	many	oneself
aught	more	other
both	most	several
each	much	some
each one	neither	somebody
each other	none	someone
either	no one	something

THE RELATIVE PRONOUN—plays two parts at once: **pronoun** and **connective**. As a pronoun it acts as subject or object in a subordinate part of the sentence. As a connective it joins the subordinate to a more important part of the sentence:

It was a silence *that* could be heard.

The relative pronoun *that* acts as the subject of one group of words (*that could be heard*) and at the same time joins it to a more important group (*It was a silence*) by referring or relating back to the noun *silence*. The noun *silence* is the antecedent of the relative pronoun.

He saw the man *who* was invisible.

The relative pronoun *who* connects two parts of the sentence by relating back to its antecedent *man*, and acts as the subject of one part (*who* was invisible).

She is the woman *whom* I heard.

Here, *whom* connects two parts of the sentence by relating back to its antecedent *woman*, and acts as the object of one part (*whom I heard*).

In the following declension, note that only *who* has different case forms, and that *which*, *that* and *what* have no distinctive possessive forms:

SINGULAR AND PLURAL

NOMINATIVE	POSSESSIVE	OBJECTIVE
who	whose	whom
which	of which	which
that	of that	that
what	of what	what

Several **compound relative pronouns** are in general use. They are formed by adding *ever* and *soever* to the simple forms *who*, *which*, and *what*:

SINGULAR AND PLURAL

NOMINATIVE	POSSESSIVE	OBJECTIVE
whoever	whosoever	whomever
whichever	of whichever	whichever
whatever	of whatever	whatever
whosoever	whosesoever	whomsoever
whichsoever	of whichsoever	whichsoever
whatsoever	of whatsoever	whatsoever

Who refers to either a masculine or a feminine antecedent: *The man who smiles* or *The woman who smiles*.

Which refers to things (or animals) only: *The bed which broke*, *The dog which snarled*.

That refers to masculine, feminine, or neuter antecedents: *The man or woman that smiles*, *The bed that broke*.

The compound relative pronouns frequently include their own antecedents: *Whoever* writes must sweat.

Whoever in the preceding sentence equals 'the one who'—the antecedent being self-contained.

What, too, though simple in form, is compound in meaning, since it equals 'that which':

What is to be will be.

THE INTERROGATIVE PRONOUN—helps ask a question.
Who will go with me to Ramoth-Gilead?
Which of you, without taking thought, can add to his stature one cubit?

SINGULAR AND PLURAL

NOMINATIVE	POSSESSIVE	OBJECTIVE
who	whose	whom
which	of which	which
what	of what	what

Note that only *who* changes the form to show case.

THE NUMERICAL PRONOUN—definitely cites a number, either a **cardinal number** (*one, two, three,* etc.) or an **ordinal number** (*first, second, third,* etc.). They are pronouns when they take the place of an understood noun:

The opposing team cut him off and *one* of them tackled him—the *eleventh* to try.

THE REFLEXIVE AND THE INTENSIVE PRONOUN—are formed by adding *-self* or *-selves* to the personal pronouns:

SINGULAR	PLURAL
myself	ourselves
yourself	yourselves
himself, herself, itself	themselves

Their usage, however, varies.

The **reflexive** pronoun is used as **object,** referring to the same person as the subject:
He loves *himself*.
Here, *himself*, the reflexive pronoun which is the object, and *he*, the personal pronoun which is the subject, refer to the same person. The subject acts on itself—the action reflecting back upon the subject.
The reflexive may also follow a linking verb:
I feel *myself* again.
The **intensive** pronoun is used simply **to emphasize:**
The people *themselves* sinned.
They sinned *themselves*.
The intensive pronoun is appositive with the noun or pronoun to which it refers.

THE RECIPROCAL PRONOUNS—represent **two or more persons or things interactive—**interchanging the action denoted by the verb:
They cheat *each other*.
They cheat *one another*.
Note: Some excessively careful people use *each other* when two people are involved and *one another* when more than two. But the distinction is generally disregarded, even by meticulous writers.

Exercise No. 9

(1) Choose the correct form of the pronouns bracketed, then name the class and case of the word chosen.

(2) Name the class to which each of the pronouns italicized belongs (personal, reflexive, demonstrative, etc.) and its case.

1 *He* was loyal to (whoever, whomever) trusted *him*.
2 He was loyal to (whoever, whomever) he was trusted by.
3 I bit (me, myself) on the elbow.
4 Psychologists know (we, us, ourselves) sometimes despise (us, ourselves).
5 There we were—*all* of us—Einstein, Fermi, and (I, me, myself).
6 The lover and his lass kissed (each other, one another).
7 I heard it from the man (who, whom) knew the porter to (who, whom) the chairman of the company had dropped a significant word.
8 He stood on a hill (whose haughty brow, the haughty brow of which) frowned at *everything*.
9 This device is a useful gadget (whose use, the use of which) *nobody* knows.
10 Let*'s* you and (I, me) kill rats.

AGREEMENT OF PRONOUNS. Pronouns agree with their antecedents— the words for which they stand—in **number, person,** and **gender.**

Agreement in Number. If the antecedent is singular, the pronoun must be singular; if the antecedent is plural, the pronoun must be plural.

Harry the Horse gave *his* smallest 'hello'.

The men bred *their* white elephants.

In the first sentence the singular pronoun *his* refers to the singular noun *Harry the Horse;* in the second sentence the plural pronoun *their* refers to the plural antecedent *men.* In sentences like those quoted, there are few difficulties —at least for those people whose native language is English. Difficulties multiply, however, in two allied situations:

1 When the antecedent is an indefinite pronoun:

Wrong: Each man gets to heaven in *their* own way.

Right: Each man gets to heaven in *his* own way.

Each is singular—and so are *either, neither, everyone, no one, everybody, nobody.* Avoid using a plural pronoun to stand for any of them.

Note: *None* may be either singular or plural.

2 When the antecedent refers to a collective noun:

Wrong: The jury were divided. *It* was unable to bring in a verdict.

Right: The jury were divided. *They* were unable to bring in a verdict.

Here *jury* seems to be plural, a deduction supported by the plural verb *were.*

When *either . . . or* and *neither . . . nor* connect two antecedents:

Wrong: Neither the Liberal Party nor the Conservative Party wants Jones as *their* candidate for Orpington.

Right: Neither the Liberal Party nor the Conservative Party wants Jones as *its* candidate for Orpington.

The pronoun *its* refers to one party or the other—not to both; the pronoun must consequently be singular.

Agreement in Person. The pronoun must be in the same person—first, second, or third—as its antecedent.

Error in person-agreement occurs principally in shifting points of view.

Wrong: The school insists on good behaviour: *we* are not Prussians, but *one* must teach children discipline or else *you* will turn out moral monsters.

Right: We insist on good behaviour at our school: *we* are not Prussians, but *we* believe that *we* must teach children discipline or else turn out moral monsters.

The first sentence shifts from third person (*school*), to first (*we*), to third (*one*), to second (*you*). The second maintains a first-person point of view throughout.

Note: *We* ought to be used with a specific antecedent, either stated or clearly understood: *we*—the editors; *we*—the authors; *we*—the people of Britain. Avoid a vague or ambiguous or shifting signification for *we*.

Agreement in Gender. Pronouns—personal pronouns—must be in the same gender—masculine, feminine, or common—as their antecedents.

The man has *his* duty, the woman has *hers*, the child has *its*.

Note that *his* corresponds in gender with its antecedent *man*, *hers* with its antecedent *woman*, *its* with its antecedent *child*.

Exercise No. 10

Correct all errors in agreement of pronoun and antecedent.
1 Everybody has a right to their own opinion right or wrong.
2 Either the marines or their gallant commander, Captain Jinks, may be relied upon for their customary rescue, to occur just before the final curtain.
3 'In Britain,' he said, 'one knows that he is free, but sometimes he becomes a little afraid that we might not put our freedom to the best use.'
4 What a sweet child it is! He seems the image of your friend Jack.
5 If the pig or the fool are of a different opinion, it is because they know only their side of the question.

CASE OF A PRONOUN—depends on its use in the sentence. The pronoun agrees with its antecedent in number, person, and gender, but not in case.

Jean loved John, but *he* spurned *her*.

The pronoun *he* is in the nominative case, whereas its antecedent *John* is in the objective case; *her* is in the objective case, whereas its antecedent *Jean* is in the nominative case.

Like the noun, the pronoun may be in the nominative, possessive, or objective case. Unlike the noun, the objective case of the pronoun undergoes a change in form—is spelt differently from the nominative case.

In the sentences *John struck Jim* and *Jim struck John*, the noun is spelt the same whether it acts as subject or as object. Only the word order shows who initiates and who receives the action.

But in the sentences *He struck John* and *John struck him*, the pronoun is spelt one way (*he*) when functioning as subject and another way (*him*) when functioning as object.

Actually, though, the variations in form to indicate change in case may be easily exaggerated. Only six pronouns, for example, have distinct forms for the objective case:

> NOMINATIVE: I, we, he, she, they, who
> OBJECTIVE: me, us, him, her, them, whom

Note: If compound pronouns (*whoever*, *whosoever*) and archaic forms (*thou*, *ye*) are counted, the number is slightly larger.

The case of pronouns depends on the same sentence-relationships as the case of nouns. The following analysis of case is therefore abbreviated.

The Nominative Case

SUBJECT OF A VERB

He strains at a gnat.

We are no braver than they [are brave].

PREDICATE NOMINATIVE

It is *I*.

DIRECT ADDRESS

You, come here!

APPOSITIVE

The captain and his company—*he and they alone*—attacked the position.

The Possessive Case

To indicate possession, source, authorship, and similar relationships.
'Twas *mine*, 'tis *his*.

Mill read Wordsworth *whose* verse he praised for *its* healing power.

The Objective Case

DIRECT OBJECT OF A VERB

Jane likes *him* although he loathes *her*.

Jane, *whom* he loathed, liked *him*.

Note: To decide whether the nominative or the objective case of the relative pronoun ought to be employed, substitute a personal pronoun for the relative:

who/whom he loathed

she/her he loathed

Few people would decide that *she* was the proper form; consequently the nominative form is incorrect and *whom* ought to be employed.

He was the detective *who/whom* found the obvious clue.

he/him found the obvious clue. Here, the nominative *he* is plainly the correct form; therefore *who* ought to be employed.

The criminal *who/whom* he sought eluded him.

he/him he sought

Here, the objective *him* is correct; therefore *whom* ought to be employed.

She likes Jane more than [she likes] him.

Note: The words in brackets complete the thought. When unexpressed, they must be silently supplied in order to determine whether the nominative or the objective form is correct. If the sentence read

She likes Jane better than he.

the meaning would be

She likes Jane better than he [likes Jane].

INDIRECT OBJECT OF A VERB

He taught *her* Esperanto.

She gave *him* a packet of cyanide.

OBJECT OF PREPOSITION

We know with *whom* we must deal.

Whom are you speaking to?

Note: The preposition may properly come at the end of a sentence, if it seems natural to place it there.

APPOSITIVE

I poisoned Wainewright, his wife, and his dog—*him*, *her*, and *it*, all three.

Exercise No. 11

Supply the correct case form of the pronoun and give the reasons for each entry.

1 Between you and (I, me) and the lamp-post, I think neither (he, him) nor (she, her) knows the time of the day.

Pronouns

PERSONAL	DEMONSTRATIVE	INDEFINITE	RELATIVE	INTERROGATIVE	NUMERICAL	REFLEXIVE AND INTENSIVE	RECIPROCAL
I; we my, mine; our, ours me; us you your, yours he, she, it; they his, hers; its; their, theirs him, her, it; them.	this; these; that; those.	all, any, anything, both, each, either, one, everyone, everything, few, many, more, neither, none, somebody, someone, something	who, whose, whom; which, of which; that, of that; what, of what;	who, whose, whom; which, of which; what, of what;	one, two, three; first, second, third.	myself, ourselves; yourself, yourselves; himself, herself, itself, themselves.	each other one another
I speak to *him,* but *he* turns *his* deaf ear towards *me.*	What is *this* or *that* to me *who* talked it out in Tartary.	In Adam's fall We sinned *all.*	This is the cock *that* crew in the morn.	*What* light is that, and *whose* hand holds it aloft?	*One* for the money, and first things *first.*	He that wrongs his friend wrongs *himself* more.	The people do not cherish *one another.*

2 Fools like (they, them) need keepers.
3 It was (we, us) children who fired the arsenal.
4 I believe (they, them) to be the villains.
5 He pointed to the most intelligent person present; namely, (I, me).
6 You are, very obviously, as ugly as (he, him).
7 (Who, whom) the gods love, they grind to dust; those (who, whom) are of the devil's party, however, receive much of the same treatment.
8 The Pope is a man (who, whom) we suppose envies no one.
9 All but (he, him) had fled from the burning deck.
10 Than (who, whom) would you say is he more audible?

THE VERB

The verb states something about the subject. Usually the verb expresses action, but also it may express condition or state of being.
He *walks, falls, gets up, continues.*
He *is, was,* and always *shall be.*

TRANSITIVE AND INTRANSITIVE VERBS. A transitive verb needs an object to complete its meaning—to receive the action or motion which it expresses:
He *struck* the board.
Here, the *board* completes the meaning of the verb; the action passes over from subject (*He*) to object (*board*). *He struck* alone would seem incomplete, the statement unfinished.
An intransitive verb needs no object to complete its meaning; the action or motion is confined to the subject:
He sleeps.
The action seems complete, the statement finished.
Note: The distinction between transitive and intransitive verbs helps solve one of the recurrent problems of usage. These verbs are transitive: *set, raise, lay* (to place); these are intransitive: *sit, raise, lie* (to recline). Thus:
I *lay* (*laid, have laid*) the book down.
I *lie* (*lay, have lain*) asleep.

LINKING VERBS. The linking verb is a special kind of intransitive, deserving special treatment. **Such a verb joins subject to predicate:**
Time *is* money.
God *is* love.
Note that *is* establishes a sort of equality between the word which precedes it and the word which follows. Nouns and pronouns following *is*, or any part of *to be*, are in the nominative case; but since they appear in the predicate rather than the subject they are termed **predicate nominatives.** The bearing on usage becomes apparent when a pronoun functions as a predicate nominative:
The man is *he.*
Note that *he* is not an object.
An adjective may follow the linking verb:
The bells are *joyful.*
Such an adjective, describing or defining the subject, is termed a **predicate adjective.**
Other verbs may serve as joining verbs: *appear, become, feel, grow, look, prove, remain, seem, turn:*

Hopes *prove* false.
All *seems* lost.
Dictators *turn* tyrants.

AUXILIARY VERBS. An auxiliary verb helps another verb express action or condition or state of being, forgoing its use as a principal or main verb for that purpose:
He *has* tried scalp massage.
Here, *has* helps *tried* make its statement, thus functioning as an auxiliary. In the following sentence, however, *has* is employed as a principal verb:
He *has* no hair.
The auxiliary verbs are: *can, could, do, did, have, had, is* (and the parts of *to be*), *may, might, must, shall, should, will, would.*
Note: The auxiliary may be separated from the other parts of the verb by a modifier:
I *can* hardly *lie* down and die.
He *has* rarely or never *exhibited* human intelligence.

Exercise No. 12

Indicate by marking them *T*, *I*, *L*, or *A*, whether the italicized verbs are transitive, intransitive, linking, or auxiliary.

1 I sometimes *sit* and *pity* Noah; but even he *had* this advantage over all succeeding navigators, that wherever he *landed*, he *was* sure to get no ill news from home. He *should be* canonized as the patron saint of newspaper correspondents, being the only man who ever *had* the very latest authentic intelligence from everywhere.
2 However good you *may* be, you *have* faults; however dull you may *be*, you *can* find out what some of them *are*; and however slight they may be, you *had* better make some—not too painful, but patient—effort to get rid of them.
3 The division of labour—and *let* us say also of play—between poets and scientists, and the cleavage of the two commodities they *make*, *does* not any more *mean* the end of poetry than of science.

STRONG AND WEAK VERBS. Strong (or **irregular**) verbs show past time by varying a vowel within the present form of the verb:

PRESENT:	s*i*ng,	dr*i*nk,	kn*o*w
PAST:	s*a*ng	dr*a*nk,	kn*e*w
PAST PARTICIPLE:*	s*u*ng,	dr*u*nk,	kn*ow*n

Weak (or **regular**) verbs show past time by adding *-ed*, *-t*, or *-d*, to the present form of the verb:

PRESENT:	talk,	feel,	love
PAST:	talk*ed*,	fel*t*,	lov*ed*
PAST PARTICIPLE:	talk*ed*,	fel*t*,	lov*ed*

Note: 'Strong verbs' acquired their name because they seemed to form the past without requiring the assistance of any endings, whereas 'weak verbs' needed such assistance.
'Regular' and 'irregular' are more meaningful (though not precise) terms. In Old English, verbs were inflected in several ways. With the passage of

---

* A participle (discussed later) is an adjective formed from a verb. The past participle generally ends in *-ed* (*climbed*), *-d* (*laid*), *-t* (*wrought*), *-n* (*mown*), *-en* (*ridden*).

time, however, most verbs assumed some regularity—that is, people began forming them according to a dominant pattern. But the irregular verbs resisted conversion because they were so commonly used that people remembered their inflection.

Of the thousands of verbs in English, fewer than three hundred are strong or irregular. Unable to withstand the process of analogy, most verbs (all verbs newly added to the language) tend to adhere to the regular models.

PRINCIPAL PARTS OF VERBS. The principal parts of the verb are the **infinitive,** the basic or root part of the verb—usually the same in form as the present form used with *I* (*hop, skip, jump*); the **past tense, first person singular** (*hopped, skipped, jumped*); and the **past participle** (*hopped, skipped, jumped*). From the principal parts, the other verb-forms are constructed:*

The **infinitive** yields the **present** and **future.**
(love)   (I *love*) (I shall *love*)
The **past tense** yields the **past tense only.**
(loved)   (I *loved*)
The **past participle** yields the **present perfect.**
(loved)   (I *have loved*)
the **past perfect,** the **future perfect.**
(I *had loved*)   (I *shall have loved*)

PRINCIPAL PARTS OF IRREGULAR VERBS. The principal parts of the irregular verbs that give the most trouble are included in the following list.

PRESENT (INFINITIVE)	PAST	PAST PARTICIPLE
awake	awaked, awoke	awaked
be (am)	was	been
bear	bore	borne
begin	began	begun
bid	bade	bidden
break	broke	broken
burst	burst	burst
dive	dived	dived
do	did	done
drink	drank	drunk
flee	fled	fled
fly	flew	flown
forsake	forsook	forsaken
get	got	got
go	went	gone
hang	hung, hanged	hung, hanged
have	had	had
know	knew	known
lay	laid	laid
lie	lay	lain
light	lit, lighted	lit, lighted
ring	rang	rung
rise	rose	risen
see	saw	seen

* The verb *be* and the defective verbs (those lacking one or more inflectional forms) *may, can, must, ought, will,* and *shall* are exceptions.

PRESENT (INFINITIVE)	PAST	PAST PARTICIPLE
sing	sang	sung
slay	slew	slain
slink	slunk	slunk
speak	spoke	spoken
sting	stung	stung
stink	stank, stunk	stunk
swear	swore	sworn
swim	swam	swum
wake	woke, waked	waked
wring	wrung	wrung
write	wrote	written

Exercise No. 13

Correct the errors in verb form. (If a form other than the given one is preferred supply it.)

1 I seen him when he busted my balloon.
2 He swum out beyond the breakers.
3 He has got gold, but the process has froze the gentle current of his soul.
4 I have laid awake on rainy mornings, wondering why I had lain away money for them.
5 When the warden rung the bell, the prisoner was hung.
6 I beared the burden that I was borne to bear.
7 Because he had drank so much, his wife wrang his neck.
8 The sun shined over Ruth as she binded the sheaves.
9 The Romans loaned Antony their ears.
10 When the bee stang him, he sprung to his feet.

VERB INFLECTION: CONJUGATION. Verbs change their form or spelling to show **person** (which tells whether the subject is speaking, is spoken to, or is spoken of); **number** (which tells whether the subject is singular or plural); **tense** (which tells whether the subject is involved in a present, past, or future action); **mood** (which tells whether the speaker regards an action as a fact, a command, or a condition); and **voice** (which tells whether the subject performs an action or is acted upon). Verb inflection is called **conjugation.**

PERSON IN THE VERB. The verb agrees with its subject in person. The verb has three persons:

FIRST PERSON:	I love	we love
SECOND PERSON:	you love	you love
THIRD PERSON:	he, she, it loves	they love

I *am* your obedient servant.
I, who *am* your obedient servant, refuse.
You *are* my ex-servant.
He *is* looking for a job.
He and I *are* looking for jobs.
John, who *seeks* a job, *finds* one.
Note: The noun is always in the third person; therefore it always takes a verb in the third person.

NUMBER IN THE VERB. The verb agrees with its subject in number. The verb has two numbers:

SINGULAR: I *love*, you *love*, he, she, it *loves*.
PLURAL: We *love*, you *love*, they *love*.

A compound subject takes a plural verb.
Nero and Caligula *need* shock therapy.
Note: When the compound subject denotes a single idea it may take a singular verb.
The tumult and the shouting *dies*.
The sum and substance of her objection *amounts* to this: she does not like him.

A subject plural in form but singular in meaning takes a singular verb.
Electronics *was* a science and *has become* an industry.
The gallows *seems* her destiny.

A collective noun takes a singular or a plural verb, depending on the way it is understood:
The class *is* unanimous.
The class *are* divided.
After a construction like *one of those who* or *which* or *that*, the temptation is to use a singular verb. The temptation should be resisted:
Wrong: He is one of those men who *gets* bitten by non-existent mosquitoes.
Right: He is one of those men who *get* bitten by non-existent mosquitoes.
The relative pronoun (serving a subject of the verb *get*) is plural, since its antecedent *men* is plural. Therefore the verb ought to be plural.
An easy test consists of relocating the troublesome group of words:
Of those men who get bitten by non-existent mosquitoes, he is one.
When the sentence is revised in such a manner, the temptation to use a singular verb disappears.
It is one of the mosquitoes that (or which) *zing* as they *sting*.
Of the mosquitoes that *zing* as they *sting*, it is one.

Exercise No. 14

Correct the errors of person and number in the verbs included below.
1 Neither John or I are utterly senseless.
2 The herd of cattle which are grazing on the field has been sold down the river.
3 He is one of those men who needs to be seen doing good.
4 There is a table, a chair and a tape-recorder: now talk!
5 The wages of sin are death.
6 He is one of those pedagogues who has given *pedantry* its meaning.
7 It is I, not he, who is at fault.
8 There's gold pieces in plenty here.
9 Seven days without water make one week.
10 The general, together with five thousand picked troops, storm the tavern.

TENSE IN THE VERB. The tense of a verb shows the time of an action—present, past, or future. There are six tenses, however—three simple and three perfect.

Simple Tenses. The present tense shows that an action takes place now:
He *fills* the cup and *drinks*.
God *is* just and *has* His reasons.

The forms of the verb in the present tense follow.
Note: The verb *fill* is regular; the verbs *drink, am, have,* are irregular.

SINGULAR	PLURAL
1 I fill, drink, am, have	We fill, drink, are, have
2 You fill, drink, are, have	You fill, drink, are, have
3 He, she, it fills, drinks, is has	They fill, drink, are, have

The past tense shows that an action took place at some previous time.

SINGULAR	PLURAL
1 I filled, drank, was, had	We filled, drank, were, had
2 You filled, drank, were, had	You filled, drank, were, had
3 He, she, it filled, drank, was, had	They filled, drank, were, had

The future tense shows that an action will take place in time to come.

SINGULAR	PLURAL
1 I shall fill, drink, be, have	We shall drink, fill, be, have
2 You will fill, drink, be, have	You will drink, fill, be, have
3 He, she, it will fill, drink, be, have	They will drink, fill, be, have

Perfect Tenses—denote that an action is completed or perfected at the present, at some past time, or at some future time. They are formed by prefixing *have (has)* or *had* or *shall have (will have)* to the past participle.

Present Perfect Tense—shows that an action is complete at present. The action indicated began in the past and extends to the present or bears on the present:

I *have tried* kindness always. Here the indication is that 'I have up to the present tried kindness always.' The implication, perhaps, is that the speaker considers altering his course (but other inferences are possible).

Compare the simple past tense:

I *tried* kindness.

Here, the indication is that 'At a specific time in the past, I tried kindness.' Note that the perfect tense may not be used to describe a definite time in the past.

Wrong: I have voted in the election last year. (Perfect)

Right: I voted in the election last year. (Past)

Compare also the following statements:

I *ate.* (Past)

I *have eaten.* (Perfect)

In the first sentence, the action indicated took place at a definite (but unstated) time in the past. In the second sentence, the action indicated took place so recently that it has some influence on the present—perhaps it means: 'I have eaten so recently that I do not want to eat now.' The perfect tense, then, implies some relationship to the present; the past tense reports only that an action is past.

SINGULAR	PLURAL
1 I have filled, drunk, been, had	We have filled, drunk, been, had
2 You have filled, drunk, been, had	You have filled, drunk, been, had
3 He, she, it has filled, drunk, been, had	They have filled, drunk, been, had

Past Perfect Tense—shows that an action was completed before another action in the past, or completed before a definite time in the past:

Before the audience *arrived* [past], he *had memorized* his impromptu speech.

When he *had finished* his second glass of brandy, he *saw* [past] things more clearly.

For twenty years they *had considered* the plunge they *have taken* [perfect].

In the last sentence cited, *they* apparently considered for twenty years the feasibility of taking the plunge, and *then* took it.

SINGULAR	PLURAL
1 I had filled, drunk, been, had	We had filled, drunk, been, had
2 You had filled, drunk, been, had	You had filled, drunk, been, had
3 He, she, it had filled, drunk, been, had	They had filled, drunk, been, had

Future Perfect Tense—shows that an action will be completed before another action in the future, or before a given time in the future.

Note: The future perfect tense is seldom employed.

They *will have hanged* the man while the committee debate.

They will try to stop you, but you *will have passed* beyond their reach.

SINGULAR	PLURAL
1 I shall have filled, drunk, been, had	We shall have filled, drunk, been, had
2 You will have filled, drunk, been, had	You will have filled, drunk, been, had
3 He, she, it will have filled, drunk, been, had	They will have filled, drunk, been, had

Exercise No. 15

Give the tense of each italicized verb in the following sentences:

1 I fell in love before I *had reached* years of discretion.

2 I wonder how many souls the devil *will have collected* before he returns to his winter home.

3 With the continued growth of specialization, the experts *have* necessarily *had* more and more to say in the affairs of industry.

4 The true friend of property, the true conservative, is he who *insists* that property *shall be* the servant and not the master of the commonwealth.

5 During the Victorian Age the standard of the best building *had risen* almost as high as it *had been* in England in any earlier period; but the mass of good buildings *had* relatively *decreased*; and the domestic dwellings in both country and city *lost* those final touches of craftsmanship that *had lingered* here and there, up to the first half of the nineteenth century.

6 Many people *believe* that it *was* a sad day indeed when Rutherford split the atom; other people *believe* that if it *hadn't been* Rutherford, it *would have been* someone else.

7 What *made* Poe particularly acceptable to the French, however, was what *had distinguished* him from most of the other Romantics of the English-speaking countries: his interest in aesthetic theory.

8 No one *can be found* who *will deny* that in the case of any single individual the greatest prosperity *can exist* only when that individual *has reached* his highest state of efficiency; that is, when he *is turning* out his largest daily output.

9 It *is* well for the world that in most of us, by the age of thirty, the character *has set* like plaster, and *will* never *soften* again.

10 In a few years the Octogenarian Club *will have been decimated*.

MOOD IN THE VERB. The mood of a verb shows the manner in which a statement is made. There are three moods: **indicative, imperative, and subjunctive.** For a statement of fact, a verb in the indicative mood is used:

I *ask* questions.

For a command or request, a verb in the imperative mood is used:

You, *ask* questions.

For an idea presented as doubtful, contrary to fact, conditional, or imaginary, the subjunctive mood is used.

Indicative Mood is the mood of fact, or rather of statement presented as fact. Though the statements which follow contradict each other, both employ the same (indicative) verb:

Rum is an alcoholic drink.

Rum is a non-alcoholic drink.

Questions employ verbs in the indicative mood (since questions expect statements of fact in reply).

Is rum an alcoholic drink?

The indicative mood is much the most important in English; perhaps ninety-eight per cent of the verbs employed in speaking and writing are in the indicative mood. Almost every function of the subjunctive may be assumed by the indicative. Thus, *If he ask questions, he will receive answers* has been instanced as subjunctive. But unquestionably the indicative alternative, *If he asks questions, he will receive answers* is equally usual. Moreover, the uses of the subjunctive shrink continually, the indicative increasingly embracing them.

The indicative forms for the six tenses are listed under **Tense in the Verb.**

Imperative Mood is the mood of command and request.

Consider the ant.

Join the army.

Hold your tongue.

Note: *You* is understood but generally not expressed in the imperative.

The imperative has only one tense and one number. It has both numbers, but the form for the singular is identical with the form for the plural.

Subjunctive Mood is the mood of doubt, condition, wish, imagination, and the like.

The forms of the subjunctive follow. Note that the subjunctive implies future time; consequently, the subjunctive, requiring no future forms, includes only four tenses. (*If,* though no part of the subjunctive, precedes each form because the subjunctive most often appears in *if*-constructions.)

PRESENT TENSE: (If) I, you, he, we, they *fill, drink, be, have.*

PAST TENSE: (If) I, you, he, we, they *filled, drank, were, had.*

PRESENT PERFECT TENSE: (If) I, you, he we, they *have filled, have drunk, have been, have had.*

PAST PERFECT TENSE: (If) I, you, he, we, they *had filled, had drunk, had been, had had.*

Note that most verbs have only one form of the subjunctive different from the corresponding indicative form—the third person singular of the present tense:

SUBJUNCTIVE: (If) he, she, it *drink, fill, have.*

INDICATIVE: He, she, it *drinks, fills, has.*

The verb *be* (the sole verb currently used in the subjunctive to any extent) has two distinctive forms:

Be for all persons of the present tense.
Were for the first and third persons of the past tense.

SINGULAR		PLURAL	
PRESENT TENSE			
SUBJUNCTIVE	INDICATIVE	SUBJUNCTIVE	INDICATIVE
1 (If) I *be*	I am	(If) we *be*	We are
2 (If) you *be*	You are	(If) you *be*	You are
3 (If) he, she, it *be*	He, she, it *is*	(If) they *be*	They are
PAST TENSE			
1 (If) I *were*	I was	(If) we *were*	We were
2 (If) you *were*	You were	(If) you *were*	You were
3 (If) he, she, it *were*	He, she, it was	(If) they *were*	They were

The subjunctive has only two live uses—and neither exhibits so much liveliness as formerly. They are:

(1) In a 'condition contrary to fact' construction:

If he *were* to fall into the pond, he would come up with a fish in his mouth.
I wish you *were* here—instead of me.

Note: If the condition is presented not as contrary to fact—untrue—but merely as doubtful or uncertain, the present subjunctive is used:

If he *be* innocent, we are all guilty.
If he *survive*, the doctor's fees will kill him.

(2) In a *that*-construction after verbs or adjectives which denote **asking, agreeing, demanding, determining, directing, enacting, insisting, ordering, proposing, recommending, suggesting,** and the like. Most such usages are formal:

He moved that the meeting *be* adjourned.
The prisoner asks that he *be* shot rather than hanged.
It is necessary that justice *be* done.
Is it just that the poor man *suffer*?

The subjunctive persists, too, in many idioms, formulae, and fossilized expressions.

Far *be* it from me.
O that it *were* possible!
Peace *be* with you.
Be it ever so humble, there's no place like home.
Though he *slay* me, yet will I trust in him.
Be that as it may.

Exercise No. 16

In the sentences following, supply the indicative or subjunctive mood, as required, of the verb in brackets.

1 If the earth ...... flat, men could perhaps sail *asquare* it. (to be)
2 Since the earth ...... round, men can sail around it. (to be)
3 If wishes ...... horses, beggars would ride. (to be)
4 Since wishes ...... not horses, beggars are pedestrians. (to be)
5 They proposed formally that he ...... admitted. (to be)
6 They will do their best to see that he ...... admitted. (to be)

7 I suggest that the student ...... carefully the shifty nature of mood. (to consider)
8 It is necessary that every voter with a small capacity for disappointment ......
   election promises. (to suspect)
9 I wish I ...... your widow. (to be)
10 Far ...... it from me to split infinitives, or hairs, to dangle participles or babies, to
    modify substantives or opinions. (to be)

VOICE IN THE VERB. The voice of a verb shows whether the subject is active or passive: the verb is active if the subject performs an action, passive if the subject receives an action.

ACTIVE: A misinformed electorate *put* him into office.

PASSIVE: He *was put* into office by a misinformed electorate.

In the first sentence the subject *electorate* acts; in the second the subject *He* receives the action.

Note: The object (*him*) of the active verb becomes the subject (*he*) of the passive verb. Since transitive verbs have objects, only transitive verbs have a passive voice.

The passive voice of the verb is made by adding its past participle to some form of the verb *be*. The following table gives the conjugation of *fill* in the passive voice for the third person singular, indicative mood.

PRESENT: It is filled

PAST: It was filled

FUTURE: It will be filled

PRESENT PERFECT: It has been filled

PAST PERFECT: It had been filled

FUTURE PERFECT: It will have been filled

The active voice is the norm in English: it is more direct and more forceful than the passive:

ACTIVE: I *pitied* him.

PASSIVE: He *was pitied* by me.

Moreover, the passive construction often leads to awkward expression, especially in long sentences: compare the passive translation of Emerson's famous sentence with the original.

Awkward Passive. If good corn *is had* by a man, or wood, or boards, or pigs *to be sold*, or better chairs or knives, crucibles or church organs *can be made* by him than by anybody else, a broad, hard-beaten road to his house, though it be in the wilderness, *will be found* by you.

Active. If a man has good corn, or wood, or boards, or pigs to sell, or can make better chairs or knives, crucibles or church organs than anybody else, you will find a broad, hard-beaten road to his house, though it be in the wilderness.

There are, however, legitimate uses for the passive:

(1) To emphasize the recipient of an action:

The fuse *was ignited* by someone.

Here, the fuse, not the igniter, is the centre of interest.

(2) To eliminate mention of the agent:

The fuse was ignited.

Much *has been written* and much *has been said*, but nothing *has been done*.

Note: Since the doers of the action are irrelevant here, the passive voice seems preferable.

Exercise No. 17

In the following sentences, several of the verbs in the passive voice are ineffective because they are awkward, unnatural or unemphatic. Convert such passive verbs into active verbs; recast the sentence if necessary.

1 A most enjoyable time was had by everybody.
2 It is believed by most teachers that sentences are written in the passive by people when the communication they intend has not been thought out before the pen has been set to the paper.
3 Eric's head is being examined by a phrenologist.
4 He saw that she wanted to be kissed, and she was kissed by him.
5 After Jonathan J. Logorrhea had spoken for an hour, nobody listened to what was being said.
6 I admit that I was impressed by the bank notes which were flashed before my eyes by her father.
7 We wandered aimlessly until we were rescued by a passing dust-cart.
8 Caesar was first conquered then cuckolded by Cleopatra.
9 Books are read by soldiers—comic books, chiefly.
10 Belloc hoped that when he died people would say: 'His sins were scarlet, but his books were read.'

OTHER VERB FORMS: THE CONTINUOUS AND EMPHATIC FORMS. A meaning somewhat different from any indicated by the tense-forms previously described can be achieved by employing the **continuous** or the **emphatic** forms of the verb.

Continuous Forms—of the verb show that an action is still continuing. They may present duration more graphically than the simple tenses.

Continuous tense-forms consist of some part of the verb *be* followed by the present participle. A synopsis in the third person singular follows. Note that only the present and past forms of the continuous are used in the passive voice.

ACTIVE

PRESENT: *He is filling*
PAST: *He was filling*
FUTURE: *He will be filling*
PERFECT: *He has been filling*
PAST PERFECT: *He had been filling*
FUTURE PERFECT: *He will have been filling*

PASSIVE

PRESENT: *He is being filled*
PAST: *He was being filled*

SUBJUNCTIVE

PRESENT: *(If) he be filling*
PAST: *(If) he were filling*
PERFECT: *(If) he have been filling*
PAST PERFECT: *(If) he had been filling*

Note: In the passive voice, the past is the only subjunctive form used: *(If) he were being given.*

Emphatic Forms—of the verb are used for emphasis or stress.

Emphatic tense forms consist of *do* or *did* followed by the infinitive without *to*. The emphatic forms are used only in the present and past tense of the active voice; they are not used at all in the passive voice.

PRESENT: *I do fill*
PAST: *I did fill*

Exercise No. 18

Keeping tense and mood constant, supply the continuous form and the emphatic form (if one exists) of each verb in the following list.

1 I *play*
2 you *fiddled*
3 it *will fizz*
4 she *has constituted*

5 they *had asseverated*
6 he *will have explained*
7 (if) he *laugh*
8 he *is accosted*

THE ADJECTIVE

The adjective modifies or qualifies a substantive (noun or pronoun), altering in some way its meaning or range.

KINDS OF ADJECTIVES. Adjectives are classified according to the work they do.

DESCRIPTIVE ADJECTIVE—describes or characterizes a substantive— renders its meaning more precise. There are two kinds of descriptive adjectives:

COMMON ADJECTIVE—applies to a class of things, rather than to a particular thing.

mauve decade, *industrious* beaver, *lone* ranger, *happy* moron, *little* man, *yellow* journalism.

PROPER ADJECTIVE—applies to one particular member of a class, rather than to the class as a whole. Proper adjectives derive from proper nouns—often proper nouns are used to modify.

Sunday punch, *Roman* holiday, *American* way, *Panama* hat, *Protestant* tradition, *English* literature.

Note: Often the proper adjective has a limiting as well as a descriptive function, as in *Panama hat;* however, *Panama hats* has become a general name for a variety of plaited hat, and the limiting function of the adjective seems to be of minor importance. Ultimately, it may be written with a small *p.* For when the origin of a proper adjective is disregarded, it is generally spelt without an initial capital:

quixotic gesture, *indian* ink, *italic* type, *venetian* blinds, *satanic* wiles, *paris* green, *pasteurized* milk.

LIMITING ADJECTIVE—limits or defines the meaning of the noun— restricts its application. There are several kinds of limiting adjective.

PRONOMINAL ADJECTIVE—is a word, commonly used as a pronoun, that modifies a substantive.

DEMONSTRATIVE
this book, *these* books
that man, *those* men

INTERROGATIVE

What directions did the doctor give?

In *which* direction does the dog point?

By *whose* direction are we held?

The italicized adjectives each modify *direction*.

RELATIVE

Select *which* rapier you like.

I selected the rapier *whose* metal had been tested.

Whose may refer either to persons or to things.

INDEFINITE

some days, *any* stick, *no* islands, *every* man, *each* age, *other* times, *neither* alternative, *both* ends

POSSESSIVE

my eyes, *mine* eyes (archaic), *your* tooth, *his* hair, *her* lips, *its* tongue; *our* bodies, *your* heads, *their* appendixes

Note: The possessive adjectives agree in number with their antecedents, not with the nouns they modify:

my word, *my* words

INTENSIVE

the *very* likeness

IDENTIFYING

the *same* story

NUMERICAL

three men (cardinal)

the *third* man (ordinal)

Exercise No. 19

Underline each adjective and indicate the kind it is.

1 The full African moon poured down its light into the wide, lovely plain.
2 O may I join the choir invisible
  Of those immortal dead who live again
  In minds made better by their presence.
3 I can tell you which lie you prefer.
4 Which lie seems better?
5 The inebriated man offered to fight any woman or any child in the house.
6 Coffee, say the Spaniards, ought to be black as the devil, hot as hell, and sweet as sin.
7 The argument, subtle and specious, convinced everyone who could not follow it.
8 He suffered (or rather, other people did) from the Holmesean delusion that the worst puns are the best.
9 He called the argument brilliant but corrupt.
10 'Like a mackerel by moonlight,' he said, 'it shines and stinks.'

ARTICLES. The definite article *the* **and the indefinite articles** *a* **and** *an* **function as limiting adjectives.**

Definite Article. *The* **particularizes the noun**; that is, it specifies a particular thing, distinct from others of the same kind.

The monkey has a beard.

The children are monsters.

He is not *the* man I thought he was.

The derives from the old form of the demonstrative *that*, and still has demonstrative force:

He is *the* George Bernard Shaw.

The preceding an adjective may form a plural noun:

Only *the* brave deserve *the* fair.

The valiant never taste of death but once.

The preceding a singular noun may have a generalizing effect, equal to the indefinite *any* or *every:*

The child is father to *the* man.

The lunatic, *the* lover, and *the* poet.

Are of imagination all compact.

Note: Repetition of *the* before the nouns of a series stresses their individual quality.

The before a proper noun converts it into a common noun.

He was *the* Solomon of our asylum.

She was *the* Jezebel of the old ladies' home.

In the sentences cited, *Solomon* equals 'wise man', and *Jezebel* 'wicked woman'.

Indefinite Article. *A* **is used before words beginning with a consonant sound:**

a boy, *a* crowd, *a* girl, *a* union, *a* European

Note: Both *union* and *European* begin with a **consonant** sound; consequently each is preceded by *a*.

An **is used before words beginning with a vowel sound.**

an apple, *an* eagle, *an* idiot, *an* omen, *an* urn

Note: *An* is preferred before 'silent' *h:*

an heir, *an* hour, *an* habitual offender

A is preferred before 'sounded' *h:*

a history, *a* hump, *a* hill, *a* horse

Note: With some words *a* or *an* is used according to whether the speaker pronounces the *h* or not.

a hotel *or an* hotel

a historical novel *or an* historical novel

A and *an* generalize the noun; that is, they point to an object as one of a general class:

And this is the sum of lasting love:

Scratch *a* lover, and find *a* foe.

Though he seemed *a* man of distinction, he acted like *an* ape.

A woman, *a* dog, and *a* chestnut tree,

The more you beat them, the better they be.

A and *an* derive from the old form of *one*, and sometimes have the force of the numeral:

A stitch in time saves nine.

A and *an* sometimes have the force of each:

Her perfume costs *a* pound *an* ounce.

He works seven days *a* week.

Exercise No. 20

Insert *a* (*an*) or *the*, whichever seems the more logical, in the following blanks. (If neither article is appropriate, make no change.)

1 Every man has ...... good angel and ...... bad angel attending on him in particular.

2 His wisdom has became ...... proverb and ...... byword, but ...... half was not told me.

3 There ...... wicked cease from troubling and there ...... weary be at rest.

4 I saw ...... very strange couple yesterday, ... monkey leading ...... man; today my occulist saw ...... same pair, ... monkey still leading ...... man.

5 It was ...... Honourable Trismagestus Q. Terwilliger.

6 ...... inn as well as ...... hotel often has ...... history.

7 Lo! Death has reared himself ...... throne
In ...... strange city lying alone
Far down within ...... dim West,
Where ...... good and ...... bad and ...... worst and ...... best
Have gone to their eternal rest.

8 ...... Thames, England's principal river, rises in Gloucestershire on ...... east slope of ...... Cotswold Hills and bounds part of Gloucestershire, Middlesex, Essex, Wiltshire, Berkshire, Surrey, and Kent.

9 ...... *h* in 'heaven' is aspirate.

10 We will now consider that charming beast, ... hippocampus.

POSITION OF ADJECTIVES. An adjective regularly precedes the noun it modifies directly:

Brave men and *fair* women
Kind hearts and *gentle* folk
Cold hands and *warm* heart

But in some relatively established phrases the adjective follows:

Streets *wide* and *narrow*
Life *everlasting*
Time *enough*

Note: An adjective coming before the noun, listing one of its attributes, is called an **attributive adjective.**

An adjective sometimes acts like a noun in apposition, following and explaining the noun.

The devil, *unholy* and *unabashed*, stood before Cotton Mather.

The Byronic hero—*passionate, tormented, world-weary*—was fashioned after Byron's own image.

He scorned our simple ways, *simple* but *joyous*.

Note: An adjective used like a noun in apposition is called an **appositive adjective.**

An adjective may complete the meaning of the verb while modifying the subject:

The sea is *calm* tonight, the tide is *full*.

The problem proved insoluble.

The child became *difficult* first, then *impossible*.

Note: An adjective that is part of the predicate but functions as a modifier of the subject, is called a **predicate adjective.**

COMPARISON OF ADJECTIVES. Most adjectives denote variable qualities—qualities that exist in various degrees. The adjective is inflected (its spelling is altered) to show the degree of the quality. Such modification is termed **comparison.**

There are three degrees of comparison, the **positive**, the **comparative**, and the **superlative.**

1 The positive degree names the simple quality:

Socrates was a *wise* man.

Shakespeare was a *great* poet.

2 The comparative degree expresses a higher degree of the quality:

Socrates was a *wiser* man than Protagoras.

Shakespeare was a *greater* poet than Jonson.

The comparative degree is used in comparing two persons or two things.

3 The superlative degree expresses the highest degree of the quality:

Socrates was the *wisest* Greek of all.

Shakespeare was the *greatest* English poet.

The superlative degree is used in comparing three or more persons or things.

FORMING THE DEGREES OF COMPARISON. The positive degree is the form the dictionary supplies; it is the simple (uninflected) form of the adjective.

Regular adjectives form the **comparative** degree in two ways:

Almost all adjectives of one syllable and many of two syllables (disyllables) form the comparative by adding *-r* or *-er* to the simple adjective:

braver, higher, lower, smaller, larger, thinner, thicker, lazier, cleverer, narrower, commoner, pleasanter.

The remaining disyllables and almost all adjectives of three or more syllables (polysyllables) form the comparative by using *more* before the simple adjective:

disyllables { more careful, more distinct, more active, more recent.

polysyllables { more beautiful, more dangerous, more practical, more primitive.

Regular adjectives form the **superlative** degree in two ways:

Almost all adjectives of one syllable form the superlative by adding *-st* or *-est* to the simple adjective:

bravest, highest, lowest, smallest, largest, thinnest, thickest.

Many adjectives of two syllables and almost all adjectives of three or more syllables form the superlative by using *most* before the simple adjective:

disyllables { most careful, most distinct, most active, most recent.

polysyllables { most beautiful, most dangerous, most practical, most primitive.

Some commonly used adjectives are compared irregularly:

bad	worse	worst
far	farther, further	farthest, furthest
good, well	better	best
late	later, latter	latest, last
little	less, lesser, smaller	least, smallest
much, many	more	most
old	older, elder	oldest, eldest

Many adjectives of two syllables may be compared by adding the suffix *-er* and *-est* to form the comparative and superlative, or by prefixing *more* and *most*.

lovely   lovelier *or* more lovely   loveliest *or* most lovely

handsome	handsomer *or* more handsome	handsomest *or* most handsome
narrow	narrower *or* more narrow	narrowest *or* most narrow
serene	serener *or* more serene	serenest *or* most serene
remote	remoter *or* more remote	remotest *or* most remote

Note: Whether the *-er, -est* method of comparison or the *more, most* method of comparison is to be preferred depends upon euphony and emphasis: if either form of the comparative or superlative sounds better than the other, or more effectively achieves the emphasis desired, it is to be preferred.

Decreased degree of a quality may be shown by using *less* and *least*.

strong	less strong	least strong
worthy	less worthy	least worthy
repulsive	less repulsive	least repulsive

Absolutes, adjectives denoting the highest or lowest degree of a quality, are theoretically incapable of being compared. When a thing is *unique*, only one of its kind exists—itself; consequently, *more unique* and *most unique* are logically impossible. The following adjectives do not logically admit of degrees:

almighty	empty	matchless	square
certain	eternal	perfect	supreme
circular	everlasting	perpetual	triangular
complete	heavenly	round	universal
dead	infinite	single	unique

However, language is often illogical, and in practice absolutes like *perfect* are frequently used as a kind of shorthand for 'more nearly perfect'.

Exercise No. 21

Insert the appropriate comparative or superlative forms of the simple (positive) adjectives italicized below.

1 Of two evils, choose the *little*.
2 My aunt is the *old* of eighteen sisters.
3 Thank you; you are *kind*.
4 Get there *first* with the *much*—that is the *fundamental* principle of tactics.
5 Cats are *clean* than monkeys, but monkeys are *intelligent* than cats.
6 He is the *wellknown* and the *bloodthirsty* of that nefarious crew.
7 Put your *good* foot forward.
8 He had rarely listened to a (an) *absurd* proposal, or to one *happy* in its phrasing.
9 He had never eaten a sausage that was *big*, *red*, *hot*.
10 He penetrated to the *in* sanctum.

THE ADVERB

The adverb modifies or qualifies a verb, an adjective, or another adverb, altering in some way its meaning or range.

He speaks *bitterly*.
The adverb *bitterly* modifies the verb *speaks*.

He speaks in an *exceedingly* bitter fashion.
The adverb *exceedingly* modifies the adjective *bitter*.

He speaks *very* bitterly.
The adverb *very* modifies the adverb *bitterly*.

KINDS OF ADVERBS. Depending on their use, adverbs are classified as simple or conjunctive.

SIMPLE ADVERB—alters the meaning of a single word in some way. The simple adverb answers one of several questions, deriving its name from the kind of answer it gives:

ADVERB OF TIME. The adverb of time answers the question *when?*

He will come *today, tomorrow, by and by*.

ADVERB OF PLACE. The adverb of place answers the question *where?*

He has gone *here, there,* and *everywhere*.

ADVERB OF MANNER. The adverb of manner answers the question *how?*

He talks *well—slowly, distinctly,* and *lucidly*.

ADVERB OF DEGREE OR MEASURE. The adverb of degree or measure answers the question *how much?*

He seemed *quite* rich, *very* knowledgeable, *hardly* enthusiastic, but *not* unenthusiastic.

ADVERB OF CAUSE OR PURPOSE. The adverb of cause or purpose answers the question *why?*

Why does the fat lady walk through the fields in gloves?

Note: *Why* in the sentence just cited may be called an **interrogative adverb** as well, since it is used to introduce a question. (Similarly, in *How pure she is!* the adverb *how* may be called an **exclamatory adverb,** since it is used to make an exclamation.)

CONJUNCTIVE ADVERB—acts like a conjunction and it acts like an adverb. As a conjunction it joins two independent clauses; as adverb, it modifies the independent clause in which it appears.

He knows nothing; *moreover,* he doesn't know that he knows nothing.

Note: *Moreover* is said to be an adverb, though it modifies the whole idea of the independent clause in which it appears, rather than a specific verb, adjective, or adverb. It is called an **adverb** for arbitrary reasons: words that do not fit into any other category are accounted adverbs—for convenience of classification.

He laughs at psychoanalysis; he believes in group therapy, *however*.

Note: The conjunctive adverb *however* modifies the whole independent clause *he believes in group therapy,* not any particular word in the clause. Compare *however* as a simple adverb:

However ridiculous psychoanalysis seems theoretically, it has proved itself clinically.

However here modifies the adjective *ridiculous*.

The more common conjunctive adverbs are:

accordingly	hence	nevertheless
additionally	however	no
also	indeed	on the contrary
at any rate	in other words	on the other hand
anyway	in short	still
besides	likewise	then
consequently	moreover	therefore
furthermore	namely	yes
		yet

Note: Unlike the conjunction, which stands first in the clause it introduces, the conjunctive adverb may stand in any position in the clause which it modifies. The italicized words in the following sentences are conjunctions.

He beat women *because* he was a cad.

He beat women, *for* he was a cad.

Neither *because* nor *for* may be displaced: each must stand first in the clause it introduces. Compare the variously placed conjunctive adverbs in the following sentences:

He beat women; *consequently*, he was a cad.

He beat women; he was, *consequently*, a cad.

He beat women; he was a cad, *consequently*.

FORMS OF ADVERBS. Most adverbs are formed by adding -*ly* to the corresponding adjective:

ADJECTIVES: *swift, slow, hot, cold.*

ADVERBS: *swiftly, slowly, hotly, coldly.*

Many adverbs (especially those long in common use) do not end in -*ly*.

very, much, little, almost, often, there

Note: The ending -*ly* is not the invariable sign of an adverb. The italicized words in the following sentence are all adjectives:

A *lovely* lady of *queenly* bearing, she married an *ugly* man of *slovenly* habits.

Note, too, that sometimes adverbs have the same form as the corresponding adjectives: their use determines their classification.

ADJECTIVE: He had a *fast* hold.

ADVERB: He held *fast*.

Exercise No. 22

In the following sentences, underline each adverb and indicate the class to which it belongs.

1 He played chess almost professionally.

2 I eat; therefore, I exist.

3 He formerly hunted mongooses.

4 Julian has gone south; his creditors, consequently, will have to wait.

5 There she blows!

6 He feels bad and behaves badly.

7 His nerve endings are anaesthetized; hence, he feels badly.

8 Yes, we have no bananas.

9 He seldom talks sensibly; she, never.

10 Well, what now?

COMPARISON OF ADVERBS. Adverbs, like adjectives, have their degrees of comparison: the **positive,** the **comparative,** and the **superlative.**

Most adverbs form the comparative degree by using *more* and the superlative degree by using *most*.

bravely	more bravely	most bravely
beautifully	more beautifully	most beautifully
seldom	more seldom	most seldom

Adverbs of one syllable generally form the comparative degree by adding -*er* and the superlative degree by adding -*est*.

fast	faster	fastest
soon	sooner	soonest
late	later	latest
hard	harder	hardest

A few adverbs are compared irregularly:

far	farther, further	farthest, furthest
ill or badly	worse	worst
little	less	least
much, many	more	most
well	better	best

Note: In standard English, *farther* expresses greater distance; *further* expresses greater degree or quantity.

Heaven is *farther* than hell.

He received *further* reports from Screwtape.

Adverbs (like adjectives) may have the degree of their quality decreased by using *less* **and** *least.*

soon	less soon	least soon
keenly	less keenly	least keenly
agreeably	less agreeably	least agreeably

Some adverbs theoretically do not admit of comparison:

fatally	quite	certainly
absolutely	entirely	

In practice, however, they are frequently compared.

Exercise No. 23

Insert the appropriate comparative or superlative forms of the simple adverbs italicized below.

1 Extremes of fortune are true wisdom's test,
   And he's of men wisest who bears them *well.*
2 The *far* we go, the *ill* we fare.
3 For men must work and women must weep,
   And the *soon* it's over, the *soon* to sleep.
4 Of them all, she spoke *distinctly.*
5 His kite went *high* of all, and he was the *highly* elated of fliers.

THE CONJUNCTION

The conjunction joins words or groups of words.

KINDS OF CONJUNCTIONS. There are two kinds of conjunctions, **co-ordinating** and **subordinating.**

CO-ORDINATING CONJUNCTION—joins words or groups that are co-ordinate—that is, of the same order or rank.

> WORDS: Jack *and* Jill
>   wind *or* weather
>   not angles *but* angels
> GROUPS OF WORDS: of cabbages *and* of kings
>   not to live in *but* to look at
>   what we want *and* what we get
>   if we live *or* if we die
>   Knowledge comes *but* wisdom lingers.
>   We must die, *for* men are mortal.

There are six simple co-ordinating conjunctions: *and, but, for, nor, or, yet*.

Because they are regularly coupled with each other, some co-ordinating conjunctions are called **correlatives:**

both . . . and	not only . . . but (also)
either . . . or	neither . . . nor
so . . . as	whether . . . or

Neither fish *nor* fowl *nor* good red herring

He *not only* marks his cross *but also* signs his name.

SUBORDINATING CONJUNCTION—joins a subordinate clause to a main clause.*

I whistle *while* he works.

The subordinate clause *while he works* is joined to the main clause *I whistle* by the subordinating conjunction *while*. The subordinating conjunction introduces its clause **(subordinating it)** and at the same time links it to the main clause upon which it depends for its relevance and force.

Before the sun rose, the first shots were heard.

The first shots were heard *before* the sun rose.

In these two sentences, note that *before* is the link-word, though in the first sentence the clause it introduces precedes and in the second sentence follows the main clause. The logic of the connexion remains the same.

The most commonly used subordinating conjunctions, together with the relations they indicate, follow:

Time: as, as long as, as soon as, often, before, since, till (until), when, while.

Reason or Cause: as, because, inasmuch as, since, why.

Supposition or Condition: although (though), if, unless, whether . . . or.

Purpose: in order that, so, that, lest.

Comparison: than.

Exercise No. 24

Pick out each conjunction in the following sentences and tell whether it is a co-ordinating or a subordinating conjunction.

1 Neither heat nor cold daunts the postman.
2 A man is shorter when he is walking than when at rest.
3 As good cooks go, she went.
4 He pores over books when it rains.
5 Though all men deny thee, yet will not I.
6 It is certain because it is impossible.
7 He maintains a discreet silence so that no one will be able to swear he is stupid.
8 Tarry, lest you be on time.
9 The conclusion must be false, for the premises are false.
10 He is not only dull himself, but the cause of dullness in others also.

THE PREPOSITION

A preposition shows the relationship between a noun or a pronoun and some other word in the sentence.

water *under* the bridge

---

* A clause is a group of words containing a subject and predicate. A main clause can stand alone; it is a self-sufficient unit. A subordinate clause cannot; it depends upon some other word or words to make its meaning clear.

age *before* beauty

dog *in* the manger

The prepositions (italicized) connect two words, like the conjunction; unlike the conjunction the preposition shows the relationship existing between them.

OBJECT OF A PREPOSITION. The noun or pronoun that the preposition introduces or governs is in the objective case.

cannon *before them*

the secret *between us*

a headache *to him*

The pronouns *them*, *us*, and *him* are all objects of the prepositions upon which they depend.

POSITION OF THE PREPOSITION. The preposition generally precedes its object (is in the *pre* position). However, it may legitimately follow, and in idiomatic expressions or commonly employed locutions it often does:

Whom are you speaking *about?*

This is the type of arrant pedantry *which* I will not put up *with*.

Peace is *what* we must prepare *for*.

In each of the sentences above the pronoun (*whom*, *which*, *what*) is the object of the terminal preposition.

Note: The object of the preposition may be omitted.

The lady [whom] we look *for*.

The ground [which] we stand *on*.

MEANINGS OF THE PREPOSITION. The preposition generally expresses the relation of one thing to another with respect to place or position:

He stood *on* a hill, looking *at* the lake; then ran *along* the valley, *between* rows of trees.

However, the preposition may express other relations as well: **time** (*before* dawn, *after* noon, *during* the night), **instrumentality** (*through* neglect, *with* swords, *by* Charles Dickens), **manner** (*with* love, *by* hook or *by* crook), **purpose** (*for* knowledge, *for the sake of* knowledge).

Exercise No. 25

Underline the preposition and the words it relates to in each of the following sentences.

1 We saw, heraldic in the heat,
   A scorpion on a stone.
2 I never thrust my nose into other men's porridge. It is no bread and butter of mine; every man for himself, and God for us all.
3 What is bred in the bone will never come out of the flesh.
4 He came from Switzerland, through France, over to England, and stayed among us some months.
5 Whom does he speak to?

THE INTERJECTION

The interjection expresses some emotion. It is an exclamation of surprise, anger, delight, grief, consternation, or the like. It is an independent element—

one without grammatical relation to the other parts of the sentence. Words normally employed as other parts of speech may, if uttered emotionally, function as interjections.

Oh!	Bang!	Welcome!
So!	Well!	Nonsense!
Help!	Hurrah!	O dear!
	Indeed!	

Note: The interjection is generally followed by an exclamation mark.

VERBALS: GERUND, PARTICIPLE, AND INFINITIVE

VERBALS. Words derived from verbs but used as other parts of speech are called verbals. There are three kinds of verbals: gerunds, participles, and infinitives. Though they function as nouns (gerund and infinitive) or as modifiers (participle and infinitive), they also have some characteristics of the *finite verb* from which they originate. (A finite verb is 'limited' in person and number by its subject. Thus *read* and *write* are finite verbs. Their corresponding verbals are *infinite*—'unlimited'.)

GERUND. The gerund derives from the verb but functions as a noun: it is a verbal noun.

The tense and voice forms of the gerund follow:

	ACTIVE	PASSIVE
PRESENT	reading	being read
	writing	being written
PERFECT	having read	having been read
	having written	having been written

Marrying is her object.
Marrying, the gerund, is the subject of the linking verb *is*.

The gerund may serve any of the functions of a noun—subject, object, complement, appositive. Compare the sentence cited with

Marriage is her object.
Marriage, the noun, serves the same function and has essentially the same meaning as the gerund *marrying*.

The other forms of the gerund are comparatively unusual.

In retrospect, he could see her object in *having married*.

Shakespeare said that *being married* means being marred.

His *having been married* makes any man a better philosopher, Socrates contended.

Verb Characteristics of the Gerund. The gerund may take an object:

Marrying *him* is her object.

The pronoun *him* is the object of the gerund *marrying*. (To determine the object of the gerund, ask *whom* or *what* after it: Marrying *whom*? The answer, *him*, supplies the object of the gerund.) The noun *marriage*, of course, never takes an object. We may not say: *Marriage him.*

The gerund may be modified by an adverb:

Though he has several times repented leisurely, he has not been cured of marrying *hastily*.

The adverb *hastily* modifies the gerund *marrying* (in the same way that the adverb *leisurely* modifies the finite verb *repented*).

Note: An adjective may modify the gerund when its naming function is more prominent than its acting function.

Hasty marrying often leads to leisurely repenting.

Hasty, an adjective, modifies *marrying* because the noun sense of the gerund is uppermost.

The gerund may take a subject; such a subject is regularly in the possessive case.

John's marrying her is a necessary prelude to his divorcing her.

John's, a noun in the possessive case, is the subject of the gerund *marrying*. (Note that the pronoun *his*, the subject of the gerund *divorcing*, is also in the possessive case.)

In several circumstances, the subject of a gerund is regularly in the objective case:

(*a*) When the subject is stressed:

Though I approve of marriage, I cannot approve of *John* (him) marrying.

(*b*) When the subject is plural:

I cannot approve of morons marrying.

(*c*) When the subject is modified:

I cannot approve of a moronic person marrying.

Exercise No. 26

In the sentences below, underline the gerunds, along with their modifiers, subjects and objects. Correct all errors in case.

1 Desperate for news, the reporter resorted to biting dogs.
2 Jojo's avid reading in abnormal psychology has served one purpose: that of making him feel normal.
3 He spurning her demonstrates his need for both a psychiatrist and an oculist.
4 He thought him gilding lilies was a sufficient career.
5 Their having read the entire contents of the public library has not raised their intelligence quotients a fraction of a point.

PARTICIPLE. The participle derives from the verb but functions as an adjective: it is a verbal adjective.

Coming round the mountain, Susannah saw more mountains.

The participle *Coming* modifies the noun *Susannah*.

The tense and voice forms of the participle follow:

	ACTIVE	PASSIVE
PRESENT	reading, writing	being read, being written
PAST	[lacking]	read, written
PERFECT	having read, having written	having been read, having been written

Tense in the Participle. The present participle always ends in *-ing*. It indicates action taking place at the same time as the action of some finite verb.

Hermione left, *scowling* but silent.

The participle *scowling* modifies the noun *Hermione* (just as the adjective *silent* modifies it). The action it describes takes place at the same time as the action of the finite verb *left*.

Scowling but silent, Hermione leaves.

Again the action indicated by the participle is simultaneous with the action indicated by the finite verb.

The past participle is the third 'principal part' of the verb. The past participle indicates action taking place before the action of the finite verb:

Neglected and unhappy, Ambrose retired to the country.

The past participle _neglected_ modifies the noun _Ambrose_ (just as the adjective _unhappy_ modifies it). The action indicated by the past participle takes place _prior_ to the action indicated by the finite verb: Ambrose was neglected and unhappy first; he retired to the country afterwards.

Note: The past participle is the third principal part of the verb. In regular verbs, the past participle has the same form as the simple past tense (_talked_, _walked_, _balked_). In irregular verbs, the participle is formed in several ways (_taken_, _rung_, _won_) which need to be learned separately. See section on Verbs, Principal Parts.

The perfect participle is formed by prefixing the auxiliary _having_ **to the past participle.** It indicates an action that has been definitely completed, or perfected, before the action of the finite verb.

Having read his Baedeker, he felt ready to penetrate historic Italy.

The perfect participle _having read_ modifies the pronoun _he_. The action indicated by the perfect participle takes place before the action indicated by the verb _felt_.

Note: The distinction between the past participle and the perfect participle is a good deal less stringent in practice than the 'rules' imply. Actually, the rhythm of the sentence rather than the rules of tense usually determines the choice.

Verb Characteristics of the Participle. The participle may take an object.

Having eaten the _missionary_, the cannibal digested Christian principles.

The noun _missionary_ is the object of the participle _having eaten_.

The participle may be modified by an adverb.

Having eaten him _hurriedly_, he digested them poorly.

The adverb _hurriedly_ modifies _having eaten_ (just as the adverb _poorly_ modifies the finite verb _digested_).

Using the Participle. The Participle, since it is an adjective, **must modify a noun or noun-substitute.** If it does not clearly and logically relate to a noun, a misconstruction known as the **dangling participle** results.

Dangling: Squirming and wriggling, I tied the little monster.

Repaired: I tied the squirming and wriggling little monster.

(Another possible repair—though a clumsy one: squirming and wriggling, the little monster was tied by me.)

Dangling: Riding round the mountain, other mountains came into view.

Repaired: When we rode round the mountain, other mountains came into view.

Repaired: Coming round the mountain, we saw other mountains.

The participle, a verbal adjective, must be distinguished from the gerund, a verbal noun.

Gerund: Four lashes stopped the infant's _squealing_.

The gerund _squealing_ is the object of the verb _stopped_.

Participle: _Squealing_, the infant received four lashes. The participle _Squealing_ modifies the noun _infant_. Compare _The squealing infant received four lashes._

Exercise No. 27

In the following sentences, underline all participles, along with their modifiers, subjects, and objects. Correct all errors.

1 Desperate for news, the reporter had bitten dogs.
2 Having avidly read books on abnormal psychology, Jojo's normality oppressed him.
3 The lady having been spurned by Jojo, proceeded to rival the several furies of hell.
4 Having gilded lilies with loving devotion, he sought roses needing varnish.
5 Having read the entire contents of the public library, their intelligence quotients remained static.

INFINITIVE. The infinitive is the first of the principle parts of the verb.
The infinitive is usually introduced by *to*, the 'sign' of the infinitive: to *read*, *to write*, *to reckon;* the sign, however, may be omitted (especially after the auxiliaries *may*, *can*, *shall*, *will*, *must*, and after the verbs *dare*, *bid*, *make*, *see*, *hear*, *feel*).

The infinitive is a **verbal noun** chiefly; but it may also function as adjective or adverb.

The tense and voice forms of the infinitive follow.

	ACTIVE	PASSIVE
PRESENT	to read, to write	to be read, to be written
PERFECT	to have read, to have written	to have been read, to have been written

The Infinitive as Noun, Adjective, and Adverb. The infinitive is primarily used as a noun:
To *see* is to *believe*.
To see is used as subject of the linking verb *is* and *to believe* as its complement (predicate nominative).
The infinitive may be used as an adjective.
W. C. Fields liked water *to bathe in* and whisky *to drink*.
The infinitive *to bathe in* modifies the noun *water*, and the infinitive *to drink* modifies the noun *whisky*.
The infinitive may be used as an adverb.
The sower went forth *to sow*.
The infinitive *to sow* modifies the verb *went* (*forth*).
Verb Characteristics of the Infinitive. The infinitive may take an object.
To see *him* is to believe *her*.
The pronoun *him* is the object of the infinitive *to see;* the pronoun *her* is the object of the infinitive *to believe*.
The infinitive may be modified by an adverb.
To spell *correctly* requires no instruction in black magic.
The adverb *correctly* modifies the infinitive *to spell*.
The infinitive may take a subject. The subject is in the objective case.
I know *them* to be burners of books.
The pronoun *them* is the subject of the infinitive *to be*. (Compare: *I know that they are burners of books*. Here the pronoun *they* is subject of the finite verb *are* and consequently in the nominative case. However, the two constructions are closely analogous. In each sentence, the group of words following *know* constitutes its object; and in each group of words the pronoun is governed by the infinitive or the verb that follows.)

Note: The subject of the infinitive *to be* (as the subject of all infinitives) is in the objective case.

Tense in the Infinitive. The present infinitive indicates action taking place at the same time as the action of the finite verb.

I considered him *to be* only three generations removed from a savage.

The action indicated by *to be* and the action indicated by *considered* take place at the same time.

The perfect infinitive indicates action taking place before the action of the main verb.

They believed the soldier *to have taken* unofficial leave.

The action indicated by *to have taken* occurs before the action indicated by *believed*.

Using the Infinitive. When the infinitive is used as a modifier (not as a noun) **it must be logically related to the word it modifies.** Otherwise the dangling infinitive results.

Dangling: To win friends and *influence* people, guile and fraud are necessary, some politicians believe.

Repaired: To win friends and *influence* people, one must employ guile and fraud, some politicians believe.

Note: The sign of the infinitive, *to*, has been omitted before *influence* because it clearly parallels *to win*. Where the parallelism is apparent, the sign of the infinitive may be omitted.

Exercise No. 28

Correct all errors in the employment of the infinitives below.

1 He wanted to have seen the headless horseman.
2 I think the criminal to be he.
3 To write with precision it is necessary to first have thought logically.
4 I know he to be a sheep in wolf's clothing.
5 To invariably be kind to children, angelic qualities are required.

PHRASES AND CLAUSES

A group of words may substitute for a part of speech. Compare the following groups:

The *green-eyed* monster.

The monster *with green eyes*.

The monster *that has green eyes*.

Clearly, *green-eyed* acts as an adjective, modifying the noun *monster*. But *with green eyes* and *that has green eyes* similarly modify *monster;* and consequently they are **adjectives** too. The group *with green eyes* is called a **phrase;** the other group *that has green eyes* is called a **subordinate clause.** Each forms a sense unit: each acts as a single part of speech expressing a **fragmentary** thought.

There is a distinction between the two elements, however. The **subordinate clause** has a subject (*that*) and predicate (*has green eyes*). The **phrase** has neither subject nor predicate, for it lacks a pivotal word—a verb.

PHRASE. A phrase is a group of words, containing neither subject nor predicate, which acts as a single part of speech.

Phrases may be classified according to use as nouns, adjectives, or adverbs.

Noun Phrase. *To do* is to *learn*.

The phrase *to do* acts as the subject and the phrase *to learn* as the complement (predicate nominative) of the linking verb *is*.

Adjective Phrase. Books *in black and red* were the clerk's delight.
The phrase *in black and red* modifies the noun *books*.

Adverbial Phrase. He shouted *on house tops*. The phrase *on house tops* modifies the verb *shouted*.

Note: Since any group of two or more related words constitutes a phrase, it is possible to distinguish:

A **Verb Phrase**—(consisting of the main verb and its auxiliaries)—*will thrust, will have thrust, will have been thrust;*

A **Phrase Preposition**—*with reference to, in preference to, in spite of, on account of, by means of;*

A **Phrasal Conjunction**—*in order that, as if, as though, in so far as, on condition that.*

However, it seems simpler to consider these as compound verbs, compound prepositions, or compound conjunctions.

Phrases may be classified, according to their introductory or pivotal word, as **prepositional, participial, infinitive,** or **gerund.** (Note that this is a classification according to form; it does not contradict the classification according to use.)

Prepositional Phrase. The time *for conversation* is not *before breakfast;* let us eat *in silence*. The prepositional phrase *for conversation* functions as an adjective, modifying the noun *time;* the prepositional phrase *before breakfast* functions as a predicate nominative after the linking verb *is;* the prepositional phrase *in silence* functions as an adverb, modifying the verb *eat*.

Participial Phrase. *Having joined the Rotary Club*, Sinclair Lewis felt like George Babbitt.
The participial phrase modifies the noun *Sinclair Lewis*. (The participial phrase may of course be used only as an adjective.)

Infinitive Phrase. *To read books* means to *enlarge one's horizons*. (Noun use of the infinitive phrase.)

He was looking for a book *to read*.
(Adjective use of the infinitive phrase.)

He read *to enlarge his horizons*.
(Adverbial use of the infinitive phrase.)

Gerund Phrase. *Reading books* enlarge's one's horizons.
(The gerund phrase may of course be used only as a noun.)

Absolute Phrase. A phrase may be **grammatically detached** from the rest of the sentence in which it occurs. Such a construction modifies no one word in the sentence, but instead the whole idea of the sentence.

A **participle**, plus the noun or pronoun it modifies, **may form an absolute phrase.**

The albatross having been slain, they were idle as a painted ship upon a painted ocean.
The italicized phrase, an absolute construction, really has an adverbial function, equalling *When the albatross was slain, they were idle . . .* The noun in the **substantive plus participle** construction is called the **nominative absolute.**

An infinitive may form an absolute phrase.

To tell the truth, I lied.

Note: Appositive and parenthetical phrases are sometimes considered absolute phrases.

Underline the phrases in the following sentences, classifying them as to use and form.

1 A bird in the hand is worth two in the bush.
2 Having seen three birds in the bush, he let the one in his hand fly away.
3 The birds in the bush having been captured, Jojo found his hands full.
4 He lived to snare birds and burn bushes.
5 To part from friends is to die a little.

CLAUSE. A clause is a group of words containing a subject and a verb. If the clause makes a statement capable of standing alone—if it 'makes a complete statement'—it is called a **main** (or **principal** or **independent**) clause. If the clause makes a statement that cannot stand alone—if it depends for its meaning on some other word or words in the sentence—it is called a **subordinate** (or **dependent**) clause.

Main Clause—is a group of words, containing a subject and a verb, which makes a complete statement.

Men come and go, but *the brook goes on for ever*.

The sentence contains two main clauses (italicized), each capable of standing alone. Note, however, that if either of the italicized parts stood alone, it would be classified as a simple sentence, not as a clause. **Clause** necessarily implies the larger whole of which it is a part.

Subordinate Clause—is a group of words, containing a subject and a verb, which depends on some other word or words in the sentence for its meaning. (It is always joined to the main clause by a joining word—a relative pronoun or a subordinating conjunction.)

Clauses are classified according to use as nouns, adjectives, and adverbs.

Noun Clause. He believes *that the devil likes angel cake*.

The noun clause functions as object of the verb *believes*.

Adjective Clause. The lady *who had two heads* could not credit the proverb *which declared* that two heads were better than one.

The first adjective clause modifies the noun *lady;* the second modifies the noun *proverb*.

Note: A relative pronoun in the objective case may be omitted:

This is the evidence [*which* or *that*] the detectives sought, and now they can arrest the men [*whom* or *that*] they have suspected.

Adverbial Clause. He cried *because he had spilt milk*.

The adverbial clause modifies the verb *cried*.

Elliptical Clause. The subject and predicate of a clause may be omitted when they can be supplied from the context:

He needs shock therapy more urgently than you [*do* or *need it*].

While [he was] eating, he kept talking relentlessly.

Note: When the elliptical (or omitted) subject differs from the subject of the main clause, a dangling construction results:

While eating, his words tumbled forth relentlessly.

Underline all the subordinate clauses below, noting the function of each.

1 She knew where she was going and how she would get there.
2 He ate when he was hungry and drank whenever he could.

3 He had but a single purpose, which he concealed from everybody, including himself.
4 Criminals who have status in their world frequently serve an apprenticeship in crime.
5 While making hay, you ought to see whether the sun is shining.

THE SENTENCE

A sentence is a group of words containing both subject and predicate and expressing a complete thought.

Sentences may be classified in two ways: by **use** and by **structure**.

Sentences Classified According to Use. Sentences may function in four ways.

Declarative sentence makes a statement.

In 1666 much of London was consumed by fire.

Note: A declarative sentence may of course make a false statement:

In 1620 the Great Fire of London occurred.

Interrogative sentence asks a question.

Where are the snows of yesteryear?

Imperative sentence issues a command or expresses an entreaty.

Give us this day our daily bread.

Note: Often, the subject of an imperative sentence is understood, not expressed. In the sentence given above, for example, the subject is *you* (understood).

Exclamatory sentence gives vent to strong feelings—of anger, sorrow, grief, surprise, or the like.

Oh, Hamlet, thou hast cleft my heart in twain!

Sentences Classified According to Structure. Four kinds of construction may be distinguished in sentences.

Simple sentence contains one subject and one predicate.

Men love.

This is the simplest form of the simple sentence, containing a noun for its subject and a finite verb for its predicate. The simple sentence may of course be lengthened by adding modifiers and a complement.

Neurotic men and women love only themselves. The compound subject (*men and women*) does not alter the simple construction: either subject or predicate or both may be compound.

Note: No matter how it is constructed (simple, compound, or complex), a sentence may be used to make a declarative, an interrogative, an imperative, or an exclamatory statement.

Compound sentence contains two or more main (principal, independent) **clauses.**

Man has his will, but woman has her way.

The independent clauses italicized are joined by the co-ordinating conjunction *but*. (A semicolon would have served as well: *Man has his will; woman has her way.*)

Complex sentence contains one main clause and one or more subordinate (dependent) **clauses.**

A woman's is the most inconsistent compound of obstinacy and self-sacrifice *that I have ever seen.*

(One main clause, not in italics, and one subordinate clause, in italics.)

Women are such a provoking class of society *because, though they are never right, they are never more than half wrong.*

(One main clause, not in italics, and two subordinate clauses: *because they are never more than half wrong* and *though they are never right.*)

Compound-complex sentence contains two or more main clauses and one or more subordinate clauses.

However great may be the love that unites them, a man and a woman are always strangers in mind and intellect; they remain combatants *who belong to different races.*

(Two main clauses, not in italics, and two subordinate clauses, in italics. The semicolon, substituting for a comma plus co-ordinating conjunction, links the two main clauses.)

Exercise No. 31

Convert the following simple declarative sentences into compound and complex sentences.

1 Jack loves Jill. Jill loves herself.
2 The pound has a diminished value. It no longer buys a good seat at the opera.
3 Ideas have consequences. The consequences are sometimes far-reaching.
4 He reached for the moon. He stubbed his toe.
5 The American way of speaking and writing differs from the English way. It is not therefore inferior.

SENTENCE ERRORS

AGREEMENT

Agreement between Subject and Verb

The verb must agree with its subject in number. Number, in English, applies to nouns, pronouns, and verbs. Number distinguishes between one and more than one: words which denote one (*tree, man*) are *singular*; words which denote more than one (*trees, men*) are *plural*. Thus, if the subject is singular, the verb that goes with it must be singular; if the subject is plural, the verb that goes with it must be plural:

The dog barks.   The singular verb *barks* agrees with the singular subject *dog*.
The dogs bark.   The plural verb *bark* agrees with the plural subject *dogs*.

Note: Most nouns form their plurals by adding *-s, -es, -ies: dogs, masses, ladies*. Most verbs form their singular by adding *-s:* he *barks*, she *walks*, it *moves*.

When the subject comes before the verb, usually no problem about agreement exists. However, there is sometimes difficulty when the word order is reversed, or when certain special constructions are used. These problems and their solutions are discussed in the sections below.

The number of the noun in a phrase introduced by the preposition *of* **does not affect the number of the verb.**

     SUBJ.   PHRASE   VERB
Right: A *list* (of many things) *has* been drawn up.
The true subject of this sentence *is* list, not *things*. Since *list* is singular, the verb agreeing with it must be singular—*has* (not *have*).

Exercise No. 32

Which of the italicized verbs is correct?

1 One of the cats (*scratch, scratches*) children.
2 The cause of typhoons (*is, are*) known.
3 Three months of my work (*was, were*) wasted.
4 Two ships of the Asiatic fleet (*is, are*) missing.
5 The longest of modern epics (*is, are*) Joyce's *Ulysses*.

Note: A plural verb follows the construction *one of those who* because the antecedent of *who* is plural (*those*).

George is one of those *men who* always *excel* in tests.

Note: Relative clauses introduced by *who, that,* or *which* take verbs agreeing with the antecedent of the pronoun.

Right: Ulysses is one of the most interesting *books that have* ever been written.

Ulysses is the subject of the linking verb *is*. The subject of the clause is *that;* its antecedent is the plural noun *books*. Therefore, the verb must also be plural—*have*.

Exercise No. 33

Which of the italicized verbs is correct?

1 Tests are one of the difficult ordeals that (*confront, confronts*) mankind.
2 Charles is one of those experienced accountants who never (*fail, fails*) to spot an error.
3 Geriatrics is one of the newest sciences that (*has, have*) commanded public interest.
4 Agreement is one of those points in grammar that always (*confuse, confuses*) me.
5 Ann is one of those mediocre singers that (*need, needs*) a less talented accompanist than Bob.

When the subject and predicate nominative differ in number, the verb agrees with the subject, *not* the complement.

SUBJ.   VERB   COMPLEMENT

Right: The *theme* of the novel *is* the *experiences* of an *au-pair* girl in London.

SUBJ.   VERB   COMPLEMENT

Right: The essential *difficulty was* the *hordes* of enemy tribes surrounding our camp.

Compound subjects (A + B) joined by *and* ordinarily take a plural verb.

A   +   B

Right: The *flower* and the *vine are* decayed.

Although each of these subjects is singular, when joined by *and* they become plural, and therefore the verb must be plural.

Note: Reversing normal word-order (that is, the subject-verb pattern) does not alter the rule about agreement between compound subjects and their verb.

A +   B

Right: Here *come John* and his *brother*.

A   +   B

Right: There *are* the *bread* and the *spice* for the stuffing.

There and *here* are always *adverbs* and can never be subjects.

Exercise No. 34

Which of the italicized verbs is correct?

1 Laughing and giggling (*irritate, irritates*) the dour man.
2 There but for the grace of God (*go, goes*) I.
3 (*Was, were*) there three patients due today?
4 Here in the desk, of all places, (*was, were*) the thermometer and the screwdriver.
5 Candlelight and white wine (*add, adds*) a touch of Venus.

Note: Compound subjects joined by *or, either . . . or, neither . . . nor, not only . . . but also* ordinarily take verbs agreeing in number with the near subject.

SUBJ.   SUBJ. VERB

Right: Neither *Norman* nor his *sister is* listening.

SUBJ.   SING. SUBJ.

Right: Not only *laymen* but also the *tax expert*

SING. VERB

makes errors.

SUBJ.   PLURAL SUBJ.

Right: Not only the *layman* but also *tax experts*

PLURAL VERB

make errors.

Exercise No. 35

Which of the italicized verbs is correct?

1 Either Bob or Ann (*has, have*) played a trick on us.
2 Here in suburbia neither Labour nor Conservative (*dominate, dominates*) local politics.
3 Neither the principal nor the teachers (*understand, understands*) John's behaviour.
4 Not only the technician in the studio but also the televiewers (*was, were*) amused by the antics of the comedian.
5 Some think that neither Amis nor Wain (*is, are*) destined for lasting neglect among novelists.

Note: Singular subjects (when followed by prepositional phrases introduced by *with, along with, together with, as well as*) ordinarily take a singular verb.

       SUBJ.

Right: Cleopatra, as well as her entire retinue,

VERB

was eager to meet Caesar.

       SUBJ.

Right: France, together with 5 other countries,

VERB

is attending the conference on Pollution.

As well as and *together with* introduce phrases which modify the subject, but are not themselves the subjects. Although formally correct, these constructions are often stilted. By substituting *and* for the preposition, a more normal sentence results. Note, however, the change in number.

      A   +   B

Right: Cleopatra and her *retinue were* eager to meet Caesar.

Exercise No. 36

Which of the italicized verbs is correct?

1 The soldier, along with his commanders, (*enter, enters*) the bivouac area.
2 Ellen, as well as the other girls in her form, (*dislike, dislikes*) classical music.
3 The suspect's attitude, together with the material evidence against him, (*was, were*) decisive in the verdict.
4 Beelzebub, as well as his Satanic cohorts, (*search, searches*) eternally new means to seduce mankind.
5 Bebop, played with Dixieland jazz in the background, (*lead, leads*) one to envy the deaf.

INDEFINITE PRONOUNS. Each of the following indefinite pronouns takes a singular verb:

anyone	everybody	nothing
everyone	somebody	anything
no one	someone	everything
each	either	neither

SUBJ.   PHRASE   VERB

Right: Each (of the men) *was* irritated by his work.

Right: Everybody here *knows* the importance of building vocabulary.

Each of the following indefinite pronouns takes a plural verb:

both   many   several   few

Right: Several were present at the meeting, but *few spoke.*

Each of the following indefinite pronouns is singular or plural depending upon the context of the sentence:

none   some   any   most   all   more

Right: None of the applicants *has* yet arrived.

Since *none*, an indefinite pronoun, is too vague to indicate number, we may safely turn to the context of the sentence. Although *applicants* is plural, the context suggests that *no one* of them has yet arrived.

But: *Some* (most, all, more) of the applicants *have* arrived.

Much of the task has been accomplished, but *some* of it still *remains* to challenge us.

All is lost.

Nouns of quantity, although plural in form, are often understood as collective units and therefore take singular verbs.

Right: Three-quarters of his talent *lies* in music.

Right: The *crowd shouts* its approval of the speaker.

Right: Seven *years is* a long time for a famine.

Right: The *jury takes* several hours to reach its verdict.

Note: If, however, the parts of the unit are considered more important than the unit as a collective whole, the verb must be plural.

Right: There *are* a *number* of men who will not accept the opinion of the majority.

Right: The *majority* of the class *are* interested in their work.

AGREEMENT BETWEEN PRONOUN AND ANTECEDENT

The pronoun must agree with its antecedent noun or pronoun in *number, person,* **and** *gender.*

Almost all errors in agreement between pronoun and antecedent result from confusion about number rather than about person or gender. Few people, for example, would write either:

The Englishman expects every man to do *her* duty. (Error in gender.)

England expects every man to do *your* duty. (Error in person.)

But many people might write:

England expects every man to do *their* duty. (Error in number.) The correct form of this sentence, of course, is:

England expects every *man* to do *his* duty.

The pronoun *his* has as its antecedent the noun *man*. Since *man* is singular in number, masculine in gender, and third person, the pronoun which refers to *man* must agree with it in each of these respects.

Note: A plural pronoun is used to refer to two or more singular antecedents joined by *and*.

Right: The *beautiful* and the *damned* have *their* place in fiction.

Right: In the modern theatre *romance* and *realism* have had *their* days.

Note: A singular pronoun is used to refer to two or more singular antecedents connected by *either . . . or*, *neither . . . nor*, *or*, *nor*, and the like.

Right: Neither Sophocles *nor* Aeschylus *has lost his* appeal.

Note: The pronoun is either singular or plural when it refers to a collective noun depending upon whether that noun is singular or plural in meaning.

Right: The jury gave *its* verdict.

Jury here means the members collectively, as a whole unit, and thus the pronoun is singular.

Right: The jury gave *their* verdict.

Jury here means the jurors individually, as if they were polled. Thus, the meaning is plural and the pronoun is plural.

Exercise No. 37

Write the correct form of the pronoun and the antecedent with which it agrees.

EXAMPLE:

Neither Goldilocks nor Red Riding Hood liked (*her*, *their*) animal friends.

CORRECT FORM	ANTECEDENT
her	Goldilocks
	Red Riding Hood

1 All must heed the laws of (*his*, *their*) land.
2 Each of the authors received (*his*, *their*) royalties.
3 The lass with the delicate air and the lad with the frightful mien went (*his*, *her*, *their*) separate ways.
4 Orwell is one of those authors who do (*his*, *their*) best to irritate the reader.
5 If anyone cries out, I'll shoot (*them*, *him*).
6 None of this material is pertinent now, but (*it*, *they*) may be later.
7 Whoever wishes to enter a claim on this property must make (*his*, *their*) wishes known at once.
8 Last week our chess team lost (*its*, *their*) final match.
9 Some stand and wait, but (*he*, *they*) also serve in the higher cause.
10 I won't join discussion groups because (*it*, *they*) take up too much of my limited time.

Note: To avoid the clumsy effect of 'he or she' or 'his or her' use the masculine pronoun except where the antecedent is clearly feminine.

Right: Each of the students wishes to have *his* say.

Although both boys and girls may be in the class, the sentence would gain little by adding 'his or her say'.

Right: Every student in the cooking class prepared *her* own batter.

Now the antecedent, although still of common gender, suggests through the context of the sentence that a feminine pronoun should be used.

Note: Maintain consistency in person between pronoun and antecedent. Shifts in person confuse the reader because they obscure point of view.

Wrong: I enjoy photography because *you* acquire a souvenir of whatever place *we* visit.

The original pronoun *I* is shifted twice in this sentence: to *you*, and again to *we*. Thus the reader no longer knows who is telling the story. Revised, the sentence reads logically.

Right: I enjoy photography because through it I acquire a souvenir of whatever place I visit.

Exercise No. 38

Rewrite the following passage so that a consistent relationship exists between the person of the pronoun and its antecedents.

Hesitantly, I approached the darkened stairwell where you could not help feeling the gloom enclose everyone. Although I was trembling, I began to mount the worn old steps we had trodden so often in the happier times of our youth. You just sensed that at the summit of those steps our whole lives would change, but I had to go on.

CASE OF PRONOUNS

The case of a pronoun depends on its use in the sentence. The pronoun agrees with its antecedent in number, person, and gender, but **not** in case. To avoid sentence errors involving case, watch for two trouble spots:

The distinct forms of the personal and relative pronouns in each of their three cases:

NOMINATIVE	OBJECTIVE	POSSESSIVE
I	me	my
he	him	his
she	her	her
we	us	our
they	them	their
who	whom	whose

The uses of the pronoun in the sentence:

Nominative
    Subject of a verb: *He* marches in the parade.
    Predicate Nominative: It is *they*.
    Direct Address: *You*, go away!
    Appositive: He who knows pain—*he* and *he* only—knows the fullness of life.

Objective
    Direct object of a verb: I admire *him*, but the others in his crowd, *whom* I know too well, I despise.
    Indirect object of a verb: I gave *him* a book.
    Object of a preposition: I know with *whom* you went. I gave it to *him*.
    Appositive: They nominated Henry for chairman—*him*, of all people.

Possessive
    To indicate possession, source, authorship, and similar relationships:
    I have read Johnson for *his* ironic wit.
    I know *whose* verse that is.
    Garlic has *its* own peculiar smell.
    Use the nominative form when the pronoun is subject of a sentence or clause, no matter what the antecedent of the pronoun is.
    Right: His family disinherited Cain because he was not a good brother.

Although *Cain*, antecedent of *he*, is in the objective case, *he* takes the nominative case because in its own clause it is the subject of the verb *was*.

Right: Cain was disinherited because his family considered him a bad brother.

Although *Cain*, antecedent of *him*, is in the nominative case, *him* remains objective because in its own clause it is the object of the verb *considered*.

After a linking verb, the pronoun usually takes the nominative case.

FORMAL: It is *I*. That is *he*. It is *they*.

INFORMAL: It's *me*. That's *him*. It's *them*.

This use of the objective case after a finite form of *to be* has become so common that it is generally considered to be acceptable.

Use the objective case when the pronoun is the direct or indirect object of a verb or preposition.

Wrong: Give that rod to James and I.

James and I is the object of the preposition *to*, but *I* is not the objective pronoun.

Right: Give that rod to James and me.

Wrong: He invited Jim and I to the dance.

Jim and I is the object of the verb, but *I* is not the objective case of the pronoun.

Right: He invited Jim and me to the dance.

Wrong: We resented the Shanes, both he and his wife.

He and his wife is in apposition with *Shanes*, and should be in the objective case after the verb *resented*.

Right: We resented the Shanes, both him and his wife.

Use the objective case when the pronoun acts either as subject of or as object of an infinitive.

Right: His instructors considered him to be promising.

Him is the subject of the infinitive *to be*.

Right: The investigators suspected the embezzler to be him.

Him is the object of the infinitive *to be*.

Before a gerund, the pronoun is usually in the possessive case.

Right: We fully approve of their marrying.

Marrying is a gerund, object of the preposition *of*. The error that may result is usually caused by the writer's assuming that the pronoun is also object of the preposition. Actually the pronoun is a possessive modifying the gerund. If the pronoun is used in the objective case—We fully approve of *them* marrying—the sentence sense is ambiguous, for it suggests that we like these young people, but leaves *marrying*, now a participial modifier, awkwardly modifying *them*.

Note: If the emphasis is intended to be on the person or thing, the pronoun should be in the objective case and should be modified by a participle.

Right: Often I worry about him working too hard.

The stress here is on *him* rather than on *working*.

Note: An indefinite pronoun cannot be used in the possessive case before a gerund:

Right: I know men who indulge in lying on occasion, but I cannot think of anyone indulging consistently.

Anyone is an indefinite pronoun.

Right: Many girls behave as she does, but I know of some behaving quite differently.

Some is an indefinite pronoun with no distinct form in the possessive.

Pronouns take the same case as the nouns or pronouns to which they are linked by co-ordinating or correlative conjunctions. Thus, if the noun or pronoun before the conjunction is in the nominative case, then the pronoun following the conjunction ought to be in the nominative case.

Wrong: Between him and I there is little to choose.

Him is object of the preposition *between*. *I*, linked to *him* by the conjunction *and*, should also be the object of the preposition and consequently in the objective case:

Right: Between him and me there is little to choose.

Wrong: Since the judges selected only one winner, neither Jim nor me won a prize.

Jim is subject of *won*. *Me*, joined to *Jim* by the correlative conjunction *nor*, should also be part of the subject and consequently in the nominative case:

Right: Since the judges selected only one winner, neither Jim nor I won a prize.

Note: *But* may act as a preposition as well as a conjunction. In its function as a preposition *but* means 'except,' and is followed by the objective case:

Right: Everyone fled but him.

Pronouns in apposition take the same case as the noun or pronoun of which they are appositives.

Right: All will attend the party—they and we. The subject of the verb *will attend* is *all. They and we* is in apposition with *all*, and therefore takes the nominative case.

Right: He murdered both of them—him and her.

The object of the verb *murdered* is *both. Him and her* is in apposition with *both*, and therefore takes the objective case.

The conjunctions *than* and *as* have no effect upon the case of the pronoun which follows them.

Wrong: You can be taller than her.

Than is a conjunction introducing the clause *than she is* (understood). The writer has misused it as a preposition and made *her* the object of the preposition.

Right: You can be taller than she [is].

Wrong: I am as happy as them.

Right: I am as happy as they [are].

Avoid substituting the reflexive for the personal pronoun.

Wrong: The Johnsons have a splendid present for Hilda and myself.

The reflexive pronoun should be used to indicate an action reflecting back upon the subject, as in *I hate myself*. In the sentence cited, no such action takes place.

Right: The Johnsons have a splendid present for Hilda and me.

The case of the relative pronouns *who* and *whom* is determined by their use in the sentence.

Nominative: This is the agent who is responsible for the sabotage.

who acts as subject of the verb *is*.

We tried to determine who she was.

who is the complement of *was*, not the object of the infinitive to *determine*.

Objective: Give the car to whomever you wish.

whomever is the object complement of *wish*.

He learned that Pennsfield, whom he despised, was an informer.
whom is the object of *despised*.
Whom are you speaking to?
whom is the object of the preposition *to*.
Note: To decide whether the nominative or the objective case of the relative pronoun ought to be employed, substitute a personal pronoun for the relative:
who or *whom* is responsible
he or *him* is responsible
He is obviously the correct answer, and the corresponding form of *he* is the relative *who;* therefore, *who is responsible* is the correct form.
who or *whom* are you speaking to?
you are speaking to *who* or *whom?*
you are speaking to *he* or *him?*
Him is correct, and the corresponding form of *him* is the relative *whom*; therefore, *whom are you speaking to?* is the proper form.
To distinguish between *whoever* and *whomever* note that
whoever the one *who*
whomever the one *whom*
Note: Parenthetic expressions like *I believe, I think*, or *he says* do not affect the case of the relative pronoun.
Wrong: He is the man whom I think pilfered the sleeping pills.
I think is merely parenthetic. The subject of the verb *pilfered* is *who*. Try substituting the personal pronoun to prove that *who* is correct; *he* or *him pilfered?* Clearly, the answer is *he pilfered*, and the relative pronoun corresponding with *he* is *who*.
Right: He is the man who I think pilfered the sleeping pills.
Wrong: That irritating fellow who they say everyone tried to avoid has finally gone abroad.
They say is parenthetic and does not influence the case of the relative pronoun. The object of the infinitive *to avoid* is *whom*. Everyone tried to avoid *him*.
Right: That irritating fellow whom they say everyone tried to avoid has finally gone abroad.

Exercise No. 39

Select the proper case for each of the following pronouns.

1 David and (*I, me*) are going to the meeting.
2 Laura is a girl (*who, whom*) may make my life difficult.
3 I cannot conceive of (*he, his, him*) accepting the post.
4 Did you hear about George and (*she, her*) eating live snails?
5 The debate between his brother and (*he, him*) ended in a draw.
6 I believe they are deliberately plotting against (*we, us*) boys.
7 Do you suspect it is (*they, them*)?
8 I cannot bear the thought of (*his, him*) going away.
9 (*Who, whom*) do you wish to send this letter to?
10 The principles he preaches convince neither (*he, him*) nor (*I, me*).
11 I refuse to talk to anyone but (*he, him*).
12 We insisted that we were as intelligent as (*they, them*).
13 Bill divided the money between John and (*he, him, himself*).
14 The reporter took the names of only two people, (*he, him*) and (*I, me*).
15 (*Whoever, whomever*) assumes his statement true is foolish.

16 Here is the fellow (*who, whom*) I believe asked about your trip.
17 The hat fitted Bob better than (*I, me*).
18 Not a single one of (*us, we*) men will support that troublemaker.
19 If only that could have been (*we, us*).
20 Did you wish the winner to be (*he, him*)?

REFERENCE OF PRONOUNS

The pronoun substitutes for the noun. Unlike the noun, the pronoun does not name, but refers to the word (antecedent) that does name the person, place, or thing being discussed:

Williams answers the door because he is a butler.

He is the pronoun which refers to the person *Williams*. Because it functions as a word of reference, the pronoun must be placed with extreme care so that no doubt exists about the noun to which it refers:

When Mary looked at her sister, she blushed.

She may refer to its immediate antecedent, or to *Mary;* consequently, the reference of the pronoun *she* is ambiguous. **To avoid ambiguous reference:**

The pronoun must be placed as near as possible to its logical antecedent:

Mary blushed when she looked at her sister.

The antecedent must be supplied or repeated:

When she looked at her sister, Mary blushed.

The sentence must be recast to achieve clarity:

Looking at her sister, Mary blushed.

The sections below discuss several problems in accurate reference of pronouns.

Avoid placing the pronoun in a position where it may refer to more than one antecedent.

Wrong: Stephen followed Tommy into a corner, where he hid.

He may refer either to *Stephen* or to *Tommy*, and is, consequently, ambiguous.

Right: Stephen followed Tommy into a corner and saw him hide there.

The related nouns and pronouns are now in parallel order.

Stephen, subject of the verb *followed*, corresponds with the understood subject of the verb *saw;* Tommy, object of the verb *followed*, corresponds with the pronoun in the objective case, *him*.

Right: Tommy hid in the corner to which Stephen had followed him.

Wrong: Bill told his friend that he would soon be home.

He may refer either to *friend* or to *Bill*. The sentence needs to be recast.

Right: Bill told his friend, 'I will be home soon'.

Wrong: Craven asked Nevins whether his car would be safe in his garage.

This sentence represents confusion worse confounded. Four meanings are possible:

Nevins' car, Nevins' garage
Craven's car, Craven's garage
Nevins' car, Craven's garage
Craven's car, Nevins' garage

The sentence must be recast.

Right: Craven asked Nevins, 'Will my car be safe in your garage?'

Note: Avoid explaining the ambiguous pronoun by placing its antecedent in brackets:

Awkward: Craven asked Nevins whether his (Craven's) car would be safe in his (Nevins') garage.

Avoid using pronouns to stand for ideas rather than for nouns. Most errors of this kind are caused by the demonstrative pronouns (*this, that*) and the relative pronouns (*who, which, that*).

Vague: Valerie brought home from school several excellent ceramics and watercolours. This made her family extremely proud.

This has no actual antecedent in the preceding sentence. The pronoun suggests only the implied idea that all of Valerie's activities brought pleasure to her family. But pronouns do not refer to implied ideas; they refer only to specific antecedents. Therefore the sentence must be recast.

Right: When Valerie brought home from school several excellent ceramics and watercolours, her family was extremely proud.

Right: The ceramics and watercolours Valerie brought home from school made her family extremely proud.

Note: The demonstrative pronouns may on occasion be used correctly without an antecedent:

Right: He eats garlic. *That* is why he gets a seat in the underground.

That refers clearly to an idea expressed by the whole clause.

Right: This is the way we wash clothes.

Right: That is Alan bowling now.

In each of these constructions the pronoun stands for a noun which follows rather than precedes the pronoun. *This* stands for *way*, *that* stands for *Alan*.

Wrong: We tried to complete the book in a month, which is why we were utterly exhausted. *Which* refers only to the implied idea of the preceding clause, not to any specific antecedent.

Avoid using the pronouns *it, you,* and *they* to stand for ideas rather than nouns.

Wrong: The employer intended to wish good cheer to each of his workers. He knew it would make a splendid impression on them.

It refers to the general notion of good wishes, but has no specific antecedent.

Right: The employer intended to wish good cheer to each of his workers. He knew that such a message would make a splendid impression upon them. A noun, *message*, has been supplied.

Right: The employer knew that sending a message of good cheer to his workers would make a splendid impression upon them.

The sentence has been recast.

Wrong: It says in my notebook that pronouns must have clear reference.

It has no specific antecedent.

Right: My notebook contains the statement that pronouns must have clear reference.

Note: Avoid repeating the same pronoun within a single sentence when the pronoun has different antecedents.

Wrong: The club was the scene of a nightly brawl; nevertheless it was patronized by men who liked participating in it.

The first *it* intends referring to *club*, the second to *brawl*. But the combination is clumsy and confusing.

Right: Though the scene of nightly brawls, the club was patronized by men who liked participating in them.

Right: The club was the scene of a nightly brawl; nevertheless, men who liked participating in it patronized the club.

Note: *It* may on occasion be correctly used without an antecedent:

Impersonal expressions. *It is raining; it is damp.*

Constructions in which *it* stands for a noun or noun equivalent which follows rather than precedes. *It is a splendid day. It* stands for the noun *day* which follows.

Wrong: If you look for the pot of gold, you may find it.

Unless the pronoun *you* refers to a specific person (as 'You George', or 'You, the reader'), avoid using the impersonal second person pronoun. Here *you* seems to refer generally to anybody.

Better: If one looks for the pot of gold, one (*or he*) may find it.

The impersonal pronoun *one* avoids the inaccuracy of impersonal *you*, but it is often a stiff and formal usage. A wiser procedure involves recasting the entire sentence:

Right: The man who searches for the pot of gold may find it.

Wrong: They say that the new group of recruits is well educated.

The indefinite use of *they* seems to refer to some far removed authority or to people generally. Use a specific antecedent.

Right: Army Officials say that the new crop of recruits is well educated.

Avoid referring to an antecedent so remote from the pronoun that the central meaning of a sentence is obscured.

Wrong: The Aztecs for centuries held great power in Mexico. The lakes were filled in and a great city developed. They brought with them many cultural patterns hitherto unknown to the natives.

They, introducing the third sentence, refers to *Aztecs*, the subject of the first sentence. But the antecedent is so remote from the pronoun that the loose reference causes obscurity.

Right: The Aztecs for centuries held great power in Mexico. They filled in the lakes, introduced cultural patterns hitherto unknown to the natives, and developed a great city.

The pronoun *they* has been brought nearer to its antecedent *Aztecs*, and the other elements of the sentence have been arranged in parallel construction.

Avoid referring to an antecedent in a subordinate construction.

Wrong: We bought copies of the publication he was selling to earn some pocket money. It was *The Exchange and Mart*.

It refers awkwardly to *publication*, object of the preposition *of*. The phrase, a subordinate construction in the sentence, is lifted to undue prominence, and the central meaning of the sentence is obscured.

Right: We bought copies of the publication he was selling to earn some pocket money. He was selling *The Exchange and Mart*. The antecedent has been repeated to clarify the reference. The revision is still slightly awkward.

Right: We bought copies of *The Exchange and Mart*, the publication he was selling to earn some pocket money.

Exercise No. 40

Rewrite the following sentences, correcting all faults in reference.

1 The Clean-up T.V. Association sent a magazine to its readers which had many wholesome suggestions.

2 If your hat does not fit your head, it should be made smaller.

3 Edward's father is returning from abroad, which will make him happy.
4 They say that everything will get better next year.
5 The Railway Board plans to increase the fare in order to reduce the annual deficit. This will be a hardship on commuters.
6 Chaucer wrote entertainingly about the Middle Ages. These were years in which feudalism and religion exercised profound influence on noble and serf alike. He tells of these matters in *The Canterbury Tales*.
7 Although it was a dull party for me, it was amazing how many there enjoyed it.
8 If you borrow material from another writer's work, it should be acknowledged.
9 In Franklin's *Autobiography*, it gives precepts on thrift.
10 Beethoven's later works are remarkable, more so when you consider that he was deaf when he wrote them.

VERBS

Sequence of Tenses

Logical sequence of tenses—adjusting the tense of the verb in the subordinate clause to the tense of the verb in the main clause—ought to be maintained. Violating tense sequence often effects awkward or ambiguous constructions.

Noun, adverbial, and adjective clauses present different problems.

NOUN CLAUSES. If the verb in the main clause is in the past perfect tense, the verb in the noun clause is generally (though not invariably) **in the past or past perfect tense.**

MAIN CLAUSE   SUBORDINATE CLAUSE

He $\begin{Bmatrix} \textit{believed} \\ \textit{had believed} \end{Bmatrix}$ that he $\begin{Bmatrix} \textit{trisected} \\ \textit{had trisected} \end{Bmatrix}$ angles

Using dates may clarify the principle involved:

He *believed* (in 1976) that he *trisected* angles (in 1976).

He *had believed* (in 1974, presumably before being disillusioned) that he *trisected* angles (in 1974).

He *believed* (in 1975) that he *had trisected* angles (in 1974).

He *had believed* (in 1973) that he *had trisected* angles (in 1972).

Note: The principle—that a past in the noun clause follows a past in the main clause—applies with especial force to indirect discourse:

He *said* that he *was* Napoleon.

If the verb in the main clause is in the present tense, the present perfect tense, the future tense, or the future perfect tense, the verb in the subordinate clause may be in any tense at all.

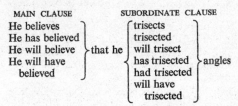

MAIN CLAUSE   SUBORDINATE CLAUSE

He believes
He has believed
He will believe ⟩ that he
He will have
    believed

⟨ trisects
trisected
will trisect
has trisected ⟩ angles
had trisected
will have
    trisected

To express some universal truth (real or supposed), **a past tense in the main clause may be followed by a present tense in the subordinate clause.**

MAIN CLAUSE		SUBORDINATE CLAUSE
He *believed*	that	angles *are* trisectable
He *had believed*	that	angels *guard* us

ADVERBIAL CLAUSES. If the verb in the main clause is in the past perfect tense, the verb in the subordinate clause is in the past or past perfect tense.

MAIN CLAUSE   SUBORDINATE CLAUSE

He $\left\{ \begin{array}{l} was \\ had\ been \end{array} \right\}$ honest although he $\left\{ \begin{array}{l} was \\ had\ been \end{array} \right\}$ rich

If the verb in the main clause is in the present, present perfect, future, or future perfect tense, the verb in the subordinate clause may be in any tense at all.

MAIN CLAUSE   SUBORDINATE CLAUSE

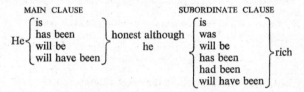

Note: In an adverbial clause of *degree* (one which tells *how much* or to what extent) or of *comparison*, any tense may be used in the subordinate clause (regardless of the tense of the verb in the main clause):

He *weighed* as much as *I shall weigh* after my diet.

He *will like* you better than he *has liked* his wife.

ADJECTIVE CLAUSES. In adjective clauses, the subordinate verb may express any time that the sense demands.

Freud formulated the theory which men *ignored* at first, which they *attack* now, and which they *will accept* ultimately.

INFINITIVES. The **present infinitive** shows action taking place *at the same time as* (or *after*) the action of the main verb.

He wanted *to read* all books, *to swim* all rivers, *to love* all women.

The **perfect infinitive** shows action taking place *before* the action of the main verb.

He wanted *to have been* rich, *to have been* rich from birth, to have had the experiences of those born rich.

They are glad *to have helped*, but they expect to be paid.

PARTICIPLES. The **present participle** shows action taking place *at the same time as* the action of the main verb.

Hating mankind, Swift nevertheless loved Tom, Dick, and Harry.

The **perfect participle** shows action taking place *before* the action of the main verb.

Having embarked for Utopia, he landed in Virginia Water.

Note: More informally, the present participle may show action taking place before the action of the main verb:

Embarking for Utopia, he landed in Virginia Water.

Exercise No. 41

Choose the correct form of the tense in each of the following:

1 The artist, plainly a better critic than painter, destroyed what he (*laboured over, had laboured over*) for ten years.
2 The man insisted that he (*had once seen, once saw*) a mermaid riding a sea-horse.
3 He declared that he (*wore, wears*) no man's mantle.
4 They never saw snakes when they (*have visited, visited*) Ireland.
5 Einstein thought Newton had missed the point, that he (*neglected, had neglected*) important data.
6 He regretted (*being born, having been born*).
7 The ambitious sergeant hoped (*to be, to have been*) a general.
8 The books were infinitely dull and Gulliver had only a small capacity for boredom; consequently he wanted (*to have read, to read*) them—reading them was too painful a task.
9 (*Having been taught, Being taught*) manners by my heavy-handed father, I suppressed my yawns.
10 (*Reaching, Having reached*) for the moon, he brought down a star.

SHALL AND WILL. In informal speech and writing, *will* **frequently does duty for all three persons.** This is an insensitive usage, however. A precise use of *shall* and *will* makes possible many delicate shades of meaning and it is well worth mastering the principles that govern their use:

Shall expresses **simple futurity** in the **first person,** singular and plural; *will* expresses **simple futurity** in the **second and third persons,** singular and plural.

SIMPLE FUTURITY

1 I shall	We shall
2 You will	You will
3 He, she, it will	They will

I *shall* drown; nobody *will* help me.
Here the speaker predicts only—he does not exhibit any determination to drown. (If he did, the sentence would read: 'I *will* drown; nobody *shall* help me'.)
He will try to make his getaway, but perhaps we shall be too much for him.
The baby's cries will grow hard to bear; I shall pop him into the frigidaire.
Will expresses **determination** in the **first person,** singular and plural; *shall* expresses **determination** in the **second and third persons,** singular and plural.

DETERMINATION

1 I will	We will
2 You shall	You shall
3 He, she, it shall	They shall

Thou *shalt* worship no other god.
The weather man says, 'It *will* rain'; God says, 'It *shall* rain'.
We *will* keep the commandments.
In questions, the form expected in the answer is used:
Shall God be denied? (God shall not be denied.)
Will you take this woman? (I will.)
Contractions
INFORMALLY:
I shall or *I will* becomes *I'll.*
You will or *you shall* becomes *you'll.*

He will or *he shall* becomes *he'll*.

We shall or *we will* becomes *we'll*.

They will or *they shall* becomes *they'll*.

The negative *will not* becomes *won't*.

The negative *shall not* becomes *shan't*.

Note: *I'd*, *you'd*, *he'd*, etc. are the corresponding contractions for *should* and *would*, the past forms of *shall* and *will*.

Exercise No. 42

Choose the correct form of the verb in each of the following sentences.

1 What (*shall, will*) we do with the drunken sailor?

2 We (*shall, will*) go to the park today if the weather remains pleasant.

3 What (*shall, will*) we do now, what (*shall, will*) we ever do?

4 If I lend you my best collection of records, (*will, shall*) you return it?

5 Yes, I promise absolutely that I (*shall, will*) return them next week.

6 'That young man,' said the future president's father, '(*shall, will*) be a famed man one day.'

7 If I die, no soul (*shall, will*) pity me.

8 These are the principles which I know (*will, shall*) have their way, no matter how formidable the attempt to defeat them.

9 The studio posted a notice which read: 'No one (*shall, will*) enter while the red light is on.'

10 Next week, I (*shall, will*) return all the books I have borrowed.

TROUBLESOME AUXILIARIES. Eight auxiliary verbs share the function of mood and show the manner in which a statement is made. These auxiliaries express:

1 **potentiality** (ability or possibility): *may, might, can, could.*

2 **condition**: *should, would.*

3 **obligation**: *must, ought.*

Note: The auxiliaries are followed by the infinitive without *to*.

Compare: Women can *play* while men *must* work.

with

Women are able *to play* while men are obliged *to work*.

These auxiliaries are frequent sources of error because their meaning shifts with shifting contexts.

May implies **permission, doubt,** or **possibility.**

You *may* rest tomorrow.

He *may* be telling the truth.

It *may* rain tonight.

Might, though the past tense of *may*, does not necessarily represent past time. Often it implies **more doubt,** a greater dependence on circumstances than *may*:

If the clouds are salted, the rains *might* come. Here *might* presents a future possibility in spite of its past form.

Can implies **ability**:

We *can* still win.

You may leave if you *can* walk.

The preceding sentence might be translated:

'You are permitted to leave if you are able to walk.'

Note: The distinction between *can* and *may* still holds in formal speech and writing, but it is sometimes disregarded in informal speech and writing. The construction *can't* frequently replaces mayn't: 'We can't leave without permission.'

Could, although the past tense of *can*, does not necessarily represent past time. Often it implies a **more uncertain condition** than *can*.

She *could* refuse, but she never does.

Note: Here *could* presents a future ability, in spite of its past form.

Should **expresses futurity from the standpoint of some past time:**

I said that I *should* help if called. *Should* is future with respect to *said*.

Note: Normally *should* and *would* are governed by the same rules that govern shall and will:

SIMPLE FUTURITY		DETERMINATION	
1 I should	we should	I would	we would
2 you would	you would	you should	you should
3 he, she, it, would	they would	he, she, it, should	they should

In reporting indirectly, *should* **may substitute for the** *shall* **of direct speech:**

Direct: 'I shall return in lilac time,' the poet declared.

Indirect: I declared that I should return in lilac time.

Usually, *should* does not represent past time; rather it implies duty or fitness; doubt or hesitancy; supposition or condition. To express these meanings, *should* is used for all three persons, singular and plural.

I *should* hardly think so.

Properly, you *should* wear a black tie.

He *should* pass his examination.

If they *should* attack, they will attack in force.

If I *should* die before I wake, I pray the Lord my soul to take.

Note: *Should* is probably used most often to express duty or condition.

Would **expresses futurity from the standpoint of some past time.**

He said that he *would* help if he could.

In reporting indirectly, *would* **may stand for the** *will* **of direct speech:**

Direct: 'There will be bloody heads,' the barman commented.

Indirect: The barman commented that there would be bloody heads.

Usually, *would* does not represent past time; rather, it implies habitual action, determination, or condition:

Charles Churchill *would* go to bed drunk night after night.

I *would* go, I decided, in spite of all their protests.

If she were shrewd, she *would* resist their offer.

Note: In the last sentence, note that *would* appears in the main clause. In standard English, *would* (unlike *should*) is not used in an if-clause.

Must **implies necessity or obligation:**

Night *must* fall.

You *must* see his new twelve-act play.

Must **may also express conviction, in the teeth of contradictory evidence:**

Mars *must* be inhabited.

Note: *Must*, originally a past tense, is used only in the present.

Ought **implies duty or obligation** (more strongly than *should*):

You *ought* not to beat your wives.

He *ought* to make the most of his small abilities.

Note: *Ought* is used with *to* plus the infinitive (unlike the other auxiliaries, which omit *to*).

Exercise No. 43

Choose the correct auxiliary in each of the following sentences.

1 We (*can, may*) still beat them if we try.
2 If a peace treaty is signed, the world (*may, might*) relax.
3 I believe that we (*can, could*) swim the channel, if it were not too rough.
4 The operator said that she (*should, would*) ring us when she had obtained our number.
5 Because she is my sister, I (*should, would*) attend her wedding.
6 I want no argument. You (*ought, should, must*) to listen when I am speaking.
7 If you (*can, may*) relax sufficiently tonight, you (*should, ought*) be in good shape for the walk tomorrow.
8 The captain insisted that he (*should, would*) lead his team to victory.
9 Do you think I (*can, may*) get permission from the principal to leave school early tomorrow?
10 He (*should, would*) not climb to the peak of Everest if he were really intelligent.

ADJECTIVES AND ADVERBS

Many errors result from failure to recognize similarities and dissimilarities between the functions of adjectives and adverbs.

Similarities. Both modify other parts of speech.

It is a *lovely* tree.

The adjective *lovely* describes or modifies the noun tree.

He followed her *rapidly*.

The adverb *rapidly* describes or modifies the verb *followed*.

Certain adverbs and adjectives have identical forms.

I have a *high* opinion of him.	Adjective
Send the kite *high*.	Adverb
Late guests are always welcome.	Adjective
But don't always come *late*.	Adverb
Edward lives a *fast* (colloquial) life.	Adjective
Edward drives too *fast*.	Adverb

Both have degrees of comparison.

	POSITIVE	COMPARATIVE	SUPERLATIVE
ADJECTIVES	good	better	best
	bad	worse	worst
	cold	colder	coldest
ADVERBS	well	better	best
	badly	worse	worst
	coldly	colder	coldest

Dissimilarities. Adjectives modify nouns or pronouns by identifying, limiting, or describing them.

Mock turtle soup is *delicious*.

Adjective *delicious* describes or modifies the noun *soup*.

He is *handsome*.

Adjective *handsome* modifies pronoun *he*.

Adverbs modify other sentence elements, generally verb, adjective, or other adverb.

The boxer *deftly* jabbed his left.

Adverb *deftly* modifies the verb *jabbed*.

This hot chocolate is *extraordinarily* sweet.

Adverb *extraordinarily* modifies adjective *sweet*.

The preacher spoke *exceedingly* well.

Adverb *exceedingly* modifies adverb *well*.

Eating *slowly* conduces to better digestion.

The adverb *slowly* modifies the gerund *eating*.

Thus: 1   Learn the conventions which govern each form.

       2   Note how the word is used in the sentence before using the adjective or adverb form.

Note: Do not allow an adjective to modify a verb:

Wrong: He eats *rapidly* and *sloppy*.

The adjective *sloppy* cannot modify the verb *eats*. Substitute the adverb *sloppily*.

Note: An adjective, not an adverb, is generally used to complete the meaning of the following verbs and to describe their subjects: *to be, become, seem, appear*.

Right: The story of Cyrano is *sad*.

Right: Suddenly he became *silly*.

Right: Their situation seems *desperate*.

Right: The plot increasingly appeared *absurd*.

Note: Adjectives are generally used after the sensory verbs: *feel, taste, sound, look, smell*, and after verbs like *remain, prove*, and *grow*.

Right: Edmond felt *happy* about winning his scholarship.

Happy describes (or modifies) *Edmond*, not the verb *felt*. Since it is the noun rather than the verb which is modified, an adjective rather than an adverb should be used.

The crêpe suzettes we ate last night tasted *sour*. *Sour* modifies the noun *crêpe suzettes*, not the verb *tasted*.

Hoagy's arrangement of Orpheus sounds *good*.

Good modifies the noun *arrangement*, not the verb *sounds*.

Now that I've seen Edwina, Julie looks *beautiful*.

Beautiful modifies the noun *Julie*, not the verb *looks*.

The brandy sauce smells *sweet*.

Sweet modifies the noun *sauce*, not the verb *smells*.

Note, however, that if the *manner* of feeling, tasting, and the like is required, an adverb should be used.

Right: After his nose was broken, George smelt *badly*.

The adverb *badly* describes George's ability to smell, not his personal effluvium.

Right: She looked *sadly* about her.

The adverb *sadly* describes the *manner* in which the girl observed her surroundings.

Note that the distinction between *bad* and *badly* falls within this category.

I feel *bad*. Adjective suggesting poor health, poor spirits or remorse.

I feel *badly*. Adverb meaning literally that the sense of touch is impaired.

A useful device to distinguish whether adjective or adverb ought to be used is this: For the sensory verb followed by the adjective substitute a form of *to be*. If the resulting construction appears sensible, allow it to stand; otherwise substitute an adverb for the adjective.

Do you feel (dizzy, dizzily)?

For the sensory verb *feel* substitute a form of *to be* (*are*) and add the adjective.

Right: Are you dizzy?

He looked (foolish, foolishly) as he wandered about the room.

For the sensory verb *looked* substitute a form of *to be* (*is*) and add the adjective: He is foolish. In this example the result is obviously nonsensical; therefore the adverbial and not the adjectival form must be used:

He looked *foolishly* about the room.

Note: After a verb and its direct object, the modifier may be either an adverb or an adjective depending upon its function in the sentence. It is an adverb if it modifies the verb, an adjective if it modifies the noun or pronoun.

Right: Kerner held the rudder *steady*. Adjective *steady* is correct, for it suggests that the *rudder* is steady.

Right: Kerner held the rudder *steadily*. Adverb *steadily* is also correct, for here the implication is that Kerner *held* steadily, and so the adverb modifies the verb.

Exercise No. 44

Select the correct form and give your reason. If more than one form is correct, explain why.

1 I can't hear the actors (*good, well*) from the last row.
2 Walcott lost the fight quite (*easy, easily*).
3 I study this book so that I can write (*proper, properly*).
4 The marlin looked (*fresh, freshly*) to the old man.
5 We thought that *Saint Joan* was a (*profound, profoundly*) serious play.
6 I can't read (*good, well*) with these glasses.
7 Violets will smell (*sweet, sweetly*) in the sitting-room.
8 The damp air (*certain, certainly*) feels (*good, well*) after that long dry spell.
9 The prospect of yet another war makes him feel (*wretched, wretchedly*).
10 She clasped the infant (*tight, tightly*) in her arms.
11 He rides his mount (*good, well*).
12 The Secretary of State stood (*firm, firmly*) in his decision.
13 The dazed victim of the accident gazed (*helpless, helplessly*) across the road.
14 Some actors speak their lines far too (*loud, loudly*).
15 Some actresses speak (*soft, softly*), but the gallery-goers hear them (*clear, clearly*) nevertheless.
16 The orchestra sounded (*cacophonous, cacophonously*) at rehearsal.
17 Most (*gentle, gently*) he stroked the cat's fur.
18 The verdict of guilty made the prisoner feel (*angrily, angry*) towards the jury.
19 I added the bill (*wrong, wrongly*) when she bought her cat's meat.
20 The aeroplane flew by too (*quick, quickly*) for me to see it, but it (*definite, definitely*) sounded (*noisy, noisily*).

Comparisons must be complete and logical. When two subjects are being compared, use the **comparative** form of the adjective or adverb.

Right: Of Orwell's two satires, I think *Animal Farm* the better.

Better is the comparative form of the *adjective*, and ought to be used here. *Best*, the superlative, would be correct if the sentence read: *Animal Farm* is the best of Orwell's works.

When the comparative degree of an adjective or adverb is used, exclude the subject of the comparison from the class with which it is compared.

Wrong: Writers are generally more neurotic than people.

Writers, the subject of the comparison, cannot logically be compared with *people*, the class or group.

Right: Writers are generally more neurotic than *other* people.

The word *other* excludes *writers* from the class with which it has been compared.

Wrong: A nuclear weapon is more destructive than any implement of warfare.

Right: A nuclear weapon is more destructive than any *other* implement of warfare.

Compare only things which can logically be compared.

Wrong: His skis are as well polished as an Olympic champion.

This sentence is absurd because it implies a comparison between *skis* and an *Olympic champion*.

Right: His skis are as well polished as *those* of an Olympic champion.

Right: His skis are as well polished as an Olympic champion's.

Wrong: Wordsworth, undeniably one of our greatest poets, is undeniably prosier than any poet in English literature.

The comparison is absurd because it suggests that Wordsworth was more prosy than anyone, including himself.

Right: Wordsworth, undeniably one of our greatest poets, is often prosier than *any other* poet in English literature.

Complete each comparison before modifying it.

Wrong: Our Bentley is as old as, if not older than, Bill's.

Right: Our Bentley is as old as Bill's, if not older.

Wrong: Muriel is as short as, if not shorter than, her brother.

Right: Muriel is as short as her brother, if not shorter.

Some adjectives are absolute and must not be compared: *unique, round, square, perfect, empty, dead, opposite, entirely.*

Wrong: This is a very unique example of a Persian ceramic cat.

Since unique means 'only one of a kind', it cannot logically be qualified. Thus, the adverb *very* must be omitted.

Note: The same principle applies to words like 'rounder', 'more square', and the like, for objects cannot logically be more round or square than what is already round or square.

Nevertheless, **in colloquial usage, these superlatives are often qualified:** *a more perfect union, roundest head, more completely*, and the like.

Avoid the vague, half-finished comparison.

Wrong: It was *so* pleasant.

So may carry meaning when the person hears the enthusiasm of the speaker, but in writing, it suggests that half a sentence has been written.

Right: It was so pleasant that we must return again.

Right: It was pleasant.

Wrong: He is such a good-hearted fellow.

Right: He is a good-hearted fellow.

Right: He is such a good-hearted fellow that people can't help suspecting him.

The adverbs *but, hardly, never, only, scarcely,* **have negative meanings, and when used in sentences require no other word of negation.**

Wrong: We did not hardly have time to eat. Since *hardly* has a negative meaning, combining it with *did not* produces a faulty double negative.

Right: We did not have time to eat.

Right: We hardly had time to eat.

Exercise No. 45

Some of the following sentences are correct; some contain errors of faulty comparison. Let those which are correct stand, but make any necessary corrections in the others.

1 Most students believe that their writing is better than their fellow students.
2 We had a larger rainfall in the South in 1900 than in any other year.
3 We think that our cat is almost as unique as any cat.
4 Keeping tropical fish is almost as time-consuming, if not more so, than growing cacti.
5 Lydia has more trouble taking care of Philip than anyone.
6 His collection of antiques is as valuable as that owned by the best museums.
7 Valerie can sing as well as anyone in her class.
8 Clumsiness is the worst of his faults.
9 Many soldiers have found that being in politics is not so simple as the army.
10 I have heard both his speeches, and I think yesterday's clearly the best.

PROBLEMS INVOLVING THE USE OF MODIFIERS

Modifiers are words, phrases, or clauses which alter the meaning of other sentence elements by limiting, describing, or emphasizing them.

I wear a coat of brocaded silk in the woodland house that I share with my friend.

of brocaded silk—phrase modifying *coat.*

woodland—word modifying *house.*

that I share with my friend—clause modifying *house.*

When each modifier is in its proper place, it adds depth to an otherwise simple statement: I wear a coat in my house. If, however, the modifiers are incorrectly placed, the sentence becomes confusing:

I wear a coat of brocaded silk in the house in the woodland that I share with my friend.

Does he share the *house* or the *woodland* with his friend?

Modifiers, then, must modify precisely; else they distort the meaning and blur the intention of the sentence.

DANGLING MODIFIERS—'dangling' when there is no word to which they can clearly and logically relate:

Having at last reached home, the door closed behind him.

The modifier *Having reached home* improperly modifies *door*, but fails in any way to describe the main subject or action. To eliminate the error, change the word-order so that the dangling element relates to an adequate subject, or expand the sentence so that an adequate subject is provided:

Having at last reached home, he closed the door behind him.

When he reached home, he closed the door behind him.

Note: Many dangling constructions may be eliminated by using the active rather than the passive form of the verb. Instead of the passive *The door closed behind him*, use the active *He closed the door*.

Dangling modifiers occur in various forms which are discussed below.

Dangling Participles—at the **beginning** of the sentence:

Dangling: Dancing and drinking every night, her reputation in the village suffered.

The modifying phrase *Dancing and drinking* modifies, illogically, (*her*) *reputation.*

Right: Dancing and drinking every night, she lost her reputation in the village.

The participial phrase has been made to relate to an **adequate subject.**

Right: Because she danced and drank every night, her reputation suffered.

The participial phrase has been expanded to a **subordinate clause.**

Dangling **participles** at the **end** of the sentence:

Dangling: Our *vacation* passed happily, swimming and playing tennis.

Our vacation did not swim or play; we did.

Right: We passed our vacation happily, swimming and playing tennis.

Right: Our vacation passed happily, for we swam and played tennis.

Note: The expressions *thus* and *thereby* often introduce loose verbal phrases:

Loose: The boys quibbled throughout their trip, thereby ruining their vacation.

Loose: I took a first-class berth, thus making my voyage more comfortable.

These sentences are illogical ('upside down' constructions) because the main idea is in the subordinate phrase and seems to dangle.

Right: The boys ruined their vacation by quibbling throughout their trip.

Right: By taking a first-class berth, I made my voyage more comfortable.

Exercise No. 46

Correct the following sentences which contain dangling participles.

1 Hanging from the bell tower, crowds watched as the fanatic prepared to leap.
2 Having entered his car, the windows were immediately opened.
3 Gingerly walking barefooted on the cobblestones, his eyes caught sight of a mangled hand.
4 Listening to the concert with rapt attention, Beethoven seemed more than ever a magnificent composer.
5 Working too hard and earning too little, my ulcer is starting to bother me again.
6 Tonight I'll not work, already tired and indisposed.
7 Leaving his flat in a violent temper, her fury mounted higher as she thought of his insolence.
8 Hanging round her neck, he saw her diamond necklace.
9 Dante spilled gravy on Beatrice's dress, thereby spoiling their evening together.
10 Entering the doss-house, his cigarette hung limply between his lips.

Dangling Infinitives

Dangling: To prepare for an examination, solitude and concentration are essential.

A person to study for the examination is the primary essential. Only then are solitude and concentration important.

Right: To prepare for the examination, *a man* needs solitude and concentration.

Right: Solitude and concentration are necessary when *one* prepares for an examination.

Dangling: To have a successful party, good conversation and food are always useful.
Good conversation and food do not give parties.
Right: To have a successful party, *one* ought to provide good conversation and food.
Right: Good conversation and food always help to make a party successful.

Exercise No. 47

Correct the following sentences which contain dangling infinitives.

1 To travel in comfort, money is a prerequisite.
2 To smoke safely, filters ought to be used.
3 To row all afternoon without getting blisters, gloves should be worn.
4 To get thirty miles to the gallon, moderate speed must be maintained.
5 To work as a pianist, constant practice is of great importance.

Dangling Gerunds

Dangling: After seeing the dentist, his teeth stopped aching.
His *teeth* did not see the dentist.
Right: After he saw the dentist, his teeth stopped aching.
Right: After seeing the dentist, he thought that his teeth stopped aching.
Dangling: In planning an Arctic expedition, careful preparations are needed.
Careful preparations do not plan Arctic expeditions.
Right: In planning an Arctic expedition, explorers need to make careful preparations.
Right: Explorers need to make careful preparations when planning an Arctic expedition.

Exercise No. 48

Correct the following sentences which contain dangling gerunds.

1 Before leaving for Rome, reservations must be made.
2 After attacking my lateness, I was dismissed.
3 On his first attempt at riding, the horse threw him heavily.
4 When entering the theatre, the clothes of the audience surprised me.
5 While turning the page, the ashtray spilt on his book.

Dangling Elliptical Clauses

Elliptical constructions from which a subject or predicate has been omitted are generally acceptable if the **subject corresponds with the subject of the main clause and if the predicate is clear:**
Right: When (I am) hunting, I always keep my gun loaded.
However, when the omitted subject does not correspond with the subject of the main clause, the elliptical clause dangles:
Wrong: While asleep in the underground, a thief picked my pocket.
The omitted subject of the elliptical clause, *I was*, does not correspond with the subject of the main clause, *thief*, and therefore the elliptical construction dangles, suggesting that it was the thief who slept.
Right: While I was asleep, a thief picked my pocket.
The elliptical clause has been supplied with subject and predicate.
Right: While sleeping, I had my pocket picked by a thief.
The main clause has been recast so that its subject and that of the elliptical clause correspond.

Exercise No. 49

Correct the following sentences which contain dangling elliptical clauses.

1 When three years old, John's mother taught him archery.
2 While visiting Wales, the weather was excellent.
3 Once relaxed, Hilda's back felt better.
4 Stephen kept watching the light till green.
5 Although famished, caviare was not his dish.

MISPLACED MODIFIERS—are 'misplaced' when they are not clearly connected with the word they modify. Misplaced modifiers occur in the various forms discussed below.

Misplaced Modifying Words

Such adverbs as: *only, nearly, almost, hardly, scarcely, just, even, quite,* **should be placed next to the words they modify.**

Wrong: I only told the jury what I had seen. The adverb *only* 'squints' looking in three directions at once. Does the writer mean: *I and no one else told the jury?* If so, then the sentence must be recast so that *only* acts as an adjective modifying the pronoun *I:*

Right: Only I told the jury what I had seen. *I told the jury what I had seen and nothing else?* If so, then *only* must be so placed that it modifies the noun clause *what I had seen:*

Right: I told the jury only what I had seen.

I told only the jury and no one else? If so—and this sentence arrangement warrants the use of *only* as an adverb—*only* must be so placed that it modifies the verb *told:*

Right: I told only the jury what I had seen.

Thus, the modifier must be placed near the word it modifies in order to avoid ambiguity.

Any other adverb may 'squint' if it is placed so that it **refers ambiguously to both the preceding and succeeding word.**

Wrong: People who teach rarely get rich.

Does *rarely* modify *teach* or *get rich?* A major difference in meaning attaches to each choice.

Right: Teachers rarely get rich.

Right: Rarely do people who teach get rich.

Note: Frequently, the difficulties caused by misplaced modifiers may be eliminated by placing them at the beginning of the sentence.

Wrong: Drivers who speed often have accidents.

Right: Often, drivers who speed have accidents.

Exercise No. 50

Revise the following sentences so that the misplaced modifying words are correctly placed.

1 Those who listen to Dr. Timothy's lectures, even the most intellectual, will be confused.
2 Vivien only reads the best in Irish literature.
3 The baby nearly walked across his playpen.
4 Eating sweets frequently ruins teeth.
5 I scarcely opened the door when his dog leaped at me.

Misplaced Modifying Phrases

Misplaced **terminal** phrases.

Wrong: Harold kept the child who misbehaved in the corner.

In the corner should modify *kept*, not *misbehaved*.

Right: Because the child misbehaved, Harold kept him in the corner.

Wrong: Stephen fed his tropical fish shrimp-eggs with eagerness at bed-time.

Two phrases are grouped erroneously at the end of this sentence to produce an absurd result.

Right: At bedtime, Stephen eagerly fed his tropical fish shrimp-eggs.

Misplaced **medial** phrases.

Wrong: I asked him the next time to invite more lively people.

The next time squints towards both *asked* and *to invite*.

Right: I asked him to invite more lively people the next time.

Wrong: The commander promised as soon as possible to send the soldier overseas.

As soon as possible squints towards both *promised* and *to send*.

Right: As soon as possible, the commander promised to send the soldier overseas.

Right: The commander promised to send the soldier overseas as soon as possible.

Exercise No. 51

Rewrite the following sentences so that the modifiers are in proper position.

1 A scream tore through the house, waking the girl in bed with a cry.
2 In eastern Mexico there is a village inhabited by Indians called Patzcuaro.
3 Columbus vowed as soon as he landed to claim the New World for Ferdinand and Isabella.
4 No cathedral have I ever seen like that one in all my travels.
5 I located the trouble with my television set in the laboratory.

Misplaced Modifying Clauses

Relative clauses.

Wrong: The face of the man looking through the window which was cruel and sardonic startled Sweeney.

Which was cruel and sardonic has as its antecedent *window* instead of its logical antecedent *face*.

To avoid confusion place the relative clause immediately after its antecedent.

Right: Looking through the window, the man's face, which was cruel and sardonic, startled Sweeney.

Right: The cruel and sardonic face of the man looking through the window startled Sweeney.

Recast the Sentence

Wrong: I heard the bees near the flowers that were buzzing.
Right: I heard the bees that were buzzing near the flowers.

Parallel Modifying Clauses

Wrong: After Oedipus, our cat, has crouched behind the chair, he leaps at our ankles, as soon as he has decided we no longer suspect him.

The two subordinate clauses are parallel in form, and should therefore be combined and placed either before or after the main clause.

Right: After Oedipus, our cat, has crouched behind the chair and has decided that we no longer suspect him, he leaps at our ankles.

Right: Oedipus, our cat, leaps at our ankles after he has crouched behind the chair and decided that we no longer suspect him.

Squinting Clauses

Wrong: Because food spoils when not in use it should always be covered. The elliptical clause *when not in use* squints toward *spoils* and *should be covered.*

Right: Because food spoils, it should always be covered when not in use.

Exercise No. 52

Revise the following sentences so that the modifying clauses are correctly placed.

1 We set out for the city beyond the rainbow in which we lived.
2 When we visited foreign lands, we tried to learn their folk-lore when we spoke with the natives.
3 He examined the specimen in the microscope that was in a glass slide.
4 He promised to visit us as we were leaving.
5 Letters can win friends that show personality and spirit.

Split Constructions. Parts of the sentence that are closely related should not be needlessly separated.

Split Subject and Verb

Wrong: David, after deceiving Uriah and sending him to the battlefield to die, repented.

Unless a good reason exists for separating them, subject and verb should remain together.

Right: After deceiving Uriah and sending him to the battlefield to die, David repented.

Split Verb and Complement

Wrong: The teacher suggested, since so many students had failed to do the exercise which had been set two weeks before, that they remain after school.

Although it is wrong to separate verb and complement to achieve emphasis, an extended modifier may, as here, destroy the clarity of the sentence.

Right: Since so many students had failed to do the exercise which had been set two weeks before, the teacher suggested that they remain after school.

Split Infinitive. Normally, the infinitive is considered to be a unit consisting of the sign of the infinitive (*to*) and the infinitive (which corresponds to the first person singular, present indicative form of the verb.) **To separate *to* from the infinitive may result in distortion of meaning or loss of emphasis:**

Awkward: The editor intended to closely and painstakingly scrutinize the manuscript.

Better: The editor intended to scrutinize the manuscript closely and painstakingly.

Sometimes, however, **clarity and emphasis are improved by separating *to* from the infinitive:**

Right: The audience was asked to kindly take its seats.

To place *kindly* elsewhere in this sentence would result in a 'squinting' construction: The audience was asked kindly to take its seats.

Right: With a lowering of the age for recruitment, the army expects to more than treble its forces.

Thus, **to attain clarity** or **to achieve emphasis, the infinitive may be split.** However, it ought not to be split without some sufficient reason:

To without reason split an infinitive disappoints the reader's sense of proper diction.

Split Comparison

Wrong: Greek ruins are as interesting, if not more interesting than, Roman ruins.

Because the modifying phrase *if not more interesting* is wrongly placed, the main clause is illogical: Greek ruins are as interesting than Roman ruins.

Complete each comparison before introducing a modifying phrase:

Right: Greek ruins are as interesting as Roman ruins, if not more interesting.

Correct, but stilted: Greek ruins are as interesting as, if not more interesting than, Roman ruins.

Exercise No. 53

Revise the following sentences whenever the split construction damages their effectiveness.

1 Dr. Johnson, although he befriended Boswell and spent many pleasant hours with his Scottish biographer, despised the Scots.
2 I warned him that, even though we had spent many years together and had shared experiences neither of us would ever forget, I would take no more of his nonsense.
3 The vicar asked his flock please to contribute to the establishment of a new youth club.
4 He tried to suddenly and violently swerve his car away from the oncoming lorry.
5 The traffic in London is as fast-moving, if not more so, than that in other cities.

SHIFTS IN POINT OF VIEW

A foolish consistency may be the hobgoblin of little minds, but stylistic consistency is not foolish. An easy mastery of varied writing techniques characterizes the mature writer; to sustain it, his writing must be resolutely consistent. Shifts in person, in number, in voice dismay the reader and consequently damn the writer.

MAINTAIN CONSISTENCY OF NUMBER AND PERSON

Wrong: We were frightened during our drive along the motorway, for one saw everywhere wreckage from previous car accidents.

Shift from first person plural *we* to third person singular *one*.

Right: We were frightened during our drive along the motorway, for we saw everywhere wreckage from previous car accidents.

Wrong: After I had the job of masseur in a Turkish bath for six months, you never knew one body from the next.

Shift from first person *I* to second, *you*.

Right: After I had the job of masseur in a Turkish bath for six months, I never knew one body from the next.

Wrong: Root filling is a standard technique to save teeth. All dentists use them.

Shift from singular *filling* to plural *them.*

Right: Root *filling* is a standard technique to save teeth. All dentists use it.

MAINTAIN CONSISTENCY OF TENSE

Wrong: We hurried to the door, but nobody is there.

Shift from past tense *hurried* to present *is.*

Right: We hurried to the door, but nobody was there.

Wrong: Limbo tells about the horrors of a cybernetic world. The novel described how a brain surgeon who was lost on a tropical island during World War III returned to what was left of America and tried to find meaning in the new order.

Shift from present tense *tells* to past tense for the rest of the passage.

Use the present tense when writing about a work of literature, music, or art.

Right: Limbo tells about the horrors of a cybernetic world. The novel describes how a brain surgeon who is lost on a tropical island during World War III returns to what is left of America and tries to find meaning in the new order.

Right: Othello is one of Shakespeare's great tragedies.

Right: The Birth of Venus, Botticelli's masterpiece, distinguishes itself among any collection of art works.

Right: Mozart's *Don Giovanni* has exquisite lyrical passages.

MAINTAIN CONSISTENCY OF MOOD

Wrong: Address the chairman first and then you will be recognized.

Shift from imperative mood *address* to indicative *will be recognized.*

Right: If you will first address the chairman, you will then be recognized.

MAINTAIN CONSISTENCY OF VOICE AND SUBJECT

Wrong: He abhorred prejudice, and all people were considered equal by him.

Subject shifts from *he* to *people;* voice shifts from active *abhorred* to passive *were considered.*

Right: He abhorred prejudice and considered all people equal.

Wrong: He visited churches in Rome, went ski-ing in Les Rousses, and night clubs were his haunts in Paris.

Subject shifts from *he* to *night clubs;* voice shifts from active *visited* and *went* to passive *were.*

Right: He visited churches in Rome, went ski-ing in Les Rousses, and haunted night clubs in Paris.

Note: Sometimes it is necessary to shift from active to passive to avoid a clumsier shift in subject:

The thief twisted through heavy traffic to elude the police. He was almost trapped between a bus and a delivery van, but squeezed through and sped on.

Although he managed to hide safely for ten minutes in a darkened hallway, he was finally cornered and arrested by three detectives.

Active: Thief *twisted, squeezed, managed*

Passive: was trapped, was cornered and *arrested*

Thus, the *thief*, central subject of the passage, sometimes acts, sometimes is acted upon. Although the principle of consistency is violated, it is wiser to shift from active to passive than to lose the centre of attention by sharing the *thief* with a *bus*, a *delivery van*, and *three detectives*.

MAINTAIN CONSISTENCY OF TONE

Wrong: 'When studying for an examination, try to achieve flexibility in handling your material: aim at insight rather than sheer memory. What you must memorize will then benefit from a reserve of reflective thought.

By this time you've probably knocked yourself out and won't be able to pass anyhow, but just in case, let's go on to some other advice. Try to anticipate the questions you may be asked. . . .'

Shift from serious, factual discussion to dubious humour disrupts rather than enhances the tone of the communication. The second paragraph would be better in this way:

'Another useful technique involves trying to anticipate the questions you may be asked. . . .'

Exercise No. 54

Correct all violations of consistency in number, person, tense, mood, voice, subject, or tone.

1 One should listen carefully to his employer if you want promotion.
2 Lorelei was a cold-hearted girl and diamonds were to her the best friends a girl could have.
3 Beethoven's *Fifth Symphony* was a famous musical achievement.
4 If he were to take an old friend's advice, he will leave his job.
5 I know that I wouldn't go out with that group unless you want to get into trouble.
6 A true democrat accepts the opinion of the majority if they disagree with it.
7 When Job heard the Voice from the Whirlwind, he knows that his moment of reckoning has come.
8 Everyone has some favourite recipe that they concoct for their friends.
9 Tom and Huck entered the cemetery and the tomb stones were enough to frighten anybody at night.
10 An experienced wrestler knows how to feign agony, and you could always tell they were not really hurt.
11 Giving directions to a stranger is not always easy but you must try to be simple and specific. What does it matter if he gets lost a little; he'll see more of the town. But in any event, it is only courteous to try to guide him as well as possible.
12 The Roundheads defeated the King and all his men were hunted down by them.
13 If I allow him enough rope, you'll hang yourself.
14 Go to Coventry, young man, and there you may find humility.
15 One must continue to practise if you wish to succeed.

PARALLELISM

To master parallelism is to control one of the principal techniques of English prose. No other single device helps more to clarify relationships between kindred ideas. **Parallelism signifies the grammatical balance of two or more logically related sentence elements:**

NOUN	ADJECTIVE	VERB	PARTICIPLE
Socrates had ability, knowledge, honesty, and courage.	Socrates was intelligent, able, honest, and courageous.	Socrates analysed, discussed, questioned, and generalized.	Socrates faced his trial fearlessly, insisting on the truth as he saw it, and rejecting expedient compromises.

GERUND	INFINITIVE	PHRASE	CLAUSE
Socrates won fame by asking embarrassing questions and by giving ironic replies.	Socrates loved to trap his friends into seemingly innocent statements and then to expose their errors in logic.	Socrates confronted his accusers with complete assurance and with unabashed candour.	Socrates believed that the ideal state should be governed by intellectual aristocrats and that democracy was a dangerous creed.

Study the parallel constructions in these passages by professional writers:

'What another would have done as well as you, do not do it. What another would have said as well as you, do not say it; written as well, do not write it.'

(Gide)

'A great nose indicates a great man—
Genial, courteous, intellectual,
Virile, courageous.' (Rostand)

'Men reject their prophets and slay them, but they love their martyrs and honour those whom they have slain.' (Dostoevsky)

Like any rhetorical device, parallelism may be abused (see section on Style). But the amateur writer, once he learns to avoid the pitfalls described below, will find parallelism indispensable to mature prose.

Parallel sentence elements linked by a co-ordinating conjunction **must be parallel in form:** noun must parallel noun, adjective must parallel adjective, phrase must parallel phrase, etc.

Nouns

Wrong: A good scholar must be precise and possess originality.
Precise is an adjective, *originality* a noun.
   Right: A good scholar must be precise and original. (Adjectives)
   Right: A good scholar needs precision and originality. (Nouns)
   Wrong: Consider the origins of man and how he has developed.
Origins is a noun, *how he has developed* a clause.
   Right: Consider the origins and development of man. (Nouns)
   Right: Consider how man originated and how he developed. (Verbs)

Adjectives

Wrong: Give me the aggressive fellow and who has initiative.
Aggressive is an adjective, *who has initiative* is a clause.
   Right: Give me the fellow who is aggressive and who has initiative. (Clauses)

Verbs

Wrong: This morning I went to the hairdresser, shopping at Harrods, and lunching at the Dorchester.

Went is a verb, *shopping* and *lunching* are *participles*.

Right: This morning I went to the hairdresser, shopped at Harrods, and lunched at the Dorchester. (Verbs).

Participles

Wrong: Nero was flattered by the courtiers, praised by the soldiers, but the people hated him. *Flattered* and *praised* are *participles, but the people hated him* is a clause.

Right: Nero was flattered by the courtiers, praised by the soldiers, but hated by the people. (Participles)

Right: The courtiers flattered Nero and the soldiers praised him, but the people hated him. (Verbs)

Gerunds

Wrong: Playing croquet is delightful, but to box is barbaric.

Playing is a gerund, *to box* is an infinitive.

Right: Playing croquet is delightful, but *boxing* is barbaric.

Right: To play croquet is delightful, but to box is barbaric. (Infinitives)

Infinitives

Wrong: The pilot received orders to bomb the target and that he would then return home.

To bomb is an infinitive, *that he would then return home* is a clause.

Right: The pilot received orders to bomb the target and then to return home. (Infinitives)

Phrases

Wrong: He hoped for an increase in salary and to get a longer holiday.

For an increase in salary is a phrase, *to get* is an infinitive.

Right: He hoped for an increase in salary and for a longer holiday. (Phrases)

Right: He hoped to get an increase in salary and a longer holiday. (Nouns)

Clauses

Wrong: The prophet warned his people of oncoming disaster and that the Assyrians would conquer them.

Main clause made parallel with subordinate clause.

Right: The prophet warned his people that disaster lay ahead and that the Assyrians would conquer them. (Subordinate clauses)

Right: The prophet warned his people of oncoming disaster and predicted the Assyrian Conquest. (Main clauses)

Note: The second element in the parallel construction need not immediately follow the co-ordinating conjunction, but it must remain parallel in form:

Right: She carried herself with poise and, when engaged in conversation, spoke with animation. *Carried* and *spoke* are separated by a clause, yet they are parallel.

Right: Jojo is a clown, winsome, hilarious, and sentimental, but more than that he is a satirist, incisive, critical, and penetrating.

Clown and *satirist* remain parallel although separated by a series of parallel adjectives and a phrase.

Exercise No. 55

Revise the following sentences so that the related sentence elements are parallel in form.

1 Some public officials are always investigating dead scandals or usually publicity hounds.
2 He believes that having courage is better than fearing and that faith is truer than doubt.
3 I want stout-hearted men and who are fighters when necessary.
4 The Indian Summer of life should be sunny and sad, like the season, and an infinity of wealth and deepness of tone.
5 The local education authority voted for improved building facilities and to enlarge the teaching staff.
6 Find time to learn goodness and giving up laziness.
7 The child eagerly awaited the hour of his birthday and that he would soon have all his new presents.
8 Saying is one thing; but to do is another.
9 What Charles needs is a doctor and rest cure.
10 We studied the life of the ant and how it operates a social community.

Parallel sentence elements linked by correlative conjunctions (either . . . or, neither . . . nor, not only . . . but also, whether . . . or) **must be parallel in form.** If an adjective follows the first conjunction, an adjective must follow the second; if a verb follows the first conjunction, a verb must follow the second, etc.

Wrong: The witness not only accused the defendant but also his entire family.

Not only is followed by *accused*, a verb; *but also* is followed by *his entire family*, a noun phrase.

Right: The witness accused not only the defendant but also his entire family.

Two nouns, *defendant* and *family*, follow the correlatives.

Wrong: We know truth either by learning to reason or by the heart.

Either is followed by *learning to reason*, a gerund phrase; *or* is followed by *heart*, a noun.

Right: We know truth either by head or by heart.

Exercise No. 56

Revise the following sentences so that the related sentence elements are parallel in form.

1 They couldn't decide whether they should leave the theatre or to hiss the performance.
2 Bill either stops mimicking me or I will bang his head.
3 Churchill was not only a skilful politician but also had a facility as an artist.
4 He neither can do as he is told, nor his parents hope to change him.
5 When Billy grows up, either he wants to be a business tycoon or an actor.

A series of two or more parallel sentence elements must be parallel in form.

Wrong: My colleague is a distinguished yachtsman, gourmet, and is also interested in entomology.

Yachtsman and *gourmet* are parallel, but the third element, a clause, is not.

Right: My colleague is a distinguished yachtsman, gourmet, and entomologist.

Wrong: E. M. Forster wrote novels, essays and *A Passage to India* has been made into a play.

Novel and essays are parallel; the third element, a clause, is not.

Right: E. M. Forster wrote essays and novels, one of which, *A Passage to India*, has been made into a play.

Note: The succeeding elements in a parallel series need not immediately follow the first element, but they must remain parallel in form:

His experiences abroad taught him patience—which he learned by watching the controlled emotions of war-agonized people suffering pain and anguish—humility, and deep compassion.

The parallel series consists of *patience, humility*, and *compassion*. The first element is followed by a clause, the second stands alone, and the third has a single modifier. Nevertheless, the structure remains parallel throughout.

To assure parallel form, repeat, where necessary, the word that introduces the parallel constructions. The words usually involved are prepositions, relative pronouns, and the sign of the infinitive: *to*.

Weak: We had to advise Edwards that to accept his offer was out of the question, to leave our farm was impossible, and to move our ailing father was dangerous.

Omission of *that* in the second and third parallel clauses confuses the meaning of the sentence.

Right: We had to advise Edwards that to accept his offer was out of the question, that to leave our farm was impossible, and that to move our ailing father was dangerous.

Weak: Electrical contractors face involved problems in estimating costs and particularly maintaining supplies.

Omission of the preposition *in* before the second element obscures the meaning of the sentence.

Right: Electrical contractors face involved problems in estimating costs and particularly in maintaining supplies.

Weak: The draughtsman had to adjust the drawing board, which had tilted too sharply, and replace the worn tracing paper.

Omission of the sign of the infinitive, *to*, before the second element obscures the meaning of the sentence.

Right: The draughtsman had to adjust the drawing board, which had tilted too sharply, and to replace the worn tracing paper.

Note: If the infinitives appear close together, repetition of *to* is generally unnecessary:

Right: He refused to listen, understand, or compromise.

Note: If the objects of the prepositions appear close together, repetition of the preposition is generally unnecessary:

Right: Their organization stands for liberty, equality, and fraternity.

Note: Change the word that introduces a series of parallel elements, if doing so is necessary to maintain correct idiomatic expression:

Wrong: He is awed and courteous to high ranking officials.

Although *courteous* and *awed* are parallel, the preposition *to* is unidiomatic and illogical when used with awed.

Right: He is awed by and courteous to high ranking officials.

Right: He is awed by politicians and courteous to them.

Note: Change any word in a series of parallel elements if doing so is necessary to maintain correct grammatical form:

Wrong: Men have always and will continue to try improving their standard of living.

Have and *will continue* are parallel, but in seeking a short cut, the writer has neglected to complete each verb properly.

Right: Men have always tried and will continue trying to improve their standard of living.

Exercise No. 57

Revise the following sentences so that the related sentence elements are parallel in form.

1 Henry Adams wrote history, fiction, and the cathedrals at Chartres and Mount St. Michel turned him to architecture.
2 Dumas always has and will continue to excite readers young and old.
3 The yokels were attentive then swindled by the confidence man.
4 The artist decided to exhibit his paintings, which hardly deserved public attention, and give lectures.
5 The doctors warned Jones that to work would prove fatal, to travel might help, but to rest would effect a complete recovery.

Sentence elements must be parallel in meaning as well as in form: action must parallel action, generalization must parallel generalization, description must parallel description, etc. If the elements are not parallel in meaning, the parallel construction must be eliminated and the sentence recast.

Wrong: The Minister suggested that the parking dilemma could be solved and that cars must not park in the streets.

The two main clauses are parallel in form, but not in meaning. The first clause, *The Minister suggested*, generalizes; the second clause, *that cars must not park*, specifies.

Right: The Minister suggested that the parking dilemma could be solved, adding that part of the solution might be to prohibit cars from parking in the streets.

Note that to preserve the sense of the sentence, the parallel construction has been excised.

Wrong: Entering the room and being good natured, Tom genially welcomed his guests.

The two participial phrases are parallel in form, but not in meaning. *Entering the room* describes an action; *being good natured* describes a quality.

Right: Being genial and good natured, Tom welcomed his guests as soon as he entered the room.

Right: Tom, a genial and good-natured host, welcomed his guests as he entered the room.

Wrong: The passenger complained of the steward's insolence and of his refusal to answer when called.

The phrases *of the steward's insolence* and *of his refusal to answer* are parallel in form but not in meaning. The first phrase describes a quality, the second an action.

Right: The passenger complained of the insolent steward's refusal to answer when called.

Exercise No. 58

Where necessary revise the following sentence to assure logical relationships in meaning as well as in form.

1 The Prime Minister warned about relaxing vigilance and about the Martian invasion of East Anglia.
2 Opening the refrigerator, and being extremely hungry, he grabbed the chicken leg.
3 He promised them that walruses would be delightful to watch, and that two of the largest specimens were in the city zoo.
4 If he takes the time to study French, and if he tries hard, he will surely succeed.
5 Timid and infuriated by his attacks on her intelligence, she fled from the room.

OMISSIONS AND MIXED CONSTRUCTIONS

In the interest of economy, good usage accepts the omission of certain words from the sentence pattern. Legitimate omissions are called *ellipses:*

'Didn't you hear what happened?'
'No. What [happened]?'
'[What happened] To Susan?'
'Well, tell me.'
'She was strangled by a maniac.'
'Where [did he strangle her]?'
'[He strangled her] on Hampstead Heath. [Do you] Want to hear the rest?'
'Yes. I do [want to hear the rest].'

However, words necessary for clear meaning or complete grammatical construction must never be omitted.

Avoid omitting articles, possessives, or connectives necessary for clearness or completeness.

Wrong: The heiress bought a gold and silver urn.
Did she buy one gold and one silver urn, or one made in part of each metal?
Right: The heiress bought a gold and a silver urn.
Right: The heiress bought a gold-and-silver urn.
Wrong: He left his money to his wife and aunt.
Right: He left his money to his wife and to his aunt.
Wrong: The school bell rang the same times as always.
Right: The school bell rang at the same time as always.

Avoid omitting any forms of main or auxiliary verbs necessary for clearness or completeness.

Wrong: Edwards is intelligent, but all the others stupid.
The elliptical construction *all the others stupid* assumes a verb, but the verb must be *is* to conform with the verb in the first clause. The number of *all the others*, however, is plural.

Right: Edwards is intelligent, but all the others are stupid.
Wrong: We work as diligently as they have or are working.
As they have what? *Work? Working?* Neither of the verb forms provided in the sentence fits.

Right: We work as diligently as they have worked or are working.

Note: Avoid using a single form of *to be* as both main and auxiliary verb.

Wrong: The violinist was in superb form and applauded by the entire audience.

Was is understood before *applauded*, but its use as an auxiliary differs from the use of *was* as the main verb in the opening clause, *The violinist was in superb form.* Therefore, the auxiliary verb must be repeated:

Right: The violinist was in superb form and was applauded by the entire audience.

Note: Only one auxiliary verb need be used to serve as predicate for two parallel subjects:

Right: I can speak as well as he (can).

Avoid omitting subordinate conjunctions or relative pronouns before clauses used as subject, object, or predicate complement.

Wrong: Caligula noted Lazarus laughed even at pain.

It is possible to mistake the noun *Lazarus* as the object of *noted* whereas it is the subject of the subordinate clause. The entire clause is object of the verb *noted.*

Right: Caligula noted that Lazarus laughed even at pain.

Wrong: The reason he failed was he refused to study.

He refused to study is an awkward predicate complement after *was.*

Right: The reason he failed was that he refused to study.

Right: He failed because he refused to study.

Note: If there is no likelihood of mistaking the subject of the subordinate clause for the object of the verb in the main clause, the subordinating conjunction may be omitted:

Right: All knew he was a drunkard. (*that* omitted after knew)

We assured him we agreed with his argument. (*that* omitted after *him*)

This is the portfolio I bought. (*which omitted* after *portfolio*)

Avoid omitting words that leave comparisons ambiguous.

Wrong: He likes Kensington as well as Alice.

Does he like Kensington and Alice, or do he and Alice like Kensington equally?

Right: He likes Kensington as well as Alice does.

Wrong: He dislikes visitors as much as his wife.

Does he dislike visitors and his wife, or do he and his wife dislike visitors?

Right: He dislikes visitors as much as his wife does.

Avoid omitting words necessary to complete the meaning of a sentence.

Wrong: One of the problems in administering Oxfam is that some countries need more than others.

Need more than others of what? More problems? More Oxfam? Or is it that some countries need from Oxfam more benefits than others? The gaps in thought must be filled in.

Right: One of the problems in administering Oxfam is that some countries need more benefits than others do.

Wrong: Gertrude Stein studied psychology at Radcliffe with William James and did research on automatic writing. Then she went to Paris and wrote a novel.

Right: After Gertrude Stein had studied at Radcliffe with William James, she went to Paris where she wrote a novel that made good use of her earlier studies in psychology and automatic writing.

Avoid shifting from one construction to another before the first construction has been completed.

Wrong: By engaging first, it changes the gear ratio of the differential, you put the car into low speed.

The writer has begun with a phrase *By engaging first;* then, without logically completing his construction, shifted to main clauses. As a result, *it* has no antecedent and *puts* has no subject.

Right: By engaging first gear and changing the ratio of the differential, you put the car into low speed.

Right: Engaging first gear changes the ratio of the differential and puts the car into low speed.

Wrong: As far as his lecture goes, often it was difficult to follow him.

The writer has confused two patterns without completing either. Both remain illogical.

Right: His lecture was often difficult to follow.

Right: As far as his lecture goes, I must admit that he was often difficult to follow.

Avoid omitting prepositions which are needed to complete the meaning of a sentence.

Wrong: No one, but no one, can be more desirous or eager for customers than Marks and Spencer.

Desirous for is not an acceptable idiomatic usage, but it is the only preposition provided in this sentence.

Right: No one, but no one, can be more desirous of customers or more eager for them than Marks and Spencer.

Wrong: The shape of his head is different yet reminiscent of a ripe cantaloup.

The preposition needed to complete *different* has been omitted.

Right: The shape of his head is different from, yet reminiscent of, a ripe cantaloup.

Exercise No. 59

Fill in any omissions in the following sentences, or recast the sentence if the constructions are mixed.

1 The house was burned, but the children saved.
2 I remember Noel Coward better than Ivor Novello.
3 I have six Jaguars but he two.
4 The teacher which I referred would not write a letter for me.
5 My dog and girl friend are going with me on my holiday.
6 He has bought as many books as any man has or can buy.
7 Our only chance was Johnson might send out an alarm.
8 The patient moaned, sweated, and other symptoms of delirium.
9 The major problem is she is not at all interested.
10 We were more familiar with the Smiths than the Joneses.
11 His recitation was highly effective and admired by all.
12 The fact is that tornadoes and typhoons are becoming more frequent, and possibly because rainmakers are 'seeding' too many clouds.
13 So far as his writing is concerned, sometimes pointless in its thinking.
14 His vision at night was almost as good as a cat.
15 Harold collected relics as well as read about Norman England.

PARAGRAPHS AND PARAGRAPHING

IMPROVING THE PARAGRAPH

THE FUNCTION OF THE PARAGRAPH. The paragraph links several related sentences, sentences that focus on the same topic, that amplify it, explain it, defend it.

THE LENGTH OF THE PARAGRAPH. Since the paragraph is a unit of a larger whole, a stage in total development, it may be one word long—or a thousand words long. If the point of the paragraph has been adequately made, the paragraph is long enough no matter how few words it contains. Today paragraphs generally average from 150 to 300 words; but the average is not the norm. The nineteenth-century paragraph was much longer, much more uniform. One scholar traces the 'decline of the paragraph' to mass production: 'When newspapers, and then magazines, began to be published for the millions, writers soon found that their readers were shortwinded. They would hold their brains together for three or four sentences, not more.' But even the relatively short paragraphs now prevailing **observe certain principles —clarity, vigour and variety,** the same principles which apply to the sentence.

DEVELOPING THE PARAGRAPH. Though the size of the paragraph has decreased, many writers still find it too long. They find it difficult to create sturdy, full-blooded paragraphs. Usually they suffer from an illness which has been diagnosed as 'paragraph anaemia'.

The cure depends on an intelligent diet: the writer must know something about the care and feeding of paragraphs. Suppose, for example, he believes that soldiers would make good Prime Ministers. First he must articulate the thought, discover how boldly he wants to state it, with what modifications he wants to hedge it. Does he mean all soldiers, or officers only? All officers, or only those who have had commands requiring administrative ability? Would they make good Prime Ministers at any time, or only in time of war or rumours of war?

Assume his winnowed thought to be: **Good generals who have commanded troops in action would make good Prime Ministers.** Then he can develop it in several ways:

By Illustration and Example. What good fighting generals have made good leaders of civil government?

By Comparison. What are the capacities and qualities which both good fighting generals and good Prime Ministers require?

By Cause and Effect. What causes (education, training, habit of mind, intelligence, and the like) make a good fighting general a good Prime Minister?

There are other ways too, of developing the paragraph about the central statement concerning generals and Prime Ministers; but those cited seem the most likely. For a reverse thesis—fighting generals would not make good Prime Ministers—a different technique of development might be enlisted: **contrast**: what qualities and capacities of good fighting generals and good Prime Ministers are inimical? And other methods of paragraph development are appropriate to other topics, especially topics which do not require a supporting argument. One might, for example, develop a paragraph on the pleasant topic of love by the method of **definition** or of **elimination**—explaining what love is or what it is not; or conceivably by the method of **analogy**—explaining how it is like something apparently very different (perhaps a bowl of cherries or a lighted cigarette).

OUTLINING. Paragraphs link sentences and are themselves linked to one another. To establish a logical union of paragraphs and to ensure proportionate development of each, most experienced writers outline their projected work. If it is a long and complex one, they will probably prefer a formal outline. Thus, an essay on the outline might be formally outlined in the following way:

I. The Outline
 A. Advantages
  1 coherence
  2 proportion
  3 order

 B. Dangers
  1 strait-jacketing
   (*a*) tendency to adhere rigidly
   (*b*) tendency to stifle initiative
  2 mechanistic

Of course, the headings and sub-headings may require more elaboration: instead of words or phrases, the writer may need sentences or even paragraphs in constructing his outline.

On the other hand, for a short and relatively simple work, he may need to jot down only a few points:

 1 definition
 2 advantages
 3 dangers

At any rate, it enables him to see what his starting point and what his terminal point will be and what route he will take from the one to the other.

CLARITY

THE TOPIC SENTENCE. You should construct a clearly defined topic sentence for each paragraph. **A topic sentence is one that states or summarizes the theme of the paragraph:** it forms the base of the well-built paragraph. Though generally the first or second sentence in the paragraph, it may be the last (particularly when the paragraph consists of details which require summary). Bacon's essay *Of Studies* begins with a model topic sentence: 'Studies serve for delight, for ornament, and for ability.' Every other sentence in the long paragraph which follows radiates from the topic sentence like spokes from a hub.

COHERENCE. You should interrelate the sentences of your paragraph. Each sentence ought to follow naturally from the impetus of the preceding one. Each ought to give the reader a 'sense of the uninterrupted flow of the mind'. Ultimately, the harmony and sequence of parts must proceed from an organic idea, a unit concept; and mechanical devices for attaining coherence are of secondary importance.

Yet they may not be wholly discounted. The following paragraph shows why:

'Fortune, we are told, is a blind and fickle foster-mother, who showers her gifts at random upon her nurslings. But we do her a grave injustice if we believe such an accusation. Trace a man's career from his cradle to his grave and mark how Fortune has treated him. You will find that when he is once dead she can for the most part be vindicated from the charge of any but the most superficial fickleness. Her blindness is the merest fable; she can espy her favourites long before they are born. We are as days and have had her parents for our yesterdays, but through all the fair weather of clear parental sky the eye of Fortune can discern the coming storm and she laughs as she places her favourites it may be in a London alley or those whom she is re-solved to ruin in kings' palaces. Seldom does she relent towards those whom she has suckled unkindly and seldom does she completely fail a favoured nursling.'   (Samuel Butler)

Hardly a perfect paragraph; but certainly an exceedingly crafty one.

Note: (1) The organizing idea, the analogy governing the disposition of sentences in the paragraph: *Fortune* is similar to a foster-mother who favours some of her children, bears animosity towards others of them.

(2) The repetition of *Fortune*—personified for the sake of immediacy.

(3) The judicious ordering of pronouns—the personal (*he, she, you, his, her, they*) especially, but also the demonstrative (*those*) and the indefinite (*such, all*)—which link with nouns in other sentences.

(4) The neat introduction of the topic sentence (the second sentence) through contrast and the concise summary in the final sentence.

The author might also have employed one or more of the conjunctive adverbs (*however, therefore, consequently, on the contrary, on the whole*, and the like). However, though they are important words for establishing the relation of ideas, they are likely to clutter prose when used too often; in any case, the *buts* serve the same connective purpose.

In addition to the other merits of the paragraph, it flows smoothly into the next:

'Was George Pontifex one of Fortune's favoured nurslings or not? On the whole I should say he was not, for he did not consider himself so; he was too religious to consider Fortune a deity at all; he took whatever she gave and never thanked her, being firmly convinced that whatever he got to his own advantage was of his own getting. And so it was, after Fortune had made him able to get it.'

Note here the use of the conjunctive adverb *on the whole* as well as of the conjunctions *for* and *and*.

FORCE AND VIGOUR

POSITION: You should place your important idea at the beginning or at the end of the paragraph, or else (rarely) isolate it in a one-sentence paragraph. Advertising men know the impact of the strategically placed sentence. In an airline advertisement, for example, one paragraph began: '1975! Abandon yourself to the sun this summer with a glorious fun-filled, sun-filled holiday, a holiday that puts every other holiday in the shade!' Another ends: 'No wonder more people fly Southern Airlines than any other airline in Europe.' And the lead paragraph consists of one sentence only: 'Southern Airlines offer you 14 carefree days in fabulous Venice for only £90.'

FOCUS. You should concentrate on one dominant idea in each paragraph. Avoid discussing anything which does not continue or exemplify your central thought: if it is worth saying, there are other paragraphs to say it in. If the central thought is a comprehensive one, of course, the paragraph may properly range in time or space:

'The Romantic Period is customarily dated from the publication of the *Lyrical Ballads* by Coleridge and Wordsworth in 1798 to the accession of Victoria in 1837. Since dates are convenient, these will do: but the tissue of tendencies called romanticism had its genesis more than half a century before the publication of the *Lyrical Ballads* and has endured up to the present day— in fact, one or another kind of "romanticism" has never been totally absent from English literature, or from any other literature.'

VARIETY

LENGTH AND STRUCTURE. You should vary the length and structure of your paragraphs. Variety spices discourse; and sometimes it is a subtle spice. Consider the two paragraphs quoted below, the first containing sixty-nine words, the second twenty-seven: they illustrate the principle of variety not merely because they differ in length or in the structure of their sentences (in fact the sentences have an apparent—not real—structural likeness). The pace and the pauses, the shifting rhythms, diverse stresses, changing cadence of the paragraph—these, rather, give them variety:

'Ours is essentially a tragic age, so we refuse to take it tragically. The cataclysm has happened, we are among its ruins, we start to build up new little habitats, to have new little hopes. It is rather hard work: there is now no smooth road into the future: but we go round, or scramble over the obstacles. We've got to live no matter how many skies have fallen.

'This was more or less Constance Chatterley's position. The war had brought the roof down over her head. And she realized that one must live and learn.'

(D. H. Lawrence)

CONCRETENESS. You should illustrate your thought concretely. 'All true merit consists in the specific concrete,' one critic writes: at any rate much true merit does. Just as it is better to say, 'They punish by hanging, burning, and torturing' than to say, 'The regulations of their penal code are severe,' it is better to describe a man's nose, ears, eyes, and skin than to call him ugly or handsome. One is definite, evokes a picture; the other is vague, evokes a blur.

Note that the author of the following paragraph does not say 'everything was in a turmoil' or 'everybody was making feverish preparations.' She specifies concretely:

'I found London agog. Scaffolds were building all along the line of march. Light horse were told off to patrol the streets. Foot guards to the number of 2,800 were assigned posts about the court. In Bow Street the magistrates issued orders for keeping the peace by day and by night. In Westminster Hall the Lord High Steward perfected a mannerly horse in the art of backing out of the Royal presence. At St. James's the young King wedded and bedded his new Queen.'   (Lillian de la Torre)

Exercise No. 60

Rearrange the following sentences so that they constitute well-ordered paragraphs. Underline the topic sentence of each paragraph.

1 (*a*) His death in 1916 left the matter of his preferences as to nationality still inconclusive. (*b*) In 1915, unhappy over American neutrality, he severed the last formal tie binding him to the country of his birth, and adopted British citizenship. (*c*) The migratory childhood of Henry and William James was the result of their father's attempt to keep them from taking premature root. (*d*) He directed that after cremation his ashes be taken to Mount Auburn Cemetery in Cambridge, Massachusetts. (*e*) Even though he permanently settled in England in 1875, he became, as he confessed to Hamlin Garland a quarter of a century afterwards, 'a man who is neither American nor European'. (*f*) He succeeded perhaps too well with Henry, for the latter remained rootless all his days.

2 (*a*) 'My next letter shall refute you,' said Lady G. (*b*) George Selwyn once affirmed in company that no woman ever wrote a letter without a postscript. (*c*) And after her signature stood: 'P.S. Who is right now, you or I?' (*d*) Selwyn soon after received a letter from her.

3 (*a*) The free people of the world look to us for support in maintaining their freedoms. (*b*) The seeds of totalitarian regimes are nurtured by misery and want. (*c*) They reach their full growth when the hope of a people for a better life has died. (*d*) They spread and grow in the evil soil of poverty and strife. (*e*) We must keep that hope alive.

4 (*a*) I [G. Bernard Shaw] claim that from the first upper cut with which Cashel Byron stops his opponent's lead-off and draws his cork (I here use the accredited terminology of pugilism) to the cross-buttock with which he finally disables him, there is not a single incident which can be enjoyed on any ground other than that on which the admittedly brutalized frequenter of prize fights enjoys his favourite sport. (*b*) I guarantee to every purchaser of *Cashel Byron's Profession* a first-class fight for his money. (*c*) At the same time he will not be depraved by any attempt to persuade him that his relish for blood and violence is the sympathy of a generous soul for virtue in its eternal struggle with vice. (*d*) Out of the savagery of your tastes you delight in it.

5 (*a*) Believe me, mankind has been doing nothing else ever since it began to pay some attention to ideas. (*b*) It has been said that a benevolent despotism is the best possible form of government. (*c*) You seek to impose your ideas on others, ostracizing those who reject them. (*d*) I do not believe that saying, because I believe another one to the effect that hell is paved with benevolence, which most people, the proverb being too deep for them, misinterpret as unfulfilled intentions. (*e*) Excuse my rambling. (*f*) I meant to say, in short, that though you are benevolent and judicious you are none the less a despot. (*g*) As if a benevolent despot might not by any error or judgement destroy his kingdom and then say, like Romeo when he got his friend killed, 'I thought all for the best!'

PUNCTUATION

TRENDS IN PUNCTUATION

Punctuation more and more rejects formal rules, becomes less and less hospitable to the commands 'thou shalt' and 'thou shalt not'. Rules found in the standard textbooks are necessarily conservative: they generally memorialize past practice; they do not often report prevailing current usage.

Today magazines and newspapers—the media influencing the practice of punctuation basically—employ about half as many points (marks of punctuation) as they did fifty years ago. Since today the average sentence is shorter and less involved than the sentence of 1900, it requires fewer points, fewer guides through its mazes. Moreover, sentence structure, diction, and grammar have also progressed towards simplicity, and that evolution has further decreased the need for an elaborate system of pointing.

The general principles governing the use of punctuation are (1) **that if it does not clarify the text it should be omitted and** (2) **that in the choice and placing of punctuation marks the sole aim should be to bring out more clearly the author's thought.** This means that punctuation must be bound to communication, not to rules. If violating any rule enhances the sense or even the grace of a sentence, one ought to violate the rule; otherwise he violates both the sentence and the reason for the rules.

Two kinds of pointing practice are in vogue: formal punctuation, which prefers to **use all marks not expressly forbidden;** and informal punctuation, which prefers to **omit all marks not definitely required.** Actually, most experienced writers strike a medium: they try to punctuate flexibly. In the following sections, formal usages will be systematically described, since they are valid for formal contexts. However, the informal alternatives will be regularly cited, since they are the ones most people exercise.

END PUNCTUATION

End marks of punctuation point out that **a sentence has come to a full stop.**

THE FULL STOP (OR PERIOD)—is used to mark the end of a declarative sentence, or of an imperative sentence that issues its command mildly rather than forcefully.

'If a man holds up a mirror to your nature and shows you that it needs washing—not whitewashing—it is no use breaking the mirror. Go for soap and water.'   (G. B. Shaw)

THE QUESTION MARK is used to mark the end of an interrogative sentence.

'Why does the blind man's wife paint herself?'   (Benjamin Franklin)

Who can refute a sneer?

Note: One or more question marks may sometimes be used **within** the body of a single sentence. Such sentence interrupters (*a*) may show the close-linked nature of the questions; or (*b*) emphasize each of the separate questions.

'How then was Abraham's faith reckoned? when in circumcision, or in uncircumcision?'   (Romans)

'Canst thou draw out leviathan with a hook? or his tongue with a cord which thou lettest down?'   (Job)

Will Stella marry John? or will Jane? or will anyone?

To show uncertainty or—amateurishly—to warn of humorous intention. (For either indication, place the question mark in brackets.)

William Dunbar, who was born in 1465 (?) and who died in 1530 (?), ranks next to Robert Burns in Scotland's literary history.

His humour (?) nauseates.

Do not use the question mark:

To mark the end of an indirect question—one implying rather than expressing a question.

Right: Poor Richard wants to know why the blind man's wife paints herself.

To mark the end of a polite or formal question.

Right: May we hear from you shortly.

Note: The interrogative force of 'courtesy questions' has diminished through frequent use, and general practice tends to omit the question mark after them.

THE EXCLAMATION MARK—is used to mark the end of an exclamatory sentence, phrase, or clause.

How the mighty have fallen!

What a mess!

God forbid!

Note: A single exclamation mark suffices.

To point a vigorous interjection, or a nominative of address when strong feeling is present.

Curses! here come Captain Jinks and the horse marines!

'Father! father! it is I! Alice! thy own Elsie!' (James Fenimore Cooper)

'But hark! what notes of discord are these which disturb the general joy, and silence the acclamations of victory? They are the notes of John Hook, hoarsely bawling through the American camp, beef! beef! beef!'

(Patrick Henry)

Note: The exclamation mark, like the question mark, may be used within the body of a sentence. Such a sentence interrupter (*a*) may show strong feeling bursting through the sentence bounds; or (*b*) may emphasize each exclamation.

Do **not** use the exclamation mark to indicate mild exclamations.

Well, we have come through.

Note: The exclamation mark ought to be used purposefully, not loosely. Over-use of the exclamation mark characterizes 'the schoolgirl style'. When hesitating between the exclamation mark and another mark, generally prefer the other mark.

Exercise No. 61

Insert the appropriate mark of end punctuation.

1 Never I would rather die
2 Die you shall
3 Jason asked why Luster had turned left
4 He exclaimed angrily that he welcomed opposition
5 'Never' did you say
6 Well played
7 May I suggest that you let us have a cheque, not later than the end of the month
8 O Scotland my dear, my native soil
9 'Heigh-ho' he exclaimed
10 Bah he's never met his deadline

INTERNAL PUNCTUATION

Internal marks of punctuation are used **within the body of the sentence to point out that the flow of thought in the sentence is being interrupted.** They warn the reader to go slow because something is added to the communication, or subtracted from it; or because the communication is making a detour or taking a short cut.

THE COMMA—separates sentence elements; it is the most frequent, and the least emphatic, of the internal marks of punctuation.

Use the comma:
To separate two independent clauses joined by a co-ordinating conjunction (*and, but, or, nor; for, so, yet, either . . . or, neither . . . nor*).

'A rabbit's foot may bring good luck to you, but it brought little to the rabbit.'   (Ambrose Bierce)

Note: If the independent clauses joined by the co-ordinating conjunction are short and closely related, omit the comma.

Right: 'They laid Jesse James in his grave and Dante Gabriel Rossetti died immediately.'   (Thomas Beer)

To separate words, phrases, or clauses in a series (that is, three or more items).

'On taking thought it seemed to me that I must aim at lucidity, simplicity and euphony.'   (Somerset Maugham)

Trollope has a thoroughly conventional mind, no discernible relevance to our times, a style with all the grace and flexibility of the Albert Memorial.

Trollope's commonplace vehicles carry us to an impossible province, where no shadow of ethical doubt glooms, where right and wrong are palpable as a clergyman's gown or a barrister's wig, where every deserving Jack ultimately gets his Jill.

Note: Dominant modern practice is to omit the comma before the *and* or *or* connecting the last two items of a series. Formal writers, however, still retain the comma in such a context. Either retain it or omit it, as you choose, but be consistent in your practice.

Alternative: A, B, C, and *D* or: *A, B, C* and *D.*

To separate two adjectives each of which modifies the noun individually.

He was a brilliant, forthright speaker.

Here the adjectives are co-ordinate modifiers of the noun: they may be linked by *and* instead of the comma:

He was a brilliant and forthright speaker.

If the conjunction *and* may be logically set between the adjectives modifying the noun, the comma is in order. However, the adjectives are not always co-ordinate; often the noun and the adjective next to it form a single unit, one thought:

He is a brilliant military analyst.

Here, the conjunction *and* may not be logically set between the adjectives. Consequently, no comma is required. Compare the following phrases.

An old, broken-down tramp.

A broken-down old tramp.

A large, spacious house.

A large brick house.

A cold, dark night.

A cold spring night.

To set off a long adverbial clause or phrase coming before the main clause.

'When a book about the literature of the eighteen-nineties was given by Mr. Holbrook Jackson to the world, I looked eagerly in the index for Soames, Enoch.' (Max Beerbohm)

'By resolute malice and unblinking devotion to the letter rather than to the spirit of the law, he managed to bring in another conviction.' (H. H. Grote)

Note: The tendency in modern punctuation, however, is to omit the comma after such clauses and phrases unless misunderstanding will result. The commas are optional, therefore, even in the sentences cited above.

To set off an introductory verbal phrase (a participial, gerund, or infinitive phrase).

Having dexterously evaded the large questions, the genteel writers trifled engagingly with a multiplicity of small ones.

To see infinity in a grain of sand, one needs vision rather than eyesight.

After riddling an opponent, you may discover that his argument is still whole.

Note: Many modern writers omit the comma after the verbal phrase, except where misreading may ensue.

Alternative: To credit many journalists it is necessary to discredit the laws of evidence.

To set off an absolute phrase in any part of the sentence—beginning, middle, or end.

Perhaps we waste our energies, *sunshine being more general than showers*, by preparing so diligently for rainy days.

Note: If the phrase in italics came at the beginning of the sentence it would be followed by a comma; if at the end it would be preceded by a comma.

To prevent misreading—even temporary misreading.

When I want to dance, well women grow sick.

In brief, dresses will be shorter.

Should you wish to swim, the ocean lies at your doorstep.

Although there were jobs for a hundred, thousands applied.

The soldier dropped, a bullet in his leg.

To separate the year from any of its divisions:

December 25, 1984.

Christmas, 1984.

December, 1984.

Note: The comma between month and year is often omitted.
Alternative: December 1984.

To separate the parts of geographical names, addresses, districts, and the like.
Kensington, London.
82 Phillimore Gardens, Kensington, London.
London, W.8.

To set off nouns in direct address.
Friends, Romans, countrymen, lend me your ears.

To follow the salutation and complimentary close of a letter.
Dear Sir,
Yours sincerely,

To indicate the omission of one or more words.
He eats no fat; his wife, no lean.
Note: Unless some misreading might ensue, current usage generally omits
the comma in such a context.
Alternative: He eats no fat; his wife no lean. (Here, too, the comma may
replace the semicolon.)

**To set off a short or informal quotation, for the purpose of distinguishing
between the speaker and what he says.**
'Stupid people,' said Michael Arlen, 'have an uncanny way of hitting the
right nail on the head with the wrong hammer.'

To set off two or more contrasting statements.
'Millions for defence, not a damned penny for tribute.'

(Charles Pinkney)

**To set off non-restrictive phrases and clauses—elements which break the
continuity of the sentence.**
Rolls-Royces, *which have four wheels*, are more expensive than Fords, *which
likewise have four wheels*.
Note: A comma precedes each of the italicized clauses because they merely
offer incidental information concerning the nouns they modify. Compare:
Rolls-Royces *that have three wheels* are not so expensive as Fords *that have
four wheels*.
Here the italicized clauses offer essential information concerning the nouns
they modify. They are called *restrictive* clauses because they restrict or limit
Rolls-Royces and *Fords:* three-wheeled Rolls-Royces are cheaper than four-
wheeled Fords. (Presumably—though the sentence does not explicitly say
so—four-wheeled Rolls-Royces are more expensive than four-wheeled
Fords.)
Phrases, too, may be restrictive.
Rolls-Royces *with three wheels* are cheaper than Fords *with four wheels*.
If a clause or phrase **restricts** (or limits or defines), **it is not set off** by commas.
If **it does not restrict**, if it merely offers information not essential to the main
communication, **it is set off** by commas. To test for restrictiveness, simply
blot out the clause: if the essential communication remains clear, the clause
is non-restrictive; if, however, blotting out the clause blots out the intended
meaning as well, the clause is restrictive.
Compare the following:
Restrictive: The man *who smiles* is the man worth while. (The clause is a
necessary part of the communication: the intent of the sentence is not that
any man is worth while, but specifically that the man who smiles is.)

Non-restrictive: My smiling uncle, *whom everybody trusts*, cheerfully cuts throats. (The italicized clause is non-restrictive: the essential communication is that my smiling uncle cuts throats; that everybody trusts him is incidental information. In the former sentence the clause identifies; in this, presumably, no identification is necessary.)

Restrictive: Women *who eat garlic* need to be beautiful.

Non-restrictive: Women, who generally possess uneducated taste-buds, rarely eat garlic.

Restrictive: The girl on the calendar was Hyacinthine Horlick.

Non-restrictive: The calendar girl, in spite of her manager's discreet silence, was Hyacinthine Horlick.

Restrictive: He will speak *if you do not*.

Non-restrictive: He will speak, *whether you do or not*. (The dependent clause in the first sentence may not be omitted without changing the communication basically; the clause is restrictive, therefore, and commas are superfluous. The dependent clause in the second sentence may be omitted, however, without radically altering the communication; the clause is non-restrictive, therefore, and commas are in order.)

Restrictive: He proved *that any part of the doughnut* is greater than the hole.

Non-restrictive: The doughnut, which is a Dutch confection, is a weak sister of the bagel.

Note: Noun clauses are always restrictive. Adjectival and adverbial clauses may be either restrictive or non-restrictive, depending on whether they are essential or unessential to the sense of the communication.

To set off parenthetical expressions, mild interjections, words or phrases in apposition, sentence modifiers.

Parenthetical Expression: The world, *it seemed to him once*, was his oyster, but later he discovered, *as many before him had*, that the oyster was inedible and contained no pearls.

Mild Interjection: *Why*, this shirt has three sleeves!

Appositive: For unto us a child is born, unto us a son is given: and the government shall be upon his shoulder: and his name shall be called Wonderful, Counsellor, The Mighty God, The Everlasting Father, The Prince of Peace.   (Isaiah 9. 6)

Sentence Modifier: His position, nevertheless, seems shaky.

Note: The sentence elements listed above are all essentially non-restrictive: they are not fundamentally necessary for the central communication.

Do not use the comma:

To separate the subject or complement from the verb (unless a non-restrictive element comes between).

'*Life is* the *art* of drawing sufficient conclusions from insufficient premises.'
                                                      (Samuel Butler)

'Our *opinions follow* our *inclinations*.'   (Goethe)

To precede the first or to follow the last item of a series.

Who believes that beans, butter, bread build biceps?

Who believes that beans, butter, and bread build biceps?

Note: The comma is optional after *butter* in the second sentence cited.

To set off an adverb or adjective from the adjacent word it modifies.

Poverty is like rain: it drops down *ceaselessly*, disintegrating the finer tissues of man, his recent, *delicate* adjustments, and leaves nothing but the bleak and *gaunt* framework.

To separate words, phrases, or dependent clauses joined by a co-ordinating conjunction (unless some purpose like contrast is to be served).

He proved ready and willing [, but not able].

He proved to be ready and to be willing.

He proved that he was ready and that he was able.

To set off restrictive elements.

'A prude is *one who blushes modestly at the indelicacy of her thoughts.*'

(Ambrose Bierce)

To break up any logically close or structurally smooth group of words.

Indeed I did.

I did indeed.

The theorem is thus proved.

Note: Whether to insert commas or not to insert them in such contexts depends on the experience and tact of the writer. If the construction without commas meets his meaning better or achieves a rhythm more consonant with his thought, he ought to employ it regardless of rules.

Exercise No. 62

Insert commas where necessary in the following passages.

1 Just as the procedure of a charity appeal must be clear-cut and definite the steps being taken with the sureness of a skilled chess player so the various paragraphs of a begging letter must show clear organization giving evidence of a mind that from the beginning has had a specific end in view.

2 In some jobs it is necessary to understand interpret and apply rules and principles. In others it is necessary also to discover principles from available data or information. These types of reasoning ability can be tested by different kinds of tests— for example questions on the relationship of words understanding of paragraphs or solving of numerical problems.

3 A plane figure consists of a square ten inches on a side and an isosceles triangle whose base is the left edge of a square and whose altitude dropped from the vertex opposite the ten-inch base of the triangle common to the square is six inches.

4 Few people take the trouble of trying to find out what democracy really is. Yet this would be of great help for it is our lawless and uncertain thoughts it is the indefiniteness of our impressions that fill darkness whether mental or physical with spectres and hobgoblins. Democracy is nothing more than an experiment in government more likely to succeed in a new soil but likely to be tried in all soils which must stand or fall on its own merits as others have done before it. For there is no trick of perpetual motion in politics any more than in mechanics. President Lincoln defined democracy to be 'the government of the people by the people for the people'.

5 I went to the woods because I wished to live deliberately to front only the essential facts of life and to see if I could not learn what it had to teach and not when I came to die discover that I had not lived.

6 In all my lectures I have taught one doctrine namely the infinitude of the private man. This the people accept readily enough and even with loud acclamation as long as I call the lecture Art or Politics or Literature or the Household; but the moment I call it Religion they are shocked though it be only the application of the same truth which they receive everywhere else to a new class of facts.

7 When Melville died on September 28, 1891 he left in manuscript a novelette *Billy Budd* which was not published until 1924 though written about 1888-1891.

8 Man was not made for any useful purpose for the reason that he hasn't served any; he was most likely not even made intentionally and his working himself up

out of the oyster bed to his present position was probably a matter of surprise and regret to the Creator.

9 Fitzgerald said 'The very rich are different from you and me.' 'Yes' Hemingway replied 'they have more money.'

10 To see how this was so let us ask ourselves why the spheres were ever supposed to exist. They were not seen or directly observed in any way; why then were they believed to be there.

11 We keep one eye open however safe we feel. Indeed some of us keep both eyes open others of us moreover wish for a third eye.

12 For him to think meant to act.

13 To die bravely fighting at first seemed good later retreat seemed better.

14 Dear Jojo

    I received your last letter. At least I hope it was your last letter.

Yours sincerely
Butch Butcher

15 The title role of *Elmer Gantry* (which Rebecca West has termed 'a sequence of sermons and seductions') is played by a profligate clergyman a ponderous monster bleater of platitudes ankle-snatcher and arch hypocrite whom we meet first as an 'eloquently drunk' student at Terwillinger College in Cato Missouri.

16 He had forgotten his wallet which reposed in his green trousers; the silver which he had in the purple pair that he was wearing didn't equal the amount of the bill.

THE SEMICOLON—functions in the area between comma and full stop—rather closer to the full stop. It separates more definitely than the comma, but not so decisively as the full stop. A formal mark of punctuation, it fills a diminished need in most contemporary writing, expecially informal writing.

Use the semicolon:

To separate two or more independent clauses not linked by a co-ordinating conjunction.

'Man can have only a certain number of teeth, hair, and ideas; there comes a time when he necessarily loses his teeth, hair, ideas.'   (Voltaire)

Note: Even though a co-ordinating conjunction links the independent clauses, a semicolon may be used to separate them more emphatically.

The 7.19 is my usual train; but I seldom make it.

'Shaw said that Socialism had made him a man; and so he endeavoured to make men socialists.'   (Maurice Elson)

To separate clauses or phrases already containing commas.

He saw Nicholas Scratch, president of the Diabolist Society; Harry Clootie, professor of moral philosophy; Lucifer Poker, public censor; and Mephisto Mammon, sales manager of the Lost Souls Merchandising Company.

'As Caesar loved me, I weep for him; as he was fortunate, I rejoice at it; as he was valiant, I honour him; but as he was ambitious, I slew him.'

(Shakespeare)

To set off a conjunctive adverb joining two independent clauses. (The conjunctive adverbs most commonly employed are *therefore, nevertheless, hence, however, moreover, consequently, thus, besides, furthermore, otherwise, accordingly*.)

There are certain and invariable deductions; consequently, the science of logic is possible.

Note: When the conjunctive adverb stands first in its clause, it is customarily followed by a comma; however, modern usage tends increasingly to omit it.

Alternative: All power corrupts; moreover absolute power corrupts absolutely.

When the conjunctive adverb is not the first word in the clause it modifies, it is preceded by a comma.

No great writer formed better sentences than Emerson; no great writer, *likewise*, constructed worse paragraphs. Thoreau was Emerson's friend; he did not especially like Emerson, however.

Note: Mistaking the conjunctive adverb for the subordinating or co-ordinating conjunction leads to many errors in punctuation.

To set off such introductory specifying words as *for example*, *e.g.* (the abbreviation of Latin *exemplum gratia*, 'for the sake of example), *that is*, *i.e.* (*id est*, 'that is'), *in other words*, *namely*, *viz.* (*videlicet*, 'namely'), *to wit*, *sc.* or *scil.* (*scilicet*, 'to wit'). **These words introduce explanations and enumerations.**

'He was a behaviourist; that is, one who extracts habits from a rat.'

(William York Tindall)

' "A Cooking Egg" (by T. S. Eliot) demands first of all that we recognize the meaning of its title; namely, the kind of egg used when the strictly fresh is not required.' (George Williamson)

Note: The semicolon after such introductory words ought to be employed sparingly; in fact, the words themselves ought to be employed sparingly. However, the semicolon legitimately precedes them when an independent clause follows them, or when the sentence is long or formal. Otherwise, prefer the comma.

Do not use the semicolon:

To set off dependent sentence elements.

Right: 'I think that common sense, in a rough, dogged way, is technically sounder than the special schools of philosophy, each of which squints and overlooks half the facts and half the difficulties in its eagerness to find in some detail the key to the whole.' (W. James)

Note: The semicolon seems especially appealing before subordinate clauses and participial phrases in long sentences. Resist its appeal. The semicolon sets off elements of equal rank.

To follow the salutation or the complimentary close of a letter.

Wrong: Dear Sir;
Right: Dear Sir,
Wrong: Yours sincerely;
Right: Yours sincerely,

Exercise No. 63

In the following sentences, replace the inappropriate commas with semicolons. (For the purpose of this exercise, prefer the semicolon to an alternate mark of punctuation.)

1 Courtship in animals is the outcome of four major steps in evolution: first, the development of sexuality, secondly, the separation of sexes, thirdly, internal fertilization, or at least the approximation of males and females, and finally, the development of efficient sense-organs and brains. (Julian Huxley)

2 They [anthropologists] wanted to know 'how modern man got this way': why some people are ruled by a king, some by old men, others by warriors, and none by women, why some people pass on property in the male line, others in the female, still others equally to heirs of both sexes, why some people fall sick and die when they think they are bewitched, and others laugh at the idea.

3 He is a man, hence, he is fallible. She is a woman, therefore she will fool him.
4 It is hard to form just ideas, wayward notions, however, come without being called.
5 A small group of people arrive: I recognize Jean Negulesco, the director, Wolfgang Reinhardt, the supervising producer, and George Amy, the cutter.

THE COLON—signals that a statement or an explanation or an enumeration follows: it is 'a mark of anticipation' primarily.
Use the colon:
To introduce a series.
There are three kinds of women: the beautiful, the intellectual, and the majority.
A salad needs three things: a miser for the vinegar, a spendthrift for the oil, and a madman for the tossing.
To stress a word, phrase or clause that follows.
Intelligently enough, he attributed his error to a single cause: stupidity.
Note: A colon may be followed by a capital letter, particularly when it introduces an independent clause:
'Some people praise art because it can improve the individual: That is like admiring roses because an eye wash can be distilled from them.'

(Remy de Gourmont)
To introduce a long or formal quotation.
Thoreau wrote: 'The mass of men lead lives of quiet desperation. What is called resignation is confirmed desperation.'
To separate clauses when the second explains or amplifies or contrasts with the first.
'She needed him just as any idol needs worshippers in order to become a god: in the empty chapel it is only a piece of carved wood, but let even one devotee enter, prostrate himself and pray, and the piece of wood is transformed into a god equal to Allah or Brahma.'   (Guy de Maupassant)
'When angry, count four: when very angry, swear.'   (Mark Twain)
Do not use the colon:
To supplement a word or words that adequately introduce a list or an explanation.
Wrong: He honoured: the wise, the witty, and the wealthy.
Right: He honoured the wise, the witty, and the wealthy.

Exercise No. 64

In the following sentences, replace the *inappropriate* semicolons and commas with colons. (For the purpose of this exercise, prefer the colon to an alternative mark of punctuation.)

1 'Will you walk into my parlour?' said the spider to the fly;
'Tis the prettiest little parlour that ever you did spy.'
2 There are two methods of curing the mischiefs of faction; the one, by removing its causes; the other, by controlling its effects.
3 Dr. Jucovy, a noted psychiatrist, writes: 'The statement, "People are stout because they eat more and consume more calories" no longer suffices. Now we ask, "*Why* do some individuals eat more?" '
4 All will be well; God is silent; he is not indifferent.
5 In *The Short Bible: An American Translation*, Professor Smith translated Psalms 19.1 thus; 'The heavens are telling the glory of God, And the sky shows forth the work of his hands.'

THE DASH—in typing, made by striking the hyphen key once, with a space each side—**has the force of a strong comma.** But it ought not to be used as a loose substitute for the comma, since it marks sharper breaks in the continuity and achieves more definite effects of suspense and abruptness than the comma.

Use the dash:

To mark a sharp or sudden turn in the thought or structure of a sentence, or an afterthought tacked to the main thought.

'Women who write always have one eye on the page and the other on some man—except the Countess Haan-Haan, who has only one eye.' (Heine)

'He seemed to have a notion that there was some sort of esoteric cookery book, full of literary recipes, which you had only to follow attentively to become a Dickens, a Henry James, a Flaubert—"according to taste", as the authors of recipes say.'   (Aldous Huxley)

To separate a parenthetical expression from the main communication.

'Bacon believed—rightly, as we now know—that science could provide a more powerful magician's wand than any that had been dreamed of by necromancers of former ages.'   (Bertrand Russell)

Note: Commas or brackets may also set off a parenthetical expression. How to choose among the three? If the parenthetical expression is relatively distant from the centre of the communication, prefer the brackets; if relatively near, the comma; if intermediate, the dash. But the choice depends on individual tact, finally.

To set off a word or words in apposition or amplification, especially when several words intervene.

'I feel that this award (the Nobel Prize for Literature) was not made to me as a man but to my work—a life's work in the agony and sweat of the human spirit, not for glory and least of all for profit, but to create out of the materials of the human spirit something which did not exist before.'

(William Faulkner)

To set off the word or words gathering or summarizing a preceding series.

'Amos on the Tekoan hills, the Great Isaiah by the waters of Shiloah and the Second Isaiah by those of Babylon, Job in the dust with his sententious friends, "physicians of no value" to him, St. John on the island of Patmos, Daniel by the river Ulai—these were men of dreams and of visions who struggled with the questions that beset us all.'   (Mary Ellen Chase)

To set off a word or words intended to effect suspense, climax, or anticlimax.

'He who laughs—lasts.'   (*Reader's Digest*)

First-year essays generally have an introduction, a body, a climax—and an anticlimax.

To mark an unfinished sentence.

'Heroes do not write epics. Heroes—'

'What do they do?'

'They die.'   (Frederick Karinthy)

Note: To mark an unfinished sentence, use the dash (one stroke of the hyphen key in typing), or three full stops (the ellipsis).

Do not use the dash:

To serve, casually, the functions of a comma or other mark of punctuation.

Schoolgirl style: There was a certain magnificence in the high-up day—a certain eagle-like royalty—so different from the equally pure—equally pristine and lovely—morning of Australia—which is so soft—so utterly pure in its softness—and betrayed by green parrots flying.

D. H. Lawrence: 'There was a certain magnificence in the high-up day, a certain eagle-like royalty, so different from the equally pure, equally pristine and lovely morning of Australia, which is so soft, so utterly pure in its softness, and betrayed by green parrots flying.'

Note: The luxuriant dashes in the first specimen distract the reader: he can focus only on discrete impressions, not on the essential integrity of the sentence. The dashed sentence is not 'wrong'; it is irritating and ineffective.

Exercise No. 65

In the following sentences, replace the inappropriate commas with dashes. (For the purpose of this exercise, prefer the dash to an alternative mark of punctuation.)

1 Persuasiveness of argument, apt examples from history and experience, inner logic, and perhaps our simple need to have a part of our experience given satisfactory meaning, these have played a far greater role in the history of theories in the social sciences than strict canons of evidence and proof.

2 Why haven't I a butler named Fish, who makes a cocktail of three parts gin to one part lime juice, honey, vermouth, and apricot brandy in equal portions, a cocktail so delicious that people like Mrs. Harrison Williams and Mrs. Goodhue Livingston seek him out to get the formula?

3 More than forty of the teachers, about half of the staff of the school, are married women.

4 My expectations were not high, no deathless prose, merely a sturdy no-nonsense report of explorers into the wilderness of statistics and half-known fact.

5 Henry's genius, if that's the word, was sometimes indistinguishable from another man's pigheadedness.

6 To be a scientist, it is not just a different job, so that a man should choose between being a scientist and being an explorer or a bond-salesman or a physician or a king or a farmer.

7 In the country there are a few chances of sudden rejuvenation, a shift in the weather, perhaps, or something arriving in the mail.

8 Why they are called comics, when people who read them, both young and old, almost always look like undertakers, eludes me.

9 Restraint, Repression, Respectability, those are the three R's that made him [Sinclair Lewis] see Red.

10 And we, well, we shut our eyes, then say, 'We can't see a thing wrong.'

BRACKETS—enclose supplementary or explanatory matter of smaller relevance to the communication than that set off by the comma or dash. The parenthetical matter is structurally separate from the sentence: the sentence ought to read as well without it, and any mark of punctuation that would be needed without brackets is needed with them too.

Use brackets:

To enclose supplementary or explanatory material relatively distant from the centre of communication.

'Most birds are monogamous, however, at least for the season (or sometimes only for a single brood—like the American wren, which as bird-banding experiments have shown, usually changes partners between the first and second broods of a single year).' (Julian Huxley)

'Perhaps the first adumbration of courtship is seen in the nuptial dances of certain marine bristle-worms (*Polychaetes*), in which at certain seasons of the year and phases of the moon the creatures swim up out of their crannies in the rocks and gather in groups, excited males wriggling round the females.'

(Julian Huxley)

Note: The full stop at the end of the first sentence quoted and the comma after *Polychaetes* in the second would be proper even if the parenthetical matter were omitted. The sentence is punctuated always as if it contained no brackets; the words in brackets are punctuated independently of the rest of the sentence. A whole sentence, or several sentences, may be in brackets:

The road seemed endless. (It was ten miles long, actually. But we were in no mood for statistics.)

Do **not** use brackets to substitute loosely for commas or to enclose words necessary to the sense of the communication.

Ineffective: The writing of a dictionary (therefore) is not a task of setting up authoritative statements about the 'true meanings' of words, but a task of recording (to the best of one's abilities) what various words have meant to authors in the distant or immediate past.

Improved: 'The writing of a dictionary, therefore, is not a task of setting up authoritative statements about the "true meanings" of words, but a task of recording, to the best of one's abilities, what various words have meant to authors in the distant or immediate past.'   (S. I. Hayakawa)

Note: If commas seem to do as well as brackets in realizing your meaning, prefer the commas. Not only can an excessively parenthetical style become irritating, but also it can obscure important features of your argument. Handle brackets with care.

Exercise No. 66

In the following sentences, replace the inappropriate dashes and commas with brackets. (For the purpose of the exercise, prefer the brackets to alternative marks of punctuation.)

1 In the days that followed, happy days of renewed vigour and reawakened interest, I studied the magazines and lived, in their pages, the gracious life of the characters in the ever-moving drama of society and fashion.

2 As the Hebrews saw their history—Genesis to Judges—it fell into several discrete sections, writes H. H. Watts; and the author—authors?—of only the first sections, Genesis 1–11, made no distinction between Hebrew and non-Hebrew fate.

3 Winchell, according to H. L. Mencken, invented *pash*, for passion, *lohengrined*, for married, and *Renovated*, for divorced.

4 If the rise over the continent of North America should amount to a hundred feet, and there is more than enough water now frozen in land ice to provide such a rise, most of the Atlantic seaboard, with its cities and towns, would be submerged.

5 Mr. W. M. Thackeray has published—under the Cockney name of 'Michael Angelo Titmarsh'—various graphs and entertaining works: *The Paris Sketch-Book*, London, 1840, *Comic Tales and Sketches*, London, 1841, and *The Irish Sketch-Book*, London, 1842.

SQUARE BRACKETS—enclose matter entirely independent of the sentence —usually comments, queries, corrections, criticisms, or directions inserted by someone other than the original writer.

Use square brackets:

To correct or call attention to an error in the text.

A thing has it's [sic] law.

Note: The *sic* ('thus') in brackets indicates that the word to which it refers was misspelt by the original writer, not by the present writer, who is merely citing what he sees.

'Shakespeare was born in 1563 [1564 is the correct date] and died in 1616.'

To mark an editorial comment or addition or explanation.

'The trouble with Harry [Henry James] seems to be that he has learned to swim without ever going near the water.'   (John LaFarge)

To enclose parentheses within brackets.

'No less a personage than Winston Churchill (once, with T. S. Eliot, Santayana, and Charles de Gaulle, a member of the [International] Mark Twain Society) has testified that Tom Sawyer and Huck Finn "represent America" to him.'   (Philip Young)

Note: Punctuation following brackets disregards their existence: any mark correct without them is correct with them; any mark incorrect without them is incorrect with them.

Exercise No. 67

In the following exercise, strike out those brackets that you think are incorrectly placed.

1 'He died on February 30 [28], 1880.'
2 'I will [applause from the Conservative benches] not [applause from the Liberal benches] say [silence].'
3 'American poets [generally speaking] have abandoned Whitman's way of writing.'
4 'They are divid'd [sic] and deject'd [sic].'
5 Though his first book (anonymously published [London, 1830]) fell flat, he refused to be defeated [and the reception of his second book justified his optimism].

INVERTED COMMAS—always in pairs, break sharply the continuity of the writer's thought. They are a shorthand way of saying *quote—unquote*.

Use inverted commas:

To enclose a direct quotation—the actual words used by a speaker or writer.

The order of placing of inverted commas and other punctuation is a matter for personal and consistent choice. The most logical method is to place stops used with words in quotation marks according to the sense.

Sidney Smith remarked, 'It is impossible to feel affection beyond 78° or below 20° Fahrenheit.'

Note: (*a*) Full stops and commas go inside the closing inverted commas where they directly relate to the matter quoted.

Compare the following sentences:

'It is impossible,' Sidney Smith remarked, 'to feel affection beyond 78° or below 20° Fahrenheit.'

He asked, 'Who has seen eternity?'

Did he say, 'I saw eternity the other night'? End marks of punctuation are not duplicated: the question mark in each of the sentences cited serves alone. Logically a full stop, too, should be used to mark the end of the declarative part of each sentence; but usage and logic are at odds here, and, as always in punctuation, usage is the guide.

(*b*) The semicolon presents a special difficulty in punctuating quotations. Compare:

'He can talk for five minutes on anything,' she commented, 'but indefinitely on nothing.'

'He can talk for five minutes on anything,' she commented; 'however, he can talk indefinitely on nothing.'

In the first of the sentences instanced, the full quotation would read: 'He can talk for five minutes on anything, but indefinitely on nothing.' Since the quotation demands no semicolon, none belongs after the interrupting words *she commented*.

In the second of the sentences, though, the full quotation would read: 'He can talk for five minutes on anything; however, he can talk indefinitely on nothing.' Here the quotation is punctuated internally by a semicolon, and therefore it must be reproduced after the interrupting words *she commented*. Logically, perhaps the semicolon belongs after *anything;* but again logic yields to usage.

(*c*) A quotation may be restrictive and consequently require no punctuation:

Bryan declared that he was 'more interested in the Rock of Ages than in the age of rocks'.

Note: The full stop goes outside the inverted commas because it relates to the main body of the sentence.

To enclose provincialisms, slang expressions, and technical terms that seem out of harmony with the general tone of the writing.

He went 'round the bend'.

The 'objective correlative' has a diminished application to the art of the dance.

It dwells mainly, we at once see, in the depths of Milly Theale's 'case'.

(Henry James)

Note: The last citation may represent another function of the inverted commas, one of which many authors are excessively fond (Henry James most notably): to enclose tongue-in-cheek expressions—those intended ironically.

To enclose titles of poems, stories, chapters, essays, or articles appearing in a larger work.

'The Whiteness of the Whale' is a key chapter in Herman Melville's *Moby Dick*.

Note: The usage described here—inverted commas for the part, italics for the whole—is that of many publishing companies. However, some still retain quotation marks for the entire work as well as for its divisions. Each publishing house has its 'house style'.

To enclose the beginning and the end of a quotation extending over several paragraphs.

Note: Each paragraph in an extensive quotation begins with inverted commas, but the closing quotation mark is placed at the end of the last paragraph only. The eccentric paragraphs which follow are from D. H. Lawrence's *Studies in Classic American Literature:*

'What do you think of the ship Pequod, the ship of the soul of an American?

'Many races, many people, many nations, under the Stars and Stripes. Beaten with many stripes.

'Seeing stars sometimes.

'And in a mad ship, under a mad captain, in a mad, fanatic's hunt.

'For what?

'For Moby Dick, the great white whale.'

A preferable method of quoting extended material is single spacing it (an indication to the printer that it is to be set in smaller type).

To enclose a quotation within a quotation.

Here double inverted commas are employed although it is a matter for personal choice whether you follow this usage or the reverse one of double inverted commas normally, with single ones for the internal quotation.

'To the demonstration of a curate who wished to hold two livings that the towns were only twenty miles apart "as the crow flies", [Bishop] Thirlwall briefly replied, "Mr. Brown, are you a crow?" '   (J. C. Thirlwall, Jr.)

For quotations further complicated—a quotation within a quotation within a quotation and so on—simply alternate single and double inverted commas as often as necessary:

'In his summation, Lord Thurlow said, "I quote the legal maxim of Sir Edward Coke: 'Corporations cannot commit treason, nor be outlawed nor excommunicated for they have no souls.' " '   (James Welch)

Do not use inverted commas:

To head an essay, story, or other composition of your own authorship— unless it is a quotation.

To enclose popularly accepted nicknames or slang expressions, technical terms that have been assimilated into the main body of the language, folk sayings or proverbs, and the like.

Right: The Gunners (Arsenal Football Club), the Fuzz (police).

Right: Think-tank, gay, stoned, chick, in drag.

Right: libido, houri, italic script, syncope, colloid

Right: right as rain, a stitch in time, cart before the horse

Note: Many popular saws have become worn out with over-use. They are no less trite because enclosed in quotation marks.

Exercise No. 68

In the following passages, place quotation marks around those words requiring them.

1 Bentley, the publisher of *Bentley's Miscellany*, said to Jerrold, I had some doubts about the name I should give the magazine; I thought at one time of calling it *Wits' Miscellany*. Well, was the rejoinder, you needn't have gone to the opposite extreme.

2 One of the old philosophers, Lord Bacon tells us, used to say that life and death were just the same to him. Why, then, said an objector, do you not kill yourself? Because it is just the same.

3   Dear Pig, are you willing to sell for one shilling
         Your ring? Said the Piggy, I will.

4 The so-called race between population and food supply has again come forward as an absorbing topic of conversation, M. K. Bennett notes.

5 William Keddie, in his *Anecdotes Literary and Scientific*, tells this anecdote: A friend of the poet Campbell once remarked: It is well known that Campbell's own favourite poem was his Gertrude. I once heard him say, I never like to see my name before the Pleasures of Hope; why, I cannot tell you, unless it was that, when young, I was always greeted among my friends as Mr. Campbell, author of the Pleasures of Hope. Good morning to you, Mr. Campbell, author of the Pleasure of Hope.

THE ELLIPSIS—three full stops is a mark of omission. It is used to let the reader know that a word or group of words has been omitted as irrelevant.

Use the ellipsis:

To mark the omission of one or more quoted words not required for the immediate purpose.

Ellipsis. Allan Devoe writes, 'The wild creatures of the earth have reacted in a variety of fashions to the coming of that unique two-legged animal . . . who made his startling appearance on their earth a few milleniums ago.'

Full Quotation. 'The wild creatures of the earth have reacted in a variety of fashions to the coming of that unique two-legged animal, gifted with a convoluted cortex and a devious will, who made his startling appearance on their earth a few milleniums ago.'

Note: If the omitted word or group of words comes at the end of a declarative sentence, the full stop ellipsis is employed.

C. S. Lewis writes: 'Now what interests me about all these remarks [the remarks made by a man quarrelling with another] is that the man who makes them isn't just saying that the other man's behaviour doesn't happen to please him. . . . Quarrelling means trying to show that the other man's in the wrong.'

To mark a thought expressed hesitantly, or one interrupted or left unfinished. (Such an ellipsis is employed in fiction more frequently than elsewhere.)

He paused. 'If . . . if I should confess, what then?' he asked.

'I thought that no girl so young and beautiful could put, you know . . . put the passion and terror into it, do you understand? . . . Sol and I were out front for that scene in the last act.'   (John Dos Passos)

Do **not** use the ellipsis to substitute loosely for more specific marks. And use only three full stops—neither fewer nor more—to mark a word or words omitted.

WORD PUNCTUATION

Several marks of punctuation are used to set apart or distinguish a word or words—particular units of speech. Word punctuation may show that two or more words are to be taken as a unit (a compound word); that a word or group of words is to be given special emphasis; that a word or group of words is to be construed possessively; that a word or group of words is to be read in a particular way (as a title, as an abbreviation, as one of several similar units).

THE HYPHEN—is essentially a combining mark. It fuses parts into a new whole, expresses a unit idea. When a combination becomes familiar, the tendency is to omit the hyphen and to consolidate it. But the hyphen is itself a half-way mark. For when words first become associated, they are generally (not always) written separately. For example, first *motor car*, later *motor-car*, and now (in *The Penguin English Dictionary*) *motorcar*. Since the hyphen is a transitional mark, its use varies. Dictionaries regularly warn that authorities disagree as to which compounds ought to be written as one word, which separately, and which hyphenated. The best principle seems to be: when in doubt consult the current edition of a good dictionary.

Use the hyphen:

To join two or more words used as a single adjective and preceding their noun.
most-favoured-nation clause
out-of-date notions
iron-clad principles
never-to-be-forgotten experience
salt-water fishing

To join two or more words used as a single part of speech.
ne'er-do-well
hero-worship
forget-me-nots
go-between
door-to-door
Note: Words like those listed are particularly troublesome, because of their instability. Many once hyphenated are now consolidated (*today, tomorrow, tonight*). Others may now be written as one, hyphenated or separately (*war monger, war-monger; folk-lore, folklore; tax-payer* or *taxpayer; man-power* or *manpower*). When in doubt (and without dictionary), consolidate.

To join two or more words when the last is a participle.
shallow-thinking journalist
worm-eaten apple
ready-made clothing
hard-working woman
battle-scarred town
Note: Some such compounds, long in the language, are consolidated (*sunburnt, thunderstruck, widespread*).

To join an adjective or noun to a noun ending in *d* or *ed*.
blue-eyed Minerva
bull-necked wrestler
bird-brained politician

To separate compound numbers, fractions used as adjectives, and compound fractions.
twenty-one years
twenty-first year
two-thirds majority (*but* two thirds of the men)
twenty-one twenty-fifths of those voting

To avoid ambiguity or confusion.
A woman-hating man needs a gun.
(*Compare:* A woman hating man needs a gun.)
re-form, re-creation, re-cover
(*Compare:* reform, recreation, recover)

To prevent three identical consonants or two identical vowels or a small letter and a capital letter from coming together.

hall-lamp	shell-like	grass-seed
re-echo	pre-eminent	semi-invalid
anti-Semitism	pro-Germanic	co-operative

Note: Some awkward words such as coefficient, coalesce and deist are now accepted in their consolidated form and others will follow.

To separate some prefixes from the rest of the compound.

self-reliance	self-reliance	non-stop
ex-Prime Minister	self-hate	pre-natal
ex-professor	self-starter	post-mortem
un-self-conscious	by-product	off-chance

To join fanciful, coined, or duplicating words.
a come-up-and-see-me-sometime glance
a know-it-all delusion

to buy on the never-never
the clomp-clomp-clomp of heavy boots
To separate two or more compounds with a common base.
bright, -er, -est
1- and 2-inch nails
To divide a word at the end of a line.

mid-dle	mid-summer
mi-cro-scope	mi-cro-scop-ic

Note: A one-syllable word ought never to be divided: *wrong, died, spared.*
A word ought never to be divided after a single letter. **Avoid:** a-broad, E-zekiel.

Words are divided by syllables, and pronunciation is the clue to syllabification. But when in doubt consult your dictionary.

Do not use the hyphen:
To join two or more words used as an adjective when they follow the word modified.

His notions were out of date years ago
His principles are iron clad
It was an experience never to be forgotten

To join a group of words acting as a unit modifier when it is enclosed by quotation marks.

'good neighbour' policy
'most favoured nation' clause
'all for love' attitude

Note: If any word or group of words was originally hyphenated, the hyphen is retained:

'*blue-pencil*' *habit,* '*actor-manager*' *duties.*

To join two words comprising a proper noun when they act as a unit modifier.

West End theatres
South American music

Note: If two proper nouns act as a unit modifier they are properly joined by the hyphen: *Latin-American music, Austro-Hungarian Empire.*

To join a prefix or suffix and a root.

antisocial	tenfold
extramural	spoonful
neolithic	clockwise
misspell	kingdom
ultramarine	womanhood

Exercise No. 69

Place the hyphen between the words requiring hyphenation.

1 He was a science fiction devotee; he had a mania for reading about space travel, time travel, martian maidens, and extragalactic supermen.
2 After an all night hunt on the moor, the police caught the thrice escaped murderer, Richardson, and the twenty two year old Watson, imprisoned for robbery with violence.
3 All cargo freighters offer dependable on time deliveries to eighty three countries and colonies on all six continents. By lighter packing, lower insurance rates, less transshipment, they can compete with other shipping media.

4 Now that the last fly over on the London Birmingham motorway is finished, it is possible to travel non stop on this up to date road.
5 His anti vivisectionism alienated the single minded fanatics.
6 Land rich but money poor, he walked unhappily through the fields of thriving, knee high corn.

THE APOSTROPHE—is a mark of omission: it indicates that a word has been contracted; that a letter or letters which belong to it (or which belonged to it at some earlier period in the history of the language) have been intentionally left out.
Use the apostrophe:
To indicate a contraction.
it's (for *it is* only)
mornin' (in colloquial speech, for *morning*)
B'ham (for *Birmingham*)
don't (for *do not*)
'tis (for *it is*)
'tisn't (for *it is not*)
ne'er (for *never*)
won't (for *will not*)
To form the possessive case of a noun.

POSSESSIVE SINGULAR	POSSESSIVE PLURAL	GROUP POSSESSIVE
John's medicine	Joneses' marriage	William and Mary's reign
Dr. John's tonic	teachers' tasks	man of straw's backbone
Jesus' life	gods' laughter	Tom and Tilly's toffee
Holmes' *Autocrat*	gentlemen's preference	men and women's approval
razor's edge	children's play	Arthur Wellesley, Duke of Wellington, the Field Marshal's death.

Note: (*a*) To form the possessive singular of a noun, add *apostrophe s* to its simple form. Add only the *apostrophe* if another *s* would cause an awkward combination of *s*-sounds.
Holmes's novel, but *Holmes' sonnet*.
(*b*) To form the possessive plural of a noun, add only the *apostrophe* to the simple plural form of the noun; but if the simple plural form does not end in *s*, add *apostrophe s: boys' books*, but *men's books*.
(*c*) To form the possessive of a group of words containing a single idea, add *apostrophe s* to the last word: William and Mary's reign (they reigned jointly), but Henry's and Elizabeth's reign (they reigned separately).
To form coined plurals, as well as standard plurals of letters, numbers, symbols, and of words referred to as words.
T.U.'s or their equivalents have sprung up.
The *x*'s equal the *y*'s.
The 1940's have been called the 'Aspirin Age'.
There are not three *two*'s in English.
Do not use the apostrophe:
To form possessive pronouns.
its (not *it's*)
hers (not *her's*)
ours (not *our's*)

116 *English Made Simple*

theirs (not *their's*)
yours (not *your's*)

To form the possessive of nouns that stand for inanimate objects, save in a few idiomatic constructions.

the value of the picture (*not* the picture's value)
the location of the comma (*not* the comma's location)
the trees of the wood (not the wood's trees)
But: duty's call, sun's beams, wit's end (all idiomatic)

Exercise No. 70

Place the *apostrophe*, or the *apostrophe s*, wherever required. (Below are given the nominative forms of those nouns to be converted into the possessive.)

1 Smith Brothers Cough Drops
2 Newton Law
3 earth surface
4 geese cackling
5 hero welcome
6 Prince of Wales horse
7 James novels
8 Queen Elizabeth II coronation
9 Achilles heel
10 anybody else word
11 princess gown
12 princesses gowns
13 Xerxes triumph
14 heres how
15 at 6s and 7s
16 *Mississippi* has four *s* s
17 six oclock
18 youll
19 theyd
20 whos

THE FULL STOP FOR ABBREVIATIONS. The full stop may mark a shortened word, an abbreviation. Abbreviations are perfectly appropriate to material requiring condensation—catalogues, for example. But in more formal contexts only conventional abbreviations ought to be employed (*Mr., Mrs., Dr., St.*). Avoid abbreviations not sanctioned by general usage.

Use the full stop to mark abbreviations.

Rev. William Baker   (formal: the Reverend William Baker,
    or   *not*
Rev. W. Baker   Rev. Baker)
Prof. R. C. Dickson   (formal: Professor R. C. Dickson or
    Professor Dickson, *not* Prof. Dickson)
Dr. French   John French, M.D.
St. Francis

etc. (*et cetera*), 'and so forth'.
e.g. (*exempli gratia*), 'for example'.
et al. (*et alii*), 'and others'.

Note: Avoid abbreviations of titles when they are not followed by a proper name and abbreviate proper names sparingly.

Do **not** use the full stop to mark abbreviations when the full stop is not part of the official name or when the full stop has been popularly discarded.

TUC	TNT (trinitrotoluol)
BBC	OED (Oxford English Dictionary)
UN	UK
USA	ERNIE (Electronic Random Number Indicating Equipment)
ANZAC	

Exercise No. 71

Abbreviate the following words.

1. *anno domini*
2. bachelor of arts
3. *post meridiem*
4. doctor
5. logarithm
6. Third verse of the fourth chapter of Saint Luke
7. radio aircraft discovery and recognition
8. tuberculosis
9. Union of South Africa
10. *videlicet*
11. square inch
12. gill
13. Seven minutes past eight o'clock in the morning
14. European Free Trade Area
15. hundredweight
16. ton
17. January
18. Monday
19. north-west (compass direction)
20. centigrade

ITALICS—(in handwriting and typewriting indicated by underlining with a single straight line) **call attention to a word or words as being distinct from other words.**

Use italics:

To emphasize or contrast.

Consider what he *is*, not what he *was*.

To set forth words in a foreign language.

We arrived, *enfin* [finally].

The latter grunted, '*C'est défendu*'. ['It is forbidden.']

Note: If the foreign word has become naturalized—absorbed into English— italics are unnecessary.

Latin: bona fide, et cetera, dramatis personae

French: café, elite, ensemble

German delicatessen, dachshund, rucksack

To set forth titles of separately published works—plays, novels, symphonies, pamphlets, magazines, newspapers, and the like.

Hamlet (play)

Lucky Jim (novel)

Lohengrin (opera)

Vogue (magazine)

The Observer (Sunday newspaper)

The Times (daily newspaper)

Titles of parts of published works are in inverted commas: 'I Begin a Pilgrimage' in E. E. Cummings' *The Enormous Room.*

To set forth names of ships or planes.

The *Titanic*

The *Sacred Cow*

To indicate a word, letter, or number as such.

The antonym of *part* is *whole.*

He knows a *p* from a *q.*

Primitive people think 7 has a magical significance.

Do **not** use italics to gain emphatic effects in a mechanical way. Excessive use of italics is one of the symptoms of the schoolgirl style.

Exercise No. 72

Italicize (underline) those words that require italicization.

1 Every Sunday morning Julia goes to bed with The People, The Sunday Times and even an Observer.
2 He sailed to America on the Europa last week.
3 'Sally Bowles', perhaps the best story in Christopher Isherwood's Goodbye to Berlin, was adapted into a mediocre play, I Am a Camera, by John van Druten.
4 Enthusiastic Anglo-Saxonists may write obstinately about starcraft or leech, instead of astronomy and doctor, but the language feels that it is already adequately supplied, though it may regret that young people are no longer betrothed, plighted or affianced, and that these beautiful words are replaced by engaged, with its automatic suggestion of a public lavatory.
5 I saw the motion picture Come Back, Little Sheba in France, with French voices dubbed in. It seemed odd to hear Shirley Booth refer to 'la petite Sheba'.

CAPITAL LETTERS—are a conventional device intended to ease the reader's way, but faulty usage impedes it. The initial capital signifies that a word is a proper noun or adjective (or to be considered as one), or that a new sentence or line of verse succeeds a former.

Use an initial capital letter:

To mark a proper noun or adjective, a title of distinction, a common noun personified, a reference to the Deity.

Proper names: Oliver Cromwell, Australia, England, Oxford

Proper adjectives: Cromwellian, Australian, English, Oxfordian

Races, ethnic groups, religions, (and the people who belong to them): Caucasian, Judaism, Catholicism, Negro, Jew, Protestant, Buddhist

Deity: God, Jehovah, Jove, Brahma, His word

Wars and battles: World War II, Battle of the Bulge

Days and months: Monday, October

Companies, organizations, clubs: Independent Television Authority, General Motors Corporation, Young Men's Christian Association, Rotary

Geographical divisions: the Thames, the West, Snowdonia, the North Pole, the East End, Knightsbridge, Piccadilly, High Street

Official bodies: the Ministry of Defence and the House of Lords

Titles of distinction: Archbishop of Canterbury, Duke of York, Earl Marshal

Personifications: There, Honour battled Ease. The Chair recognizes nobody

Specific courses: Economics I, Mathematics II

To mark the first word of every sentence, line of verse, and full quotation.

A man must eat.

'Hope springs eternal in the human breast:
Man never is, but always to be, blest.'
                                        (Pope)

'Do not hack me,' said the Duke of Monmouth to his executioner, 'as you did my Lord Russell.'

To mark the pronoun *I* and the interjection *O*.

It was I.

'Who could have thought such starkness lay concealed
Within thy beams, O Sun!' (Blanco White)

To mark a word signifying family relationship when used as a name.

Yes, Father said he would.

(But: My father said he would.)

Do not use the initial capital letter:

To mark general or class names.

Every boy wants to be prime minister.

The Queen is an honorary colonel.

Though he was a liberal in principle, he did not belong to the Liberal Party.

To mark a point of the compass, except where it refers to a recognized geographical division.

Lars Porsena sent his men north, south, east, and west.

(But: The South has become an industrial area.)

To mark the seasons of the year.

spring, summer, autumn, winter.

Exercise No. 73

Provide initial capital letters where necessary.

1 the anglo-saxon language was the language of our saxon forefathers though they never gave it that name. they called it english. thus king alfred speaks of translating 'from book-latin into english'; abbot aelfric was requested by aethelward 'to translate the book of genesis from latin into english'; and bishop leofric, speaking of the manuscript (the 'exeter manuscript') he gave to exeter cathedral calls it 'a great english book'.

2
                        upon saint crispin's day
                        fought was this noble fray,
                        which fame did not delay
                        to england to carry.
                        o when shall english men
                        with such acts fill a pen,
                        or england breed again
                        such a king harry?

3 *stories in the modern manner*, edited by philip rahv and william phillips, was published by avon books. perhaps the best story in it is gide's 'theseus'.

4 the lion is a kingly beast.
  he likes a hindu for a feast.

5 it is the grace of god that urges missionaries to suffer the most disheartening privations for their faith. This grace moved saint isaac jogues to say (when ye came to canada), 'i felt as if it were a christmas day for me, and that i was to be born again to a new life, to a life in him.'

SPELLING

THE DILEMMA

Weak spellers are at a serious disadvantage. They may be intelligent and educated, but their errors in spelling cause others (often erroneously) to consider them a trifle backward. Until he faces the reality of his problem, the weak speller depends upon a poor compromise. Afraid to try spelling the effective word, he uses the one he knows how to spell and hopes that it means almost the same thing. The dangers of this method are clear:

STUNTED VOCABULARY:

The girl in the tight red dress *walked* across the street.

INSTEAD OF *slithered, undulated, jiggled, strutted.*

INCORRECT USAGE:

That boy xylophonist is a *progeny.*

INSTEAD OF *prodigy.*

THE CAUSES

In part the spelling problem results from **illogical relationships between the sound and the spelling of English words.** These inconsistencies are due to:

Changes in pronunciation without changes in spelling.

EXAMPLE: In the Middle Ages *meat* rhymed with *neat,* but *sweet* did not rhyme with *eat.*

Changes in spelling without changes in pronunciation.

EXAMPLE: The Old English word *bough* remains today as a noun; but the verb exists as *bow.*

Changes in both spelling and pronunciation.

EXAMPLE: Old English *skip* has become modern *ship;* yet Old English *skipper* remains unchanged.

Thus, in modern English spelling, we have troublesome sounds like:

oo (*a*) m*oo*n, d*o*, cr*ui*se,   (*b*) g*oo*d, l*oo*k, r*oo*f.
      rendez*vous,* Hind*u,*   (*c*) d*oo*r, fl*oo*r.
      rag*ou*t, s*ue.*   (*d*) z*oo*logy.
k (*a*) li*k*e, *q*uery.   (*d*) anti*q*ue.
  (*b*) li*qu*or.   (*e*) hibis*c*us.
  (*c*) ex*c*ept.   (*f*) a*cc*umulate.

ough rough thorough cough
silent letters autum*n* *w*riter *p*neumonic

120

Because of such phonetic confusion, absurdities like the following may easily be constructed:

> We had *ghoti* on *phraideigh*.
>
> *ghoti* = fish   gh as in *cough*
> o as in *women*
> ti as in *vacation*
>
> *phraideigh* = Friday   ph as in *philosophy*
> ai as in *aisle*
> eigh as in *neighbour*

With certain sounds in English, no rules are effective. One has no choice but to learn the word.

Other causes for poor spelling lie with **the individual.**

He has not learned **to read** carefully.

He has not learned **to listen** carefully.

He has not learned **to memorize.**

He has not learned **to work** in order **to learn.**

THE DILEMMA SOLVED

The **ideal solution** is to reform English spelling. In Spanish and Italian, words are spelt as they sound—each letter has its fixed correspondent in sound. Although attempts have been made to modernize English spelling, the weak speller ought not to await the outcome of these experiments before solving his spelling problem.

Thus, the best **practical** solutions may be summarized:

Analyse the Difficulty—does it stem from:

1 Carelessness in writing, reading, listening?
2 Groups of similar words differently spelt?
3 Varied sorts of 'special' complexities?

Eliminate the Difficulty—by:

1 Learning the 'Rules'.
2 Using Mnemonic Devices.
3 Using the Dictionary.
4 Drilling on words over and over until they are absolutely learnt.

Copy each word neatly, carefully, using the dictionary as a double check for accuracy.

Limit the spelling list to *twenty words* at a time. It is easier to learn smaller groups of words.

LEARNING THE RULES. Memorizing the spelling of a word is better than memorizing the 'rule' for spelling. But rules do help: to explain how certain groups of words are spelt; to indicate what exceptions to the rules must be learned. Thus, a few rules and the words which illustrate them will help the weak speller to conquer almost all of his difficulties.

Note: Only those rules which are most helpful have been included in this section. Exceptions to almost every rule are frequent. One has no recourse save to learn them. Where there have been too many exceptions to make a rule practical, that rule has been omitted.

Learn each rule before proceeding to the next.

IE and EI

Rule: **When pronounced as** *ee* **(as in** *week* **or** *meek***),** *i* **is followed by** *e*, **except after** *c*.

Place I before E
Except after C

EXAMPLES:

IE pronounced as EE

achi*e*ve	cash*ie*r	gri*e*f	shri*e*k
api*e*ce	chi*e*f	ni*e*ce	si*e*ge
beli*e*f	fi*e*ld	pi*e*ce	thi*e*f
beli*e*ve	fi*e*nd	pi*e*rce	ti*e*r
bi*e*r	fi*e*rce	repri*e*ve	wi*e*ld
bri*e*f	fri*e*ze	shi*e*ld	yi*e*ld

Typical exceptions:

*ei*ther, n*ei*ther, s*ei*zure, sh*ei*k, w*ei*rd.

EI (pronounced as ee) after C

c*ei*ling	dec*ei*ve	rec*ei*ve	rec*ei*pt
conc*ei*ve	conc*ei*t	perc*ei*ve	dec*ei*t

Typical exceptions:

speci*e*, speci*e*s

EI is generally used:
If sounded as *ā* **(as in** *neighbour* **or** *weigh***)**

f*ei*nt	r*ei*gn	w*ei*ght
fr*ei*ght	sk*ei*n	v*ei*l

If sounded as *ĭ* **(as in** *hĭt***)**

counterf*ei*t	forf*ei*t	sover*ei*gn
for*ei*gn	surf*ei*t	

Exceptions: *si*eve, misch*ie*f, misch*ie*vous

If sounded as *ī* **(as in** *ice***)**

*ei*der	h*ei*ght	sl*ei*ght

Except for the variations above, the order is **IE** in almost all other sound combinations:

fri*e*nd, li*eu*tenant.

Note: If *i* and *e* do not form a **digraph** (two letters used to represent a single sound), the rules discussed have no effect.

cloth*ie*r	d*ei*ty	hygi*e*nic
fi*e*ry	glaci*e*r	sci*e*nce

EXPLANATION: *fiery* breaks into *fi ery*. Since the *i* and *e* have independent sound values, they cannot be considered a digraph. The same principle applies to other words in this group. Thus, such words must simply be memorized.

Do not proceed to the next rule before completing the exercise below.

Exercise No. 74

Complete the spelling of the following words by filling in *ie* or *ei* in the blank spaces:

1 w–rd	4 s–ge	7 f–nt	10 for–gn	13 w–ld
2 glac–r	5 l–utenant	8 anc–nt	11 cash–r	14 d–ty
3 fr–nd	6 financ–r	9 conc–ve	12 p–rce	15 hyg–ne

Silent *e*

Dropping the silent *e*

Rule: Final silent *e* is usually dropped before an ending (suffix) beginning with a vowel.

EXAMPLES:

argue	arguing	grieve	grievance
become	becoming	judge	judging
change	changing	shine	shining
conceive	conceivable		

Retaining the silent *e*

Rule: Final silent *e* is usually retained before an ending beginning with a consonant.

EXAMPLES:

achieve	achievement	like	likely
bare	barely	live	liveliness
definite	definitely	love	lovely

Note: There are several exceptions to the rules governing final silent *e*, especially those about *dropping* the vowel.

1 Final silent *e* is retained after SOFT *c* and SOFT *g* before endings (suffixes) beginnings with *a* or *o*.

EXPLANATION:

Soft *c* as in fan*c*y
Hard *c* as in *c*ome
Soft *g* as in ran*g*e, *g*ist
Hard *g* as in *g*amble, *g*ut
Thus, C and G are generally SOFT before *e*, *i*, and *y*, but HARD before *a*, *o*, and *u*.

So, to keep the soft sound of *c* and *g* before *a* and *o*, the final silent *e* is retained. If the *e* were not retained, *peaceable* (to rhyme with *peekable*) would be the result, instead of *peaceable*.

EXAMPLES:

notice	noticing	noticeable
change	changing	changeable
manage	managing	manageable

2 Final silent *e* is retained in some words before the suffix *-ing* to prevent mispronunciation or ambiguity.

EXAMPLES:

singe   singeing = to scorch
BUT
sing   singing = to chant

dye	dyeing	= to colour
die	dying	= to cease to live
tinge	tingeing	= to colour.
ting	tinging	= to make a high-pitched sound

3 Final silent *e* is retained when the endings *ye*, *oe*, *ee* precede the suffix *-ing*.

EXAMPLES:

hoe	hoeing	eye	eyeing
agree	agreeing	see	seeing
decree	decreeing	shoe	shoeing

Do not proceed to the next rule before completing the exercise below.

Exercise No. 75

Complete the spelling of the following words by filling in *e* where necessary. If no *e* is needed, leave the space blank.

1 judg–ing	3 peac–able	5 courag–ous	7 lov–ly	9 sens–ible
2 ey–ing	4 din–ing	6 manag–ing	8 chang–able	10 ho–ing

Final Y

Changing final *y* to *i*.

Rule: When preceded by a consonant and followed by a suffix (other than one beginning with *i*), final *y* changes to *i*.

EXAMPLES:

beauty	beautiful	lonely	loneliness
busy	business	marry	marriage
easy	easily	mercy	merciful
envy	envious	rely	reliance
	BUT		
carry	carrying	occupy	occupying
	carried		occupied
ply	plying	try	trying
	plies		tries

EXPLANATION:

Since the suffix *-ing* appears in the present participles *carry*, *ply*, *occupy*, and *try*, the *y* is retained—the initial letter in the suffix is *i*.

Retaining the final *y*.

Rule: If it is preceded by a vowel, the final *y* is usually retained.

EXAMPLES:

attorney	attorneys	monkey	monkeys
boy	boys	play	plays
chimney	chimneys	trolley	trolleys

Typical exceptions:

day	daily
lay	laid
pay	paid
say	said
slay	slain

Note: Before several suffixes the final *y* is retained.

EXAMPLES:

dry—dryness	joy—joyous
employ—employment	sly—slyness
enjoy—enjoyment	play—playful

Before the suffix *-ly*, the final *y* of monosyllables is sometimes dropped and sometimes retained. Either form is permissible.

EXAMPLE:

dry   drily   dryly

Do not proceed to the next rule before completing the exercise below.

Exercise No. 76

Complete the spelling of the following words by filling in the blank space with *y* or *i* (or *ie*).

1 occup–ing	6 tr–s
2 lonel–ness	7 ke–s
3 trolle–s	8 bus–ness
4 dr–ness	9 rel–ance
5 turke–s	10 occup–d

Final Consonants

Rule: A final single consonant is doubled when:

It is preceded by a single vowel (b*a*t).

It is followed by a suffix beginning with a vowel (sitt*i*ng).

It appears in a monosyllabic word (*hit, run*).

OR

It appears in a word accented on the last syllable (*o mit'*).

EXAMPLE AND EXPLANATION:

1 lop   lo*pp*ing

Final single consonant *p* is preceded by single vowel *o*.

Final single consonant *p* is followed by suffix beginning with vowel *i* (-ing).

lop is a monosyllabic word.

THUS, final single consonant is doubled–lo*pp*ing. Note that the doubled consonant keeps the preceding vowel short. Compare *lopping* with *lōping*.

2 omit   omi*tt*ed

Final single consonant *t* is preceded by single vowel *i*.

Final single consonant *t* is followed by suffix beginning with vowel *e* (-ed).

Accent is on the second syllable–o mit'.

THUS, final single consonant is doubled—omi*tt*ed. Other words whose final consonants are doubled include:

MONOSYLLABLES		POLYSYLLABLES	
beg	ship	acquit	equip
drop	stop	allot	forget
quit	swim	begin	occur
quiz		commit	permit
(Note: *qu*: *u* after *q* is not		compel	transfer
a vowel, but has the con-		confer	
sonant sound of *w*.)			

The final single consonant is NOT doubled when:

1 The accent is shifted to a preceding syllable when the suffix is added.

EXAMPLES:

confer′ confe*rr*′ing BUT *con*′ference
prefer′ prefe*rr*′ing BUT *pre*′ference

EXPLANATION:

Conferring and *preferring* fulfil the provisions of the rule for doubling the final consonant. *Con′ference* and *pref′erence* shift their accents to the first syllable, and so do not meet the rule that accent must be on the final syllable.

MORE EXAMPLES:

refer reference benefit benefited conquer conquerable

2 The final consonant is already doubled.

EXAMPLES:

start started
rela*x* rela*x*ing (*x* is equivalent to the double consonant *ks*)

3 The final consonant is preceded by two vowels.

EXAMPLES:

be*a*t be*at*ing *boi*l *boi*ling

REVIEW TEST ON RULES INVOLVING:
ie or *ei*, **final *e*, final *y*, final consonants.**

Exercise No. 77

Complete the spelling of the following words according to one of the four rules.

1 bugs on the c–ling.
2 no more worr–s.
3 f–ld of dais–s.
4 circus monk–s.
5 hop–ng to see you.
6 angry arg–ment.
7 sun is shin–ng.
8 nin–y years old.
9 he rec–ved a letter.
10 refer–ng to you.
11 unbel–vable story.
12 s–zed the gun.
13 what's your prefer–nce?
14 what occur–d?
15 th–ves in the night.
16 notic–able gap.
17 merc–less enemy.
18 s–ge of the fort.
19 dark, narrow all–s.
20 stud–ous scholar.
21 stud–ng all night.
22 benefit–d from rules.
23 rel–f from hunger.
24 I perc–ve.
25 yours tru–y.

K Added to Words Ending in C

Rule: Words ending in *c* add *k* before an ending (suffix) beginning with *e*, *i*, or *y*, to preserve the hard sound of *c*.

EXAMPLES:

frolic frolic*k*ed frolic*k*ing
mimic mimic*k*ed mimic*k*ing
picnic picnic*k*ed picnic*k*ing
traffic traffic*k*ed traffic*k*ing

-cede, -ceed, and sede

Rule: Learn the four words and eliminate the innumerable errors.

THE FOUR WORDS:
 SUPERSEDE—the only word in English that ends in *-sede*.

EXCEED
PROCEED } these three are the only words in English that end in *-ceed*.
SUCCEED

Thus, all other words having this sound end in *-cede*.

EXAMPLES:

accede	intercede	recede
concede	precede	secede

Plurals

Regular plurals.
Rule: Nouns form plurals by adding *-s* to the singular.

EXAMPLES:

boys	girls	homes
books	Greeks	lemons

Irregular plurals.
The plural of some nouns ending in *o* preceded by a consonant is formed by adding *-es*.

EXAMPLES:

echoes	tomatoes	Negroes
heroes	tornadoes	torpedoes
innuendoes	mosquitoes	vetoes
potatoes		

TYPICAL EXCEPTIONS:

albinos	gauchos	provisos
altos	halos	quartos
banjos	lassos	solos
cantos	pianos	tobaccos
dynamos	piccolos	zeros

For plurals of nouns ending in *y*, see Rule on Final *y*.
If noun ends in *y* preceded by consonant, change *y* to *i* and add suffix *-es: sky—skies; enemy—enemies.*
If noun ends in *y* preceded by a vowel, add *s: chimney—chimneys; day— days; play—plays; monkey—monkeys.*
Foreign plurals.
Most of these words, having entered the English language late, **do not fall into the usual categories and must simply be learned.**

EXAMPLES:

addendum	addenda
alumnus	alumni
axis	axes
basis	bases
datum	data

ellipsis	ellipses
erratum	errata
memorandum	memoranda
synopsis	synopses

Note: Some nouns in English retain archaic forms in their plural:
ox—oxen; deer—deer, child—children. Such words must be checked in a dictionary.

Exercise No. 78

Underline the one correctly spelled word in each of the following groups:

1 froliced, frolicked, froleced, frollicked
2 addenda, adenda, adendda, addinda
3 pimentos, pimmientos, pimientoes, pimentoes
4 synopsus, synoppsis, synopsis, synoppsus
5 innuendo, inuendo, inuenddo, innuindo
6 superside, supercede, superceed, supersede
7 succeed, succede, suceed, sucsede
8 mosquitoes, mosuito, mosquitos, mosquittoes
9 interceed, intersede, intercede, interseed
10 mimiced, mimmiced, mimicked, mimmicked
11 seceed, sesede, secede, seseed
12 Negros, Negroes, Neggros, Nigras
13 excede, ecsede, exceed, exseed
14 enemmys, enemys, enemmies, enemies
15 dynamos, dynamoes, dymanos, dymanoes

Possessives. Don't confuse contractions with the possessive forms of pronouns. Possessive pronouns do not take an apostrophe.

EXAMPLES:

Possessive Pronouns	*Contractions*
its (The door has its knob)	it's (it is)
Note: *its*' does *not* exist	
their (They went their way)	they're (they are)
your (Have your supper?)	you're (you are)
whose (Whose book is this?)	who's (who is)

Note: No apostrophes are used with the other possessive and relative pronouns either: *his, hers, ours, yours, theirs*.

If the singular or plural noun does not end in *s*, form the possessive by adding *apostrophe s* to the simple (nominative) form of the noun.

SINGULAR: Bill's book   boy's game   Joan's hat
PLURAL: oxen's yokes   men's clothes   children's games

To form the possessive plural of nouns ending in *s*, add only the apostrophe: *ladies' coats, soldiers' guns, hostesses' etiquette, princes' privileges*.

In compounds, the last word uses the sign of the possessive.

EXAMPLES:

mother-in-law's house
attorney general's office
brother-in-law's car
commander-in-chief's army

Indicate joint possession by placing the sign of the possessive on the last item in the series; indicate individual possession by placing the sign of the possessive on each item.

EXAMPLES:

Joint	*Single*
Bill and Dick's house	Bill's and Dick's trials
(they own it together)	(each has undergone a trial)
Joint Chiefs-of-Staff's opinion	Army's and Navy's opinion

Apostrophes are often omitted in well-known firm names, geographic names, names of organizations.

EXAMPLES:

United Nations Secretariat
United States Air Force
St. Pauls Cathedral
Heals furniture

Homonyms—are words similar (although not necessarily exactly alike) in sound but different in meaning and often in spelling. To eliminate the innumerable errors in spelling which result from confusion about homonyms, learn the meanings of each member of the related group of words, create sentences using each word correctly, and repeat until all confusion has disappeared.

access	way of approach; admission
excess	superabundance
advice	noun (pronounce as *ice*)
advise	verb (pronounce *-ise* as *eyes*, or *ize*)
aisle	a passageway
isle	an island
all ready	everything is ready
already	previously
all together	everyone in company
altogether	completely, without exception
allusion	a reference, as 'an *a*llusion to the Bible'
illusion	a false impression or deception
altar	place of worship (*noun*)
alter	to change (verb)
brake	a device to arrest motion by friction
break	to separate violently into parts
bridal	pertaining to a bride (*bride + al*)
bridle	headgear used to control a horse
cite	to quote or refer
sight	noun: a view; verb: to see, aim
site	location or *sit*uation
coarse	gross, unrefined
course	used for all other purposes of spelling
council	group of people organized to consider affairs
consul	government official handling affairs of his nation in an alien country
counsel	noun: advice; verb: to advise
dessert'	a sweet served after the main course of a meal (accent on last syllable)

desert	used as noun and verb for all other purposes of spelling (noun has accent on first syllable: de′sert; verb has accent on last syllable: desert′)
device	noun (pronounce as *ice*)
devise	verb (pronounce -*ise* as *ayes* or *ize*)
dining	eating (pronounce first *i* as *eye*)
dinning	making a loud noise (din) (pronounce first *i* as *i* in *hit*)
formally	in a formal manner
formerly	previously
forth	onward
fourth	number after third; one of four parts
foul	ugly, evil
fowl	a winged bird
idle	lazy, doing nothing
idol	a pagan god
idyll	a poem or prose work describing joys of country life
ingenious	clever (pronounce *e* as in *eat*)
ingenuous	naïve, forthright, simple, as in 'the ingénue's ingenuous belief that the villain meant her no harm' (pronounce *e* as in *hen*; note *u*, which is pronounced as *you*)
its	possessive pronoun of *it*
it's	contraction of *it is*
lead	noun: a metal (rhymes with *head*); verb: to conduct (rhymes with *bead*)
led	verb: the past tense of verb *lead*
loose	adjective: not tightly fastened; verb: to release, set free
lose	verb: to suffer loss of
passed	past tense of verb to pass, as 'we *passed* her school'
past	adjective, as 'this *past* week was ended too soon' or preposition, 'he walked *past* the house'
peace	freedom from disturbance
piece	a portion
personal	belonging to a particular person. Pronounced per′sonal
personnel	people engaged in a service. Pronounced per son nel′
persecute	to oppress or injure
prosecute	to try by law
practice	noun (pronounce -*iss*)
practise	verb (same pronunciation)
principal	chief, as in 'the principal of a school', or 'principal source of income'
principle	a general truth or rule. See MNEMONICS
prophecy	noun. See also *advice* and *device*
prophesy	verb
quiet	calm, still. Note two syllables: *qui* + *et*
quite	entirely, truly. Note one syllable
rain	water
rein	device used to guide horses
reign	the rule of a monarch
stationary	fixed position, as 'a ship in dry-dock is *stationary*'
stationery	writing materials
to	preposition, as 'he went to the store'; or sign of the infinitive, as 'to sing'
too	adverb meaning more than enough, as 'too long', 'too soft'
two	the number after one
weather	climate
whether	conjunction introducing an alternative, as 'he did not know whether or not to go'

Exercise No. 79

Underline the correct word in each of the following sentences.

1 I want your (advice, advise) in a legal matter.
2 Will the truce have any (affect, effect) on food prices?
3 I want you here (all together, altogether), not one at a time.
4 Please sit (beside, besides) me at the dinner table.
5 His manners are too (coarse, course) to allow him to play with refined children.
6 Shall we have (desert, dessert) in the (dinning, dining) room?
7 I asked our foreign (council, consul) to get me a visa.
8 I (cited, sited) him the place on the blueprint where I had selected the (site, sight, cite) for our house.
9 We must (device, devise) a new plan to capture Mary's affection.
10 Every pound invested returns (its, it's) value in gold.
11 He (lead, led) his horse to water, and it drank.
12 During the (past, passed) six months, her life has been miserable.
13 The (foul, fowl) of the air, and the fish of the sea, and whatsoever passeth through the paths of the seas.
14 Why do you continue to (persecute, prosecute) that poor kitten?
15 If you will remain (quiet, quite) still, you will hear the echo from Forest Mountain.

MNEMONICS. (pronounced nemon′iks)—the art of developing the memory (Greek, to remember).

In addition to the rules of spelling, the student has at his disposal **mnemonic devices.** These techniques of memory association can and do help so long as the student never forgets that the word to be spelt is more important than the mnemonic device.

The best methods may be grouped as SIGHT SPELLING and SOUND SPELLING.

Sight Spelling. Repetition of associated visual images aids memory.

Wherever possible, reduce the troublesome word to simple words.

sergeant = *serge* + *ant*
battalion = *batta* (atta boy) + *lion*
or
battle and battalion have double *t* + single *l*
business = *sin* in bu*sin*ess
separate = *pa* + *rate* or *a rat*

Group words which are spelt alike. (See HOMONYMS)

useful	earful
hopeful	cupful
careful	handful

No adjective ends in FULL (except full itself)

man-*wo*man	All right
men-*wo*men	All wrong
	All night

Sheer trickery

cem*e*t*e*ry	We get there with ease (E's).
*e*xp*e*ri*e*nc*e*	These are
*e*xist*e*nc*e*	*E*asy words.
deve*lop*	*lop* off the final e.
grammar	Write *gram*, then spell it backwards, but drop the g.
indispensable	That which one is not *able to dispense* with.
principle	A princip*LE* is a ru*LE*.

Summary of Spelling Rules

	RULE	EXAMPLES	EXCEPTIONS
IE AND EI	I before E, except after C.	achi*e*ve, but c*ei*ling	1 Use *EI* when: (a) Sounded as *a*: n*ei*ghbour, w*ei*gh (b) Sounded as *i*: forf*ei*t (c) Sounded as *i*: h*ei*ght 2 Use *IE* for almost all other sounds: fr*ie*nd. 3 If *i* and *e* do not form a digraph, rules do not apply: f*ie*ry, d*ei*ty.
FINAL SILENT E	1 **Drop** before suffix beginning with a vowel. 2 **Retain** before suffix beginning with a consonant.	grieve—grievance absolute—absolutely	1 Retain *e* after soft *c* and soft *g* before suffixes beginning with *a* or *o*: peaceable, manageable.
FINAL Y	1 **Change** final *y* to *i* if *y* is preceded by a consonant and followed by any suffix except one beginning with *i*. 2 **Retain** final *y* if it is preceded by a vowel.	beauty—beautiful BUT carry—carrying boy—boys; valley—valleys	dry—dryness; sly—slyness. day—daily; pay—paid
FINAL CONSONANTS	**Double** final consonants when: 1 Preceded by a single vowel. 2 Followed by a suffix beginning with a vowel. 3 The consonant terminates a monosyllabic word. 4 The consonant terminates a polysyllabic word accented on the last syllable.	1 drop—dropped; beg—beggar 2 quit—quitting; swim—swimmer 3 hit—hitter; run—running 4 omit—omitted; transfer—transferred	Final consonant is not doubled if: 1 Accent shifts to preceding syllable when suffix is added: confer—confer'ring BUT con'ference. 2 Final consonant is already doubled: star*t*—star*t*ed. 3 Final consonant is preceded by two vowels: beat—beating; boil—boiling.
K added to words ending in G	**Add** *k* to words ending in *c* before a suffix beginning with *e, i, y*.	frolic—frolicking—frolicked; picnic—picnicking—picnicked	

Summary of Spelling Rules (continued)

	RULE	EXAMPLES	EXCEPTIONS
-CEDE -CEED -SEDE	Except for *supersede, exceed, proceed, succeed,* all words having this sound end in -cede.	accede, precede, recede, concede	
PLURALS	1 Regular noun plurals add -s to the singular.	boy—boys; book—books	
	2 Irregular plurals:		(a) Piano—pianos; zero—zeros; solo—solos.
	(a) Add -es if noun ends in o preceded by consonant.	(a) echo—echoes; Negro—Negroes	
	(b) Change y to i and add -es if noun ends in y preceded by consonant.	(b) sky—skies; enemy—enemies	
	(c) Add -s if noun ends in y preceded by vowel.	(c) play—plays; day—days	
POSSESSIVES	1 Don't confuse contractions with possessive pronouns.	Contraction Possessive Pronoun 1 it's (it is) its they're their (they are)	
	2 Use no apostrophes with possessive or relative pronouns.	2 *his, hers, ours, yours, theirs, whose*	
	3 If singular or plural noun does **not** end in s, add **apostrophe** and s.	3 prince—prince's (Sing.), princes' (Plur.) soldier —soldier's (Sing.), soldiers' (Plur.)	
	4 If singular or plural noun **does** end in s, add apostrophe.	4 Hostess—hostess' (Sing.), hostesses' (Plur.); Jones— Jones' (Sing.), Joneses' (Plur.)	

Sound Spelling. Repetition of associated auditory images aids memory.
Many words are spelt exactly as they sound. *Therefore, break the word into syllables, carefully pronounce each syllable, and write the word as you say it.*

op po nent	crit i cism	tem per a ture
o mit ted	oc ca sion	eve ry bod y
prom i nent	dis ap point ed	

Do not omit vowels.

bound *a* ries	in *ter* ested
a ver *a*ge	su p*er* in tend ent

Do not omit consonants.

re co*g* nize	prob a *b*ly
par*t* ner	gov er*n* ment
can *d*i date	

Do not transpose letters.

vil l*ai*n	g*ua*rd
mar r*ia*ge	we*i*rd
p*er* spi ra tion	tra ge *dy*

Work out your own mnemonic devices for the following words:

stretched	opinion	led
until	immediately	appearance
together	existence	forty

Learn the following list of words often misspelt because mispronounced. The source of error in pronunciation is italicized.

abomi*n*able	chara*ct*eristic	heigh*t*
accident*a*lly	cri*ti*cism	inte*r*esting
ar*c*tic	cru*e*lty	ir*rele*vant
a*th*lete	*e*very	labor*a*tory
bellig*er*ent	extra*o*rdinary	perco*la*tor
bene*v*olent	Febru*a*ry	re*cog*nize
choco*l*ate	gri*e*vous	

THE DICTIONARY

A good dictionary is an invaluable tool. Even a small desk edition gives the spelling, pronunciation, usage, and meaning of thousands of words.

For each entry, the dictionary provides the correct spelling, variant spellings (when more than one is acceptable), spellings or irregular inflected forms, and syllabication. The principal parts of verbs, plurals of nouns, and the comparative and superlative forms of irregular adjectives and adverbs are often listed.

Pronunciations are given for each entry and for difficult inflected forms. The pronunciation key at the front of the dictionary explains the letter symbols and letters with diacritical marks that are used in the pronunciations.

Definitions, etymologies (origins of words), synonyms, and antonyms give a clear picture of a word's meaning.

In addition, usage notes show how a word should be used: whether it is in general use or a colloquial term, whether it is archaic or current, correct for formal writing or slang, what its position and function in a sentence are, and more.

Study the sample pages from the *Concise Oxford Dictionary* on pages **136–7**. When you know how and where to locate information in a dictionary, use your own dictionary to do these exercises.

1 Syllabize the following words:

illustration	geography	pronunciation
dictionary	poliomyelitis	dream
equivocate	definition	plateau
privilege	question	transference
collegiate	board	language

2 Pronounce the following words:

literature	rapine	singing
scallop	hauteur	fuselage
dirigible	drama	machination
phthisis	benign	vitiate
plethora	tomato	gladioli

3 Give the correct spellings of the principal parts of the following verbs:

sit	fly	sting
set	bleed	slay
lie	fight	dwell
lay	wring	cleave
drink	write	thrive

4 Which of the following words ought to be given capitals?

history	negro	kingdom
english	indian	chaucer
french		fascism

5 Study the definitions of the following words and discriminate between:

(*a*) satire, sarcasm, irony, parody.
(*b*) wit, humour.
(*c*) town, village, hamlet.
(*d*) flaunt, flout.
(*e*) claim, assert.

6 Learn the etymology of the following words:

epidermis	ubiquitous	eliminate
demagogue	curfew	pyjama

7 Give at least one *synonym* and one *antonym* for each of the following words:

talkative	benevolent
abhor	consent
able	narrow

8 Indicate the correct 'label' (provincial, archaic, etc.) for each of the following words:

kinky	shark	stook
glycogen	swain	epicycle
gobbledygook	surplice	pub

English Made Simple

GUIDE WORD
Two guide words at the top of each page indicate the first and last entries on the page.

ILLUSTRATIVE PHRASE
Illustrative sentences and phrases place main-entry words in a context to clarify meaning and exemplify usage.

HOMOGRAPHS
Words with the same spelling but with different meanings and indicated by a small number placed after the entry.

SYLLABICATION
Main-entry words are divided into syllables, the parts of a word that are pronounced as units.

ACCENT
Accents show how to pronounce and stress the word.

RUN-ON ENTRY
Run-on entries are formed by adding or replacing a prefix or suffix of a main entry word. They are not defined since their meaning is clear from the sense of the main-entry word.

PRONUNCIATION
Pronunciation is listed immediately after the main entry and follows a pronunciation key.

of wh. to Rom. collaterals & OF *compasser* (see foll.) is obsc.]

com'pass² (kŭm-), v.t. Go round; hem in; grasp mentally; contrive; accomplish. Hence ~ABLE a. [ME, f. OF *compasser*, f. Rom. *°compassare* measure (COM-, *passus* PACE)]

compă'ssion (-shn), n. Pity inclining one to spare or help, as *have~ on us.* [ME & OF *compassion*, f. LL *compassionem* f. LL COM(*pati pass-* suffer), see -ION]

compă'ssionate¹ (-sho-), a. Sympathetic, pitying; ‖ ~ *allowance* (granted when an ordinary pension or allowance is not admissible under official rules); ‖ ~ *leave* (granted out of compassion). Hence ~LY² (-tl-) adv., ~NESS (-tn-) n. [latinized f. F *compassionné* (-ATE²)]

compă'ssionăte² (-sho-), v.t. Regard, treat, with compassion. [f. prec.]

compăt'i|ble, a. Consistent, able to co-exist, (*with*). Hence or cogn. ~BIL'ITY n., ~bLY² adv. [F, f. med. L *compatibilis* (COM*pati* suffer with, -BLE)]

compăt'ri|ot, n. Fellow-countryman. Hence ~ŏt'IC a. [f. F *compatriote* f. LL COM(*patriota* PATRIOT)]

compeer', n. Equal, peer; comrade. [ME & OF *comper*; see COM-, PEER¹]

compĕl', v.t. (-ll-). Constrain, force, (*to do, to* a course); bring about (an action) by force, as ~ *submission*; (poet.) drive forcibly; ~*ling* a., rousing strong interest or feeling of admiration. Hence ~l'ABLE a. [ME, f. L COM(*pellere puls-* drive)]

cŏm'pend, n. = COMPENDIUM.

compĕn'dious, a. Brief but comprehensive (of works & authors). Hence ~LY² adv., ~NESS n. [ME, f. LL *compendiosus* (foll., see -OUS)]

compĕn'dium, n. (pl. -*ums*, -*a*). Abridgement; summary; abstract. [L, lit. what is weighed together f. COM(*pendĕre* weigh)]

cŏm'pĕnsăt|e, v.t. & i. **1.** Counterbalance; make amends (*for* thing, *to* person, *with, by,* another thing, or abs.); recompense (person *for* thing). **2.** (mech.). Provide (pendulum etc.) with mechanical compensation. Hence cŏmpĕn'satıve a. & n., ~OR n.‖ cŏmpĕn'satory‖ a. [f. L COM(*pensare* frequent. of *pendĕre* pensweigh)]

compĕnsā'tion, n. Compensating; thing given as recompense; ~-*balance*, ~-*pendulum*, of chronometer (neutralizing effect of temperature). Hence ~AL a. [ME, f. OF, or f. L *compensatio* (as prec., see -ATION)]

cŏm'père (-pâr), n., & v.t. **1.** Organizer of cabaret or broadcast entertainment who introduces the artistes, comments on the turns, etc. **2.** v.t. Act as ~ to. [F, = gossip]

compēte', v.i. Strive (*with* another *for* thing, *in* doing, or abs.); vie (*with* another

These pages are reproduced from
by permission of

slabber

slabber. = SLOBBER. [16th c., prob. of Du. or LG orig., cf. Du., LG *slabber(e)n*]

slăck, a., adv., n., & v.t. & i. **1.** Sluggish, remiss, relaxed, languid, loose, inactive, negligent, (~ *water*, about turn of tide, esp. low tide; ~ *in stays*, naut., slow in going about; *a* ~ *rope*, not taut; *keep a* ~ *hand* or *rein*, ride, or fig. govern, carelessly; ~ *trade, business, market*, with little doing; ~ *weather*, inclining to indolence); ~ *lime*, slaked lime; hence ~'EN⁶ v.t. & i., ~'LY² adv., ~'NESS n. **2.** adv. (In comb. w. *dry, bake*, etc.) slowly, insufficiently, (~-*dried hops; to* ~-*bake bread*). **3.** n. ~ part of rope (*haul in the* ~); ~ time in trade etc.; (colloq.) spell of inactivity or laziness[(*I'm going to have a good* ~ *this afternoon*); (dial.) cheek, impertinence; (pl.) trousers; coal-dust used chiefly for making briquettes etc. **4.** vb.~en; make loose (rope; often *off, away*); (colloq.) take a rest, be indolent, whence ~'ER¹ n.; = SLAKE (lime); ~ *off*, abate vigour; ~ *up*, reduce speed of train etc. before stopping. [OE *sleac, sliec*, adj., = MDu., MLG *slak*, OHG *slach*, ON *slakr*, cogn. w. L *laxus*; the sense 'coal-dust' is of obsc. orig.]

slăg, n., & v.i. (-gg-). **1.** Dross separated in fused state in reduction of ores, vitreous smelting-refuse, clinkers; BASIC ~; volcanic scoria; ~*wool*, = *mineral* WOOL; hence~g'Y² (-g-) a. **2.** v.i. Form~, cohere into ~like mass. [16th c., f. MLG *slagge* of obsc. orig.]

slain. See SLAY.

slāke, v.t. Assuage, satisfy, (thirst, & rhet. revenge etc.), whence ~'LESS (-kl-) a. [(poet.);](also *slack*) combine (lime) chemically with water. [OE *sleac-, slacian* f. *sliec* SLACK adj.]

sla'lom (-ah-), n. Ski-race down course defined by artificial obstacles; obstacle race in canoes. [Norw.]

slăm, v.t. & i.[(-mm-),]& n. **1.** Shut (t. & i., of door etc; often *to* adv.) with loud bang; put *down* (object) with similar sound; [(sl.)] hit, beat, gain easy victory over. **2.** n. Sound (as) of ~med door; gaining of every trick in whist, bridge, etc. (*grand, little,* ~, winning of 13, 12, tricks in bridge). [perh. f. Scand., cf. Sw., Norw., Icel. *slamra*]

sla'nder (-ah-), n., & v.t. **1.** False report maliciously uttered to person's injury; uttering of such reports, calumny; (law) false oral defamation (cf. LIBEL, SCANDAL); hence or cogn. ~OUS a., ~OUSLY² adv., ~OUSNESS n. **2.** v.t. Utter ~ about, defame falsely; hence ~ER¹ n. [ME *sclaundre* f. AF (OF) *escla(u)ndre*, alt. f. OF *escandle* f. LL SCANDALum]

slăng, n., & v.t. **1.** Words & phrases in common colloquial use, but generally considered in some or all of their senses to be outside of standard English; words & phrases either entirely peculiar to or used in special senses by some class or profession, cant, (*racing, thieves', artistic,*

DEFINITION NUMBERS
Consecutive definition numbers mark each different sense in which an entry word is used.

IDIOM
A main-entry word may be used with another word or words to form a phrase with a different meaning from the literal interpretation of the separate words of the phrase.

ETYMOLOGY
Etymologies (word origins) are placed after the definition or definitions of entry words. In this dictionary they are always enclosed in square brackets.

USAGE LABELS

GUIDE TO SPELLING IN OTHER FORMS

MAIN ENTRY
Main entries are easily recognizable by their bold type. They are not only words and phrases but abbreviations, prefixes, suffixes and combining forms.

PART OF SPEECH
The part or parts of speech. An entry word is most often used as are entered before the definition of the word.

The Concise Oxford Dictionary
the Clarendon Press, Oxford

SPELLING LIST

These are words that are frequently misspelt. They are taken from lists that have been compiled by a number of different teachers and examiners.

absence
accept
accidentally
accommodation
acquaintance
across
aggravate
all right
amateur
appearance
argument
athletic
auxiliary

beginning
believed
beneficial
benefited
buoyant
business

catalogue
cemetery
character
choose
chosen
committed
committee
competition
complete
comptroller
convenience
conscientious
conscious
council
counsel
criticise
criticism

deceive
decision
definite
descendant
description
desert
dessert
develop
difference
disappear

disappointed
dividend
doesn't
don't

eighth
embarrassed
environment
equipped
equipment
exaggerate
excellent
excite
exciting
exercise
existence
expedient
experience

familiar
fascinate
February
finally
foreigner
fourth
friend

government
grammar
grievance

hadn't
height
heroes
heroine
humorous
humour

imagination
imagine
immediately
indispensable
interested
inveigle

knowledge

laboratory
latter

literature
lonely
loose
lose
losing

maintenance
marriage
meant
mischievous
monetary
municipal

necessary
necessity
noticeable

occasionally
occur
occurred
occurrence
o'clock
omitted
opinion
opportunity

parallel
parliament
performance
personnel
pleasant
possess
precede
prejudice
president
principal
principle
privilege
probably
proceed
professor
promissory
pronunciation
prophecy
prophesy
purchasable

quiet
quite

received
recommend
referred
regrettable
relieved
responsibility
restaurant
rhythm

schedule
seize
sense
separate
similar
simplified
society
stationery
stop
stopping
strength
studies
studying
succeed
successful
superintendent
supersede
surprise

tendency
thousandth
together
too
tragedy
transferred
transient
tries
truly

villain

Wednesday
weird
where
whether
woman
writ
written

yield

Exercise No. 80

Fill in the missing letters to complete the spelling.

1 wearing new cl . . . s. 2 benef . . . d from his industry. 3 army serg . . . nt,
4 suffered no ill . . . fects. 5 will not rec . . . mend his friend. 6 super . . . tendent
of the apartment house. 7 old law omit . . . ed too much. 8 new law super . . . edes
it. 9 legal proc . . . dure. 10 buy a new diction . . . ry. 11 was . . . fected by the
climate. 12 added money to his princip . . . . 13 the prophe . . . y did not come true.
14 an inter . . . ting play. 15 parli . . . t consists of two Houses. 16 sadness and
lon . . . liness. 17 correct pron . . . ciation. 18 easy consc . . . nce. 19 cold in the
Ar . . . tic. 20 cold in the w . . . rd cem . . . t . . . y.

Exercise No. 81

Spell correctly such of the following words as are misspelt below (ignore words
spelt correctly).

innocuous	nemonic	accessible
inoculate	morgenatic	agrandize
embarassed	cemetary	plagiarize
harassed	hypocracy	transferrable
inuendo	questionaire	repellant
dessicate	manouvre	scurrulous
mimicing	tranquility	

Exercise No. 82

Following is a list of nouns. Supply the adjective derived from the same root as the
given noun.
(a) opacity, inchoation.
(b) satiety, abrasion.
(c) cacophany, calumny, condignity.
(d) acerbity, anomaly, assiduity.
(e) contiguity, contumacy, garrulity.
(f) misogyny, poignancy.
(g) recalcitration, viscosity.
(h) viscidity, salubrity, peccancy.
(i) onus, parabola, plethora.

Exercise No. 83

Indicate the correct spelling by inserting the vowel or vowels necessary:

invulner . . . ble	forc . . . ble
aberr . . . nt	portent . . . s
irrefrag . . . ble	domin . . . nce
collaps . . . ble	enforc . . . ble
confection . . . ry	adapt . . . ble
invid . . . s	adjust . . . ble
concommit . . . nt	admis . . . ble
coher . . . nce	dut . . . s
feas . . . ble	instantan . . . sly

BUILDING A VOCABULARY

THE IMPORTANCE OF A GOOD VOCABULARY

In Goethe's *Faust*, Mephistopheles gives this advice to a student:

> To words hold fast!
> Then the safest gate securely pass'd,
> You'll reach the halls of certainty at last.

At least this once we ought to listen to the Devil's counsel. Without in any way trying to raise the devil, psychologists have reached the same conclusions: that **size** and **accuracy** of vocabulary provide two of the most reliable guides to a man's **general ability.**

To just how many words do men hold fast? All answers have been debated. Estimates of the average vocabulary range from 4,000 words to 12,000. Those who read extensively may, however, have **recognition vocabularies** exceeding 50,000 words. None debate this fact: whatever the number of words in a man's vocabulary, he can easily add to it—and benefit from the addition. Before studying the steps by which vocabulary can be improved, it will be useful to understand the differences between the kinds of vocabularies.

Speaking Vocabulary—most limited of the vocabularies, it consists of the words used in conversation.

The cat is a self-centred animal, thinking only of itself, almost never of the world about it.

Writing Vocabulary—more extensive than the *speaking* vocabulary, it consists of the words used in conversation and, if the writer has a wide reading background, many thousands more.

The cat is an *egocentric* creature , *tranquil* in its *self-assurance*, *oblivious* of the world about it.

Reading Vocabulary—larger than either the *speaking* or *writing* vocabularies (both of which it includes), it contains words which the reader can define when he sees them, even though he neither speaks nor writes them.

'The cat understands *pure being*, which is all we need to know and which it takes us a lifetime to learn. It is both *subject* and *object*. It is its own *outlet* and its own *material*. . . . The cat has a complete *subjective unity*. Being its own centre, it *radiates* electricity in all directions. It is *magnetic* and *impervious*.'

(Van Vechten, *Peter Whiffle*)

Recognition Vocabulary—largest of the vocabularies, it contains, in addition to the other three, those words which he has seen or heard previously, but cannot clearly define. He may recognize them in *context* (how they are used in the sentence), but he lacks assurance about their actual meaning.

140

When you notice a cat in *profound* meditation,
The reason, I tell you, is always the same:
His mind is engaged in a *rapt* contemplation
Of the thought, of the thought, of the thought
    of his name:
    His *ineffable effable*
    Effanineffable
Deep and *inscrutable singular* Name.
          (T. S. Eliot, *The Naming of Cats**)

The *erudite partisan* of cats understands that on the rare occasions when *felines* gather, they do so in a '*clowder*' and kittens in a '*kendle*'.
          (adapted from a letter to *The Times*)
Thus, anyone who intends to improve his vocabulary must learn how to transfer into his speaking and writing vocabularies, appropriate words from his reading and recognition vocabularies. To effect the transfer involves work, but the reward is proportionate to the effort.

FOR PRACTICE: The following sentences have been selected from newspapers, speeches, magazines, books, and the like. How many of the italicized words can you define or provide a synonym for?

Next to each word, indicate to which of your four vocabularies (**speaking, writing, reading, recognition**) it belongs. Then note at the end of the exercise the sources from which the material was taken. Evaluate your own vocabulary.

1 Television is here with us, for understanding and wise *application*.
2 Although Italian wines of honourable *lineage* are relatively available, wine-drinkers know little about them beyond the *ubiquitious Chianti*.
3 Those days were gone, the old brave innocent *tumultuous*, *eupeptic tomorrowless* days.
4 Study of *scriptural* teachings, *unencumbered* by *ecclesiastical dogma*, may help to determine a *criterion* of convincing faith.
5 That *subtle* something which *effuses* behind the *whirl* of *animation*, a happy and joyous public spirit, as *distinguish'd* from a *sluggish* and *saturnine* one.

SOURCES:

1 Speaker at a public meeting.
2 Article on wines in New York *Times Magazine*.
3 William Faulkner, *Requiem for a Nun*.
4 Letter to member of radio panel.
5 Walt Whitman, *Specimen Days*.

METHODS OF BUILDING VOCABULARY

Many roads lead to a strong vocabulary and in this section we will map several of them, first indicating some well-paved routes and some dangerous soft shoulders.

Make your study of words a **passionate pursuit**, not a **painful prowl**. When

---

* From *Old Possum's Book of Practical Cats*, by T. S. Eliot. Reprinted by permission of Faber and Faber Ltd., London.

you see *denim* advertised as one of the more popular fabrics for summer wear, do you wonder why it goes by that name? If you turn eagerly to the dictionary to discover the answer, you have an affection for words that will inevitably lead to a better vocabulary.

But if, when you come upon a sentence like this:

How can the party leaders predict victory when most of the electorate are *Mugwumps?* you pass on in ignorance to the next sentence or grudgingly look up *Mugwump* in the dictionary, you are not even on a **painful prowl**—you are in **ignoble ignorance.**

Learn words that you intend to use in speaking, writing, and reading. **Don't try to learn mere lists of words.**

A Poor Method

ephemeral	short-lived
acrimonious	bitter
ubiquitous	omnipresent
clandestine	secret
obdurate	stubborn

Lists provide ineffectual study aids because:

They fail to tell whether the word is suitable for speaking, writing, or reading (since they give no reference to where or how the word was used).

They become too long and cannot easily be memorized.

They mistake **quantity** as the purpose of vocabulary building; **quality** (usefulness, relevance) is quite as important.

An Effective Method

1 Enter in a small notebook or on 3 × 5 index cards only those you want to use. Discuss only one word on a page or card.

2 List the following information from the dictionary:

(*a*) Meanings of the word.

(*b*) Spelling, pronunciation, syllabication, part of speech.

(*c*) Origin (etymology), roots.

(*d*) Use as other part of speech.

(*e*) Synonyms, antonyms.

Note: Re-read the passage about the dictionary in Section 5: **Spelling.**

3 Copy out the sentence in which you found the word. Leave space for other sentences you may come upon.

4 Jot down examples of how you have used the word in speaking or writing.

5 Keep your notebook or pack of cards handy, and study it daily. Find occasions where you can use the word in speaking and writing. (See below.)

word	EPHEMERAL
part of speech	adjective
pronunciation	i fem'ar al
syllabication	e-phem-er-al
origin	Greek: *ephēmeros*, of or for only one day
meaning	Defin.—lasting but a short time, short-lived, transitory

other uses   *ephemera*—noun; *ephemerally*—adverb

synonym, antonym   Synonyms: *fleeting, evanescent, transient*
    Antonyms: *permanent, lasting, eternal*

how it is used   'All is *ephemeral*—fame and the famous as well.'
          (Marcus Aurelius, *Meditations*)

space for other
  examples

Student's use of   We waste too much time fretting about *ephemeral* things like clothes and outings. We ought to pay more heed to lasting matters. (Letter to his college chaplain)

USING THE FAMILY OF TONGUES. The word *mother* has cognates (words related in origin) in many languages:

mutter—German	*mētēr*—Greek
moeder—Danish	*madre*—Spanish
modhir—Icelandic	*mère*—French
mater—Latin	

After many centuries of examining interrelationships of this kind, scholars have recently discovered that men living in countries ranging from Central Asia to Western Europe speak languages derived from a parent or source language whose origin dates back about 4,000 years. This parent language is commonly known as Indo-European and gave rise to the following languages:

Eastern

Sanskrit (now dead); neo-Sanskrit languages of India: Hindi, Bengali, etc.
Indo-Iranian: Persian
Armenian

Western

Celtic: Irish, Scottish, Welsh, Breton, Cornish
Italic: Latin (and other dialects like Umbrian, Etruscan); Modern Romance languages: Italian, French, Spanish, Portuguese
Hellenic: Greek
Baltic:
  EAST: Russian, Ukrainian
  WEST: Polish, Czech, Slovene
Teutonic: ENGLISH, Dutch, German, Scandinavian
Modern English passed through several stages before becoming what it is today:

Old English (Anglo-Saxon), A.D. 450–A.D. 1100.

Typical Anglo-Saxon contributions:

ARTICLES: *the, a, an*
PRONOUNS: *that, which*
PREPOSITIONS: *in, for, to, from, without*
CONJUNCTIONS: *and, but*
VERBS: *are, have, could, sit, see, run, send*
NOUNS: *mother, father, wife, husband, house, door, bed*

SOME ENGLISH BORROWINGS FROM FOREIGN COUNTRIES (Latin and Greek will be taken separately)

ITALY	SPAIN	MEXICO	GERMANY	RUSSIA	HUNGARY	NETHERLANDS
incognito	renegade	lasso	kindergarten	vodka	goulash	skipper
salvo	corral	ranch	strafe	czar	vampire	schooner
gusto	peccadillo	mesa	blitz	sable	tokay	yacht
confetti	flotilla	canyon	waltz	polka	hussar	sloop
vendetta	Negro	coyote		steppe		dock
balcony	mosquito	tomato				hull
ditto	tornado					
bandit						
contraband						

AFRICA	PERSIA	ARABIA	SANSKRIT	HEBREW	TURKEY	EGYPT
oasis	pyjama	alcohol	indigo	amen	angora	gypsy
tangerine	jackal	algebra	chintz	seraph	fez	gum
gorilla	bazaar	coffee	ginger	jubilee	ottoman	paper
chimpanzee	divan	nadir		balsam	horde	
canary		zenith		Sabbath		
		cipher		cherub		

INDIA	AMERICAN INDIAN	JAPAN	CHINA	MALAYA	POLYNESIA	AUSTRALIA
polo	tomahawk	kimono	tea	ketchup	tattoo	kangaroo
coolie	wigwam	geisha	chop suey	gingham	taboo	boomerang
khaki	skunk	jiu-jitsu	joss	caddy		
curry	tobacco		sampan	gong		
			soy	junk		

Note: Many Latin words survived from the earlier period of Roman occupation, and yet more were added when Roman missionaries began to arrive in the sixth century. About these words, more will be said later.

A Danish invasion in the eighth century added yet more monosyllabic words to the English vocabulary: *leg*, *sky*, *skin*, and the pronoun, *they*.

Middle English, 1100–1500

The Norman Conquest in 1066 introduced the French language to England. French has since that time deeply influenced English vocabulary, particularly words about food, clothing, law, government, and the like:

mauve	felony	debris	adroit
grimace	intrigue	grotesque	clique
ingénue	ennui	denouement	svelte
chauvinism	renaissance	silhouette	cliché
detour	genre		

Modern English, 1500–present

Early Modern English: Sixteenth to seventeenth centuries
Later Modern English: Eighteenth to nineteenth centuries
Contemporary English: Since 1900

From 1500 forward, as commerce increased, and England's contacts with the Continent and the East grew, the vocabulary of the English language expanded tremendously. The preceding list merely suggests some of the borrowings which have entered our vocabulary from foreign sources.

Language knows no boundaries and English as it is known and spoken today is a composite of many foreign tongues. If, therefore, you build vocabulary from your knowledge of words borrowed from these foreign tongues, you can prove even better to yourself and to those about you that no man is alone.

Exercise No. 84

PART I Make a list of words borrowed from the Italian for the following subjects:

	MUSIC	PAINTING	LITERATURE
EXAMPLE:	*solo*	*chiaroscuro*	*sonnet*

PART II One word has been omitted from each of the following sentences. From the list of foreign borrowings below, select the appropriate word to complete each sentence. Check the meaning and pronunciation of each word in your dictionary.

(*a*) Surely not for this, merely whistling at the passing parade, a trifle, a ......, not for this can you hang me.

(*b*) Blindly, zealously patriotic, ignoring his own safety, Corporal Essex, a ...... to the end, gave his life for Zanzibar.

(*c*) Wedgwood china is famed for the delicate ...... patterns which adorn it.

(*d*) Stop wheedling! She is not the type you can ...... into making you the beneficiary of her will.

(*e*) What might have been a happy marriage between Romeo and Juliet became instead a tragedy because of a ...... between their families.

(*f*) No further misfortunes can befall Stella Dallas, for she is already at the ...... of her luck.

(*g*) When Senator Flannellip really gets warmed up to his speech—about ten hours from now—we can be sure that the ...... will last for at least a week.

(h) His yawl has two masts; our ...... has but one.
(i) Love is the state in which man sees things most widely different from what they are. The force of illusion reaches its ...... here, sweetened and transfigured to new heights.
(j) Fame pursues me, but I wish only to be obscure, to be nameless, to move ...... among the throng.

vendetta (Italian)	nadir (Arabic)
bas-relief (French)	sloop (Dutch)
incognito (Italian)	peccadillo (Spanish)
zenith (Arabic)	chauvinist (French)
cajole (French)	filibuster (Spanish)

BUILDING VOCABULARY WITH ROOTS. A root (or *stem*) is that part of a word which contains the core of meaning:

fin—meaning 'end', 'limit', 'boundary' is the root of such words as:

finish—to bring to an end (or, to bring to the boundary)
finite—measurable (or, having bounds)
in*finity*—having no bounds
de*finite*—precisely bounded

aster, meaning 'star', is the root of such words as:

asterisk—the star-shaped figure used in writing as a mark of reference
astronomy—the law (or, the study of the scientific laws) of the stars
disaster—an unfortunate event (literally, hostile star or fate)

The greatest number of roots in English derive from the classical languages, Latin and Greek (*fin-*, in the example above, is a Latin root; *aster* is a Greek root). By learning several Latin and Greek roots (there are about 160 in all, but you need not try to learn every root), you increase your mastery of words in two important ways:

You will understand more clearly the essential meaning of each part of a word by observing how roots are combined to form words:

nostos, return home +, *algos*, pain = nostalgia
tele, far off + *phoné*, voice, speech = telephone
epi, upon + *-derm*, skin = epidermis
dia, through + *therme*, heat = diathermy
peri, around + *skopos*, watcher = periscope
khronos, time + *metron*, measure = chronometer

You will learn words in groups by observing how several words relate to a common root:

aequ-, Latin for equal, level, like

equal	inequality	equivocable
equate	equity	equinox
equable	adequate	equilibrium
equality	inadequate	equivalent

voc-, Latin for call

vocation	avocation	revoke
vociferate	invocation	provoke
vociferous	convoke	evoke

You do not need to know Latin or Greek to profit from the tables printed below any more than you need to know Old English, Danish, or French to speak and write effective English. Learn a few roots at a time and put them to work, first in the exercises, and then in your reading. When you come upon an unfamiliar word like *bicephalous*, don't turn immediately to the dictionary. Ask:

What does it seem to mean in context?

What is the meaning of *bi*? The answer is *two*. What is the meaning of *cephalous*? The answer is *head*.

Thus, you combine reading in context with a knowledge of roots, a significant advance towards word mastery.

A SELECTED LIST OF WORDS DERIVED FROM LATIN ROOTS (A)

ROOT	MEANING	CURRENT WORDS
AG- agere	do, drive, act	agent, coagulate, actor
AM- amo, amare	love	amorous, amatory, amour
ANIM- animus	mind, soul, breath, life; intention	animal, animate, unanimous, magnanimous, pusillanimous; animadversion, animosity
BELL- bellus	beautiful, fair	belle, belladonna, belle-lettres
BELL- bellum	war	bellicose, belligerent, rebel
CED-, CESS- cedere, cessus	go, yield	succeed, cede, secede, recede, process, excess, recess, abscess
CENT- centum	hundred	century, centennial
CIT- citare	summon arouse	recite, excite, cite, incite
CIV- civis	citizen	civic, civilization, civil, civilian
COGNIT- cognoscere, cognitus	know	cognizant, incognito, cognition
COR, CORD- cor, cordis	heart	accord, concord, discord, cordial, courage
CORP- corpus	body	corpse, corps, corporal (punishment), corporation
CRED- credere	believe, credit	credit, creditor, discredit, credible, credence, incredible, incredulous
CULP- culpa	offence, fault	culprit, culpable
CUR-, CURS- cursor, currere	run	current, concourse, cursory, precursor, discursive

Exercise No. 85

Note: Complete these exercises before proceeding to the next group of roots.

PART I For each of the LATIN ROOTS (A) above, add at least two current words not already listed.

PART II Complete the following sentences by selecting the appropriate choice from the list of CURRENT WORDS.

(All words are selected from the LATIN (A) roots and derivatives above.)

(a) In 1933, to mark a century of progress, Chicago held its ...... Exposition.

(b) The speaker used harsh, fiery language in his effort to ...... the mob to fury.

(c) The ...... man turns away from his enemy in craven and abject fear; the courageous man, although ...... of the dangers ahead, faces the enemy and taunts him.

(d) to prevent the ...... agitated autograph-hunters from becoming too ...... in their attentions, the actor, although generally cordial and ...... towards his admirers, was compelled to disguise himself and mingle ...... among the wildly ...... throng.

(e) A hasty, ... study of roots will result in failure. If, however, one approaches them with diligence and enthusiasm, not ......, his vocabulary will ...... rather than ....

CURRENT WORDS

succeed	recede	cursory
animadversion	belligerently	animated
incognito	magnanimous	incite
centennial	pusillanimous	cognizant
incredibly	amorous	

A SELECTED LIST OF WORDS DERIVED FROM LATIN ROOTS (B)

ROOT	MEANING	CURRENT WORDS
DEXTER dexter	right hand	dexterous, ambidextrous
DIC-, DICT- dicere, dictus	say, speak	dictate, predict, contradict
DIGN- dignus	worthy	dignify, condign, indignity
DUC-, DUCE- ducere, ductus	lead, bring	ductile, induce, deduce, product, duke, conduit
DUR- durus	hard	duress, endure, obdurate
FAC-, FACT- facere, factus	do, make, act	fact, factory, facsimile, effect, manu-facture, factitious, factotum.
FALL— fallere	deceive, err, be deceived	fallacious, fallacy, fallible, infallible
FERR- ferre	bear, carry, bring	ferry, infer, transfer, refer, fertile, suffer, defer
FERV- fervere	boil	fervid, effervesce, fervour
GEN-, GENER- genus, generis	class, kind, race	genus, generic, general, engender, gen-erate
GRAD-, GRESS-, gradi, gressus	walk, go, step	gradual, digress, egress, graduate, trans-gress, aggression

ROOT	MEANING	CURRENT WORDS
GRAND-, grandis	great	aggrandize, grandiose, grandeur
IT-, ire, itus	go	exit, circuit, itinerant
JECT-, jacere, jectus	throw, hurl	deject, inject
JUR-, jurare	swear	jury, abjure, perjure
LABOR- labor	work	laboratory, elaborate, collaborate, laborious

Exercise No. 86

Note: Complete these exercises before proceeding to the next group of roots.

PART I For each of the LATIN ROOTS (B) above, add at least two current words not already listed.

PART II Complete the following sentences by selecting the appropriate choice from the list of CURRENT WORDS:

(a) The central ...... in his reasoning lies in his hard-headed, ... assumption that ...... poets write better verse than those who can use only their left hand.

(b) Although it is a ...... metal, gold would be too expensive to use in laying ....

(c) Jeeves, ... extraordinary, was held in ...... because he ...... himself before a jury to support a clearly absurd, ... defence.

(d) Ants, ... in their eagerness to build an empire, raid weaker foes expecting through victory to ...... their holdings in land and slaves.

(e) To ...... one's solemnly dictated vow not only contradicts but also ...... the laws of human decency.

CURRENT WORDS

ambidextrous	conduit	ductile
duress	obdurate	factitious
factotum	fallacy	fervid
transgress	aggrandize	abjure
perjure		

A SELECTED LIST OF WORDS DERIVED FROM LATIN ROOTS (C)

ROOT	MEANING	CURRENT WORDS
LOQU-, LOC- loquor, locutus	talk, speak	elocution, loquacious, grandiloquent, soliloquy, colloquial, obloquy
MEDI-, medius	middle, between	immediate, mediaeval, mediate, medium
MIT-, MISS-, MISE- mittere, missus	send, throw	emit, permit, commit, omission, permission, dismiss, demise, missile, missive
MON-, MONIT- monere, monitus	warn, advise, remind	monument, admonition, premonition
MOR-, MORT- mors, mortis	death	mortal, immortal, mortgage, mortify
NASC-, NAT- nascitur	to be born	nascent, natal, nature, renascence
NOMIN- nomen	name	name, nomenclature, cognomen, nominate, ignominious, nominal
NOV- novus	new	novel, innovate, novice, novitiate, renovate, novelty

ROOT	MEANING	CURRENT WORDS
OMNI- omnis	all	omniscient, omnipotent, omnipresent, omnibus
PLIC- plicare	twine, twist	complicate, implicate
PONDU- pondus	weight	ponderous, imponderable, preponderance
PORT- portare	carry, bring, bear	portable, transport, porter, export, importance
RAP-, RAPT- rapio	seize, grasp	rape, rapine, rapture, rapacious

Exercise No. 87

Note: Complete these exercises before proceeding to the next group of roots.

PART I For each of the LATIN ROOTS (C) above, add at least two current words not already listed.

PART II Complete the following sentences by selecting the appropriate choice from the list of CURRENT WORDS:

(a) Whether her diction is literary or ......, the ...... Bluestocking female makes herself unpleasantly audible at all times. It is impossible to insult or ...... her, for she heeds no ...... to be silent. Conscious only of what she stupidly believes to be her supreme ......, she proceeds to analyse and to ...... the weighty, ... problems of the universe.

(b) So long as man's ...... desires for wealth and glory persist, the hopes of the world for a spiritual ...... must suffer ...... defeat, even as they did five hundred years ago in ...... times.

	CURRENT WORDS	
loquacious	colloquial	mediaeval
admonition	mortify	renascence
ignominious	omniscience	explicate
imponderable	rapacious	

A SELECTED LIST OF WORDS DERIVED FROM LATIN ROOTS (D)

ROOT	MEANING	CURRENT WORDS
SED-, SESS- sedere, sessus	sit	sedentary, reside, sedate, sedan
SPEC-, SPECT- spectare	look, see, appear	spectacle, prospectus, specie, spectator, conspicuous, introspect, perspicacious
STRING-, STRICT- stringere, strictus	bind, draw tight	strict, stringent, constrict, restrain, strait, distress
TANG- tangere	touch	tangible, contact, tangent
TEN-, TIN- tenere	hold	tenable, tenure, pertinacity, tenant, tenet
TORT-, TORQ- torquere	twist	torque, tortuous, distort, retort, torture, contortion
TRACT- trahere	draw	abstract, attract, detract, traction, tractor, protract
VERS-, VERT- vertere	turn	avert, aversion, adversary, controversy, extrovert, introvert
VIR- vir	man	virago, virile virtuous

ROOT	MEANING	CURRENT WORDS
VOC- vocare	call	convoke, vocalize, advocate, vociferous, avocation, evoke
VOL- velle	wish	volition, benevolence, voluntary, volunteer, malevolent

Exercise No. 88

Note: Complete these exercises before proceeding to the next group of roots.

PART I For each of the LATIN (D) roots above, add at least two current words not already listed.

PART II Complete the following sentences by selecting the appropriate choice from the list of CURRENT WORDS.

(a) I doubt whether Tom Wolfe, for all his self-concern and ......, ever gained the kind of insight and ...... that makes for a truly great novelist.

(b) Paul's daughter was an evil, ... foul-mouthed ......

(c) The ...... of our creed may seem harsh and ......, but if we hold ...... to them, the danger we face from our ...... will diminish.

(d) Kaye's collection of empty Scotch bottles was ...... evidence that he had lied when he ...... insisted that he had an ...... to alcohol.

CURRENT WORDS

introspection	perspicacity	stringent
tangible	tenaciously	tenets
vociferously	malevolent	virile
adversary	virago	aversion

A SELECTED LIST OF WORDS DERIVED FROM GREEK ROOTS (A)

ROOT	MEANING	CURRENT WORDS
AESTH- aisthanomai	feel, perceive	aesthetics, aesthete, anaesthetic
AGOG- agōgos	lead, bring	demagogue, synagogue
AGON agōn	contest, struggle	protagonist, antagonist, agony
ANTHROP- anthrōpos	man	anthropology, misanthrope, philanthropist, anthropomorphic
ARKH- arkhos, arkhe	rule, chief, beginning, origin	anarchy, archives, archetype, oligarchy, hierarchy
BIBL- biblion	book	bible, bibliophile, bibliography, bibliomania
BIO- bio	life	biology, biography, biotic, biophysics
KHRON- khronos	time	chronicle, chronic, chronology, synchronize
DEM- dēmos	people	democrat, demagogue, demotic, epidemic, endemic
DUNAM- dunamis	power	dynamic, aerodynamics, dynamometer, dynamo, dynamite
GAM- gamos	marriage	monogamy, polygamy, bigamy, amalgam
GE geō	earth	geography, geology, geometry
GRAPH- graphein	write	autograph, biography, graphic, stenography, phonograph, orthography, graph

Exercise No. 89

Note: Complete these exercises before proceeding to the next group of roots.

PART I For each of the GREEK ROOTS (A), above, add at least two current words not already listed.

PART II Complete the following sentences by selecting the appropriate choice from the list of CURRENT WORDS:

(a) The ......, obsessed with beauty, often leads a contemplative, ... existence, devoid of physical activity.

(b) A society that permits itself to settle into ......, forgetting that nations are an ...... of different peoples and ideas, is ripe for a ....

(c) For the ...... of perhaps his most celebrated play, Moliére chose a thoroughly unpleasant ......, the very ...... of a man-hater.

CURRENT WORDS

amalgam	sedentary	aesthete
misanthrope	demagogue	protagonist
archetype	homogeneity	

Note: Almost all the sciences append the suffix -LOGY, from logos meaning speech or discourse:

anthropology	criminology	geology
archaeology	demonology	histology
bacteriology	entomology	meteorology
biology	genealogy	mythology
morphology	philology	theology
ornithology	physiology	zoology
pathology	psychology	

Not all words that end in *-logy*, however, refer to sciences: e.g. analogy, tautology, eulogy, trilogy. How many others can you name?

A SELECTED LIST OF WORDS DERIVED FROM GREEK ROOTS (B)

ROOT	MEANING	CURRENT WORDS
IDIO- idios	own's own, peculiar	idiom, idiosyncrasy, idiot
ISO- isos	equal	isosceles, isotope, isobar
KOSM- kosmos	universe, order, adornment	cosmos, cosmic, cosmography, cosmetic, cosmopolitan
KRAT- kratia	power	democracy, aristocrat, plutocrat, theocrat, bureaucrat
LOG- logos	word, speech, reason	logic, eulogy, etymology, philology, psy- chology
METER, METR- metron	measure	diameter, metronome, symmetry
MON, MONO monos	alone	monogamy, monosyllable, monomania, monogram, monocle, monolith
NOM- nomos	law, custom	deuteronomy, economy
NEO- neos	new	neologism, neolithic, neophyte
NEUR- neuron	nerve, tendon	neuralgia, neurasthenia, neuritis, neurotic, psychoneurosis

ROOT	MEANING	CURRENT WORDS
ONOM- onoma	name	pseudonym, homonym, anonymous
ORTHO- orthos	correct, upright, just, straight	orthodontia, orthography, orthodox
PATH- pathos	feeling	sympathy, pathos, apathetic, antipathy
PHIL- philos philein—to love	friend	philanthropist, philosophy, philharmonic, philology
PHONE phōnē	voice, speech	phonetic, telephone, phonology, euphony, cacophony
PHUSI- phusis	nature	physiology, physicist, physic, physiognomy

Exercise No. 90

Note: Complete these exercises before proceeding to the next group of roots.

PART I For each of the GREEK ROOTS (B), above, add at least two current words not already listed.

PART II Complete the following sentences by selecting the appropriate choice from the list of CURRENT WORDS:

(a) When a ......, fresh to the art of word study, begins to delve into ......, each prefix, suffix, and root assumes ...... importance.

(b) Each man, proud of his quirks, ..., and ......, regards himself as sane, the other fellow as ....

(c) Journalists, unimportant as their efforts are, nevertheless do on occasion act as ...... of sorts, adding to our vocabularies ...... like 'escalate', 'breathalyser' and similar terms common to our ...... social life.

(d) ...... towards the need for ...... in diction, many writers clutch indifferently at any word and thus submit their readers to harsh, ... prose.

CURRENT WORDS

idiosyncrasies	cosmic	etymology
neologisms	neophyte	apathetic
euphony	cacophonic	neurotic
monomanias	cosmopolitan	philologists

A SELECTED LIST OF WORDS DERIVED FROM GREEK ROOTS (C)

ROOT	MEANING	CURRENT WORDS
POLI- polis	city	metropolis, politician, police, policy, cosmopolitan
PSUKH- psukhē	mind	psychology, psychiatry, psychoanalysis, psychotic, metempsychosis
PUR- pur	fire	pyre, pyromaniac, pyrotechnics
SKOP- skopein	see	scope, telescope, stereoscopic, stethoscope, microscope, bishop
SOPH- sophos	wise	philosophy, sophist, sophisticate, theosophy
TELE- tēle	far, off	telescope, telephone, telegraph, teleology, telepathy

ROOT	MEANING	CURRENT WORDS
THERM- thermē	heat	thermal, thermometer, thermostat
TYP- tupos	model, impression	typical, archetype, antitype, atypical
TOP- topos	a place	topography, topic, topical
ZO- zōon zōos	animal living	zoo, zoology, zodiac, protozoa

Exercise No. 91

PART I For each of the GREEK ROOTS (c), above, add at least two current words not already listed.

PART II Complete the following sentences by selecting the appropriate choice from the list of CURRENT WORDS below:

(a) If many more people seek help for the future on the leather couch of the ......, advocates of the ancient art of reading the ...... will have to close shop.

(b) The ...... of York was not a ...... cleric. With a group of 'Friends of the Cathedral', he experimented with ...... and was, for a time, attracted by ....

CURRENT WORDS

theosophy	telepathy	zodiac
psychoanalyst	archbishop	typical

BUILDING VOCABULARY WITH PREFIXES AND SUFFIXES. A prefix is a syllable or syllables placed (*fixed*) before (*pre-*) a word to qualify its meaning:

vocation means an occupation or trade, or, literally, *a calling*.
avocation means a hobby, a secondary occupation, or, literally, *away from a calling*.

The meaning of *avocation* has been changed, modified, or qualified by placing before it the prefix *a-*(*ab-*) meaning *away from*.

A suffix is a syllable or syllables placed after a word to qualify its meaning:
measure means dimension, size, or quantity.
measurable means capable of being measured.

The meaning of *measurable* has been modified by adding to *measure* the suffix *-able* (*-ible*) meaning *capable of being measured*.

Note that the suffix does not change the meaning of a word as drastically as does the prefix, but it does change the grammatical function. Both *avocation* and *vocation* are nouns, but the noun *measure*, because of the addition of the suffix, has become an adjective, *measurable*. Likewise, the adjective *loose* becomes an adverb when the suffix *-ly* is added (*loosely*), and the verb *commit* becomes a noun when the suffix *-sion* is added (*commission*).

Note: Certain minor changes in spelling frequently occur. These are intended to make pronunciation easier.

Most of the prefixes and suffixes in modern English derive from Old English, Latin, and Greek. They are so numerous that it is impossible to list all of them, and almost futile to try to learn every one that is listed. However, by learning the strategic affixes, you take another long stride towards improving your vocabulary:

By combining your knowledge of roots with knowledge of prefixes and suffixes, you can analyse a surprisingly large number of words:

inscription, for example, breaks down into:
ROOT: *scrip-*, meaning write (Latin, *scribere*)
PREFIX: *in-*, meaning on (Latin, *in*)
SUFFIX: *-tion*, meaning act of, state of, that which (Latin, *-tion*)

Thus (note that the definition emerges as you work *backward* from SUFFIX to ROOT to PREFIX) *inscription* means literally *the act of writing on*. The context in which the word appears usually makes the meaning more specific:

Walter found the author's *inscription* on the fly-leaf.

The tombstone bore the *inscription* of the dead man's date of birth and of death.

By observing the effect suffixes have on the words you study, you add depth to your vocabulary by learning several parts of speech derived from a single word:

rational—adjective
rationalism—noun (*-ism* means state of being)
rationalize—verb (*-ize* means to make)
rationally—adverb (*-ly* means similar, or having the quality of)

Some Techniques for Changing Parts of Speech by Using Prefixes and Suffixes

To derive from nouns:

Add the suffix *-ize* or *-ise*

terror—terrorize	drama—dramatize
economy—economize	anaesthesia—anaesthetize

Add the prefix *-en* or *-in*

slave—enslave	franchise—enfranchise
trench—entrench	grain—ingrain

To derive nouns from verbs:

Add the suffixes *-tion, -ion, -sion, -ation*

denounce—denunciation	compile—compilation
compel—compulsion	transpose—transposition

Add the suffixes *-al, -se, -ment, -iture, -ance*

refuse—refusal	expend—expense
govern—government	persevere—perseverance

Add the suffixes *-er, -or, -ant, -ent*

audit—auditor	labour—labourer
expedite—expedient	supply—supplicant

To derive adjectives from nouns:

Add the suffixes *-ful, -less, -ious, -ous, -y*

hope—hopeful	end—endless	beauty—beauteous
sorrow—sorrowful	chill—chilly	ambition—ambitious

Add the suffixes *-al, -ic, -ish, -an, -ary, -ed*

nature—natural	fever—feverish
psychosis—psychotic	Sweden—Swedish
imagination—imaginary	America—American

To derive nouns from adjectives:

Add the suffixes *-ness, -ity, -ce, -cy*

happy—happiness	loquacious—loquacity
romantic—romance	fragrant—fragrance

To derive verbs from adjectives:

Add the suffixes *-ize, -en, -fy*

fertile—fertilize	liquid—liquefy
thick—thicken	solid—solidify

To derive adjectives from verbs:

Add the suffixes *-able, -ible, -ive*

reverse—reversible	evade—evasive
manage—manageable	repair—reparable

To derive adverbs from adjectives:

Add the suffix *-ly*

handy—handily	excitable—excitably
angry—angrily	false—falsely

Add the suffix *-wise*

likewise, lengthwise

Note: Other suffixes related to parts of speech are listed in the tables below.

By observing the effect *prefixes* have on the words you study, you add depth to your vocabulary by learning *antonyms* (words opposed in meaning, as *good–bad, right–wrong*) for any given word:

rational—irrational (*ir-* means 'not', 'against')
practical—impractical (*im-* means 'not')
ordinary—extraordinary (*extra-* means 'in addition to')
territorial—extraterritorial

Learn a few prefixes and suffixes at a time. Put them to work first in the exercises and then in your reading.

Remember:

1 What does the word seem to mean in context?
2 What is the meaning of the root?
3 What is the meaning of the prefix? the suffix?

Combine these bits of knowledge and within a short time, the word will be yours.

A SELECTED LIST OF PREFIXES FROM LATIN (A)

PREFIX	MEANING	CURRENT WORDS
AB-, (a-, abs-)	from, away from	abnormal, abduct, absent, avert
AD- (a-, ac-, af-, ag-, al-, an-, ap-, ar-, as-, at-) (these varied forms are used to effect euphonious combinations with the several roots)	to, towards	adage, adapt, aggravate, admit, adjust
AMBI-	both	ambidextrous, ambivalent, ambiguous
ANTE-	before	antedate, anteroom, antecedent
BI- (bis-)	two, twice	biped, bicycle, bi-monthly, bisect
BENE-	good, well	beneficial, benevolent
CIRCUM-	around	circumstance, circumvent, circumnavigate, circumlocution
CON- (com-, co- col-, cor-)	with	congress, colloquy, co-education, correlate
CONTRA- (contro-, counter-)	against	contradict, controversy, countermand
DE-	from, down (negative meaning)	denounce, decry, decapitate, debase, degrade
DI- (dis-, dif-)	from, away (negative meaning)	divert, dispel, dismiss, dishonest, differ, diffuse
EQUI-	equal	equanimity, equilateral, equation
EX-	former	ex-president, ex-governor
EX- (e-, ef-, ec-)	out, from, away	exotic, exit, enervate, effulgent, ecstasy
EXTRA-	outside, beyond	extracurricular, extraordinary, extravagant, extraneous
IN- (il-, im-, ir-)	in, into, on (used with verbs and nouns)	intrude, induce, illuminate, import, imbibe, irrigate
IN- (il-, im-, ir-, ig-)	not (used with adjectives)	indecent, illiterate, improper, irreducible, ignoble, ignominious

A SELECTED LIST OF PREFIXES FROM LATIN (B)

PREFIX	MEANING	CURRENT WORDS
INFRA-	under, beneath	infra-red, infracostal
INTER-	between, among	inter-urban, international, interchange, interfere, interpose
INTRA-	inside, within	intramural, introvert, introspect, intravenous
MAL- (male-)	bad	malefactor, malevolent, malformed, malady
MULTI-	much, many	multiply, multitude, multicolour
NON-	not (*in-* and *un-* are usually more emphatic)	non-existent, nonsense, non-Christian
OB- (o-, oc-, of- op-)	against, out	obstruct, obdurate, obsolete, omit, occult, offend, oppose
PER-	through, throughout	persist, pertinent, perceive, perennial
POST-	after	postpone, postscript, post-graduate
PRE-	before (in *time* or *place*)	precede, predict, prevent, pre-war, prepay

PREFIX	MEANING	CURRENT WORDS
PRO-	forward, in favour of	proceed, provoke, project, propose, pro-noun, pro-British
RE-	again, back	repeat, return, remind, recall, refulgent, rebuild, reaffirm
RETRO-	back, backward	retroactive, retrospect, retrogress, retrograde
SINE-	without	sinecure
SUB- (suc-, suf-, sug-, sup-, sus-)	under, beneath	submarine, submerge, succinct, succumb, suffer, suggest, supplant, suspect
SUPER- (sur-)	above, over	superimpose, superficial, surpass, surfeit
TRANS- (tra-)	across, over	transport, transfer, transmit, traduce, traverse
TRI-	three	triangle, triumvirate
ULTRA-	beyond, outside, unusual, extreme	ultra-modern, ultra-Conservative, ultra-marine
UNI-	one	unity, uniform, unilateral, university

Exercise No. 92

Use a selected list of prefixes from LATIN (A).

PART I Separate the **prefix** from the **stem** of each of the following words. Give the meaning of the **prefix**, and then of the **entire word.**

EXAMPLE: tri/angle   tri–three
triangle: a figure whose lines intersect at three points to form three sets of angles

avert	equanimity
aggravate	equivocal
ambivalent	enervate
benefice	extraneous
colloquy	ignominious

Check your answers in the dictionary.

PART II Give the **negative** form of the following words. Use those prefixes which mean 'not', 'away from', 'against'. EXAMPLE: enchanted-disenchanted; literate-illiterate

congruous	plot
noble	quiet (verb)
ingenuous	proper
normal	inter (verb)
	engage

Note: Do not proceed to the next group of prefixes until you have mastered the foregoing.

Using a selected list of prefixes from LATIN (B) separate the **prefix** from the **stem** of each of the following words. Give the meaning of the **prefix**, and then of the **entire word.**

EXAMPLE: intermediary   inter-between
intermediary: one who goes between, a mediator

introvert	obdurate
malevolent	pertinacious
refulgent	sinecure
retrogress	surfeit
traduce	unilateral

Check your answers in the dictionary

Using prefixes from the LATIN (A) and LATIN (B) groups, give a related word for each of the following words. Give the meaning of the related word.

EXAMPLE: pertinent—impertinent
          ordinary—extraordinary
          grade—degrade, retrograde
                       Meaning

turn
urban
introvert
provoke
circumspect

Check your answers in the dictionary

SUFFIXES

Noun suffixes from different sources:

GROUP I: Abstract nouns. These suffixes signify **state of, act of, quality of.**

SUFFIX	CURRENT WORDS
-ACY	celibacy, democracy
-AGE	bondage, salvage, vassalage, marriage
-ANCE (-ancy, -ence, -ency)	severance, repentance, buoyancy, diligence, emergency
-ATION (-tion, -ion, -sion)	civilization, flirtation, union, dissension
-DOM	freedom, kingdom, serfdom
-HOOD	boyhood, manhood, falsehood
-ICE	avarice, cowardice
-ISM	communism, invalidism, Fascism, baptism
-MENT	government, agreement, statement, payment
-NESS	happiness, lewdness, deafness
-SHIP	partnership, penmanship
-TY (-ity)	security, modesty, femininity

GROUP II: Concrete nouns. These suffixes signify **one who does.**

SUFFIX	CURRENT WORDS
-AN (-ant, -ent)	partisan, artisan, participant, equestrian, vagrant, student
-ARD (-art, -ary)	drunkard, braggart, notary
-EE (-eer, -ess)	legatee, auctioneer, tigress
-ER (-ar, -ier, -or)	labourer, scholar, clothier, auditor
-IC (-ist, -ite, -lyte)	nomadic, sadist, Jacobite, acolyte

Exercise No. 93

Using the **noun suffixes** change the following words to **nouns:**

EXAMPLE: endure + ance = endurance

constitute	avaricious	till (verb)
frequent	masculine	spoil
delicate	denounce	lucid
eloquent	convoke	invert
terror	supplicate	superficial
free	lag	clothe
unite	devote	

Adjective suffixes from different sources:

GROUP I: These suffixes signify **resembling, full of,** or **belonging to.**

SUFFIX	CURRENT WORDS
-AC (-al, -an, -ar, -ary)	cardiac, seasonal, vernal, Russian, circular, imaginary
-FUL	spiteful, vengeful, hateful
-IC (-ical)	anaemic, inimical, maniacal
-ISH	foolish, English, childish
-IVE	restive, furtive, secretive
-ORY	admonitory, hortatory
-OUS	mendacious, gracious, efficacious
-ULENT	succulent, fraudulent

GROUP II: These suffixes signify **capable, able to.**

-ABLE	movable, curable, peaceable
-IBLE	irresistible, visible
-ILE	ductile, puerile, fertile

Verb suffixes from different sources:

These suffixes signify **to make.**

-ATE	procreate, animate, perpetuate, facilitate
-EN	moisten, deepen, loosen, quicken
-FY	qualify, fortify, stupefy
-IZE (-ise)	magnetize, criticize, sterilize, fertilize

A SELECTED LIST OF PREFIXES AND SUFFIXES FROM GREEK

PREFIXES

PREFIX	MEANING	CURRENT WORDS
A- (an-)	not, without	apathetic, aseptic, atheism, anarchy
AMPHI-	about, around, on both sides	amphitheatre, amphibious
ANA-	again, up, against	anachronism, analogy, analogue
ANTI- (ant-)	opposed, against	antonym, anticlimax, antidote, anti-war
ARCH- (arkhi-)	chief, beginning, origin	architect, archbishop, archangel
AUTO-	self	autocrat, automobile, autochthonous
CATA-	down, downward	cataclysm, catastrophe
DIA-	through, between	diathermy, dialogue, diagram, diameter, diagonal
EC-	from, out of	eccentric, ecstatic
EPI- (ep-, eph-)	upon, beside	epidemic, epilogue, ephemeral, epileptic
EU-	good, happy, well	euphony, eugenic, euthanasia, eulogy
HETERO-	different	heterogeneous, heterodox
HOMO-	the same	homogenous, homonym, homosexual
HYPER-	extreme, over, above	hypersensitive, hyperbole
HYPO-	under, below	hypocrite, hypodermic, hypochondriac, hypothesis
META-	after, between, among	metathesis, metaphysics, metabolism
NEO-	new	neologism, neophyte, neo-classical
PARA-	from, beside	paraphrase, paradox, parallel
PERI-	around, about	perimeter, periscope, peripatetic
POLY-	many	polygamy, polygon, polysyllable

PREFIX	MEANING	CURRENT WORDS
PRO-	to, towards, before	prologue, proselyte, programme
SYN- (sym-, syl-)	with, together	synagogue, synonym, synopsis, symmetry, sympathy, symphony, syllogism, syllable

SUFFIXES

SUFFIX	MEANING	CURRENT WORDS
-IZE (-ise)	to act, treat in a specified way	synthesize, tantalize, criticize
-OID	like, in the form or shape of	spheroid, negroid, anthropoid

A SELECTED LIST OF PREFIXES AND SUFFIXES FROM ANGLO-SAXON

PREFIXES

PREFIX	MEANING	CURRENT WORDS
A-	at, in, on, to	ahead, asleep, afoot, aground
BE-	(original meaning *about*. It now makes intransitive verbs transitive and acts as an intensifier.)	bedaub, bedeck, besmudge, beseige, beset, bemoan, befoul
FOR-	away, off, apart	forbid, forbear, forlorn
FORE-	in front, in advance	foretell, foreground, forehead
MIS-	error, defect, wrong	mistake, mislay, misbehaviour, misconduct
OUT-	beyond, far-lying, remote	outdo, outside, outbreak
UN-	not	untie, undo, uninspired
UNDER-	beneath, below	underwrite, undertow, underrate
UP-	high	upshot, uplift, upset
WITH-	from, against	withstand, withdraw, withhold

SUFFIXES

SUFFIX	MEANING	CURRENT WORDS
-DOM	authority, jurisdiction, abstraction	freedom, wisdom
-FOLD	number, quantity	tenfold, manifold
-LESS	lacking, wanting, false	helpless, thoughtless
-LING	(used to form diminutives or to express disparagement)	yearling, gosling, foundling, princeling, underling
-LY	like, similar	hopefully, meagrely, evenly, closely
-MOST	(indicates superlative degree)	foremost, hindmost, inmost
-TH	state of, quality of	wealth, dearth, warmth
-WARD	in the direction of	northward, inward, outward
-WISE	way, manner	lengthwise, crosswise, otherwise
-Y	full of, having the qualities of	greedy, nosy, bony, slimy, angry, slangy

Exercise No. 94

PART I Using the **adjective suffixes** change the following words to **adjectives**.

EXAMPLE: America—Americ*an*

satire   admonish   deride

mania	work	access
virus	continue	fallacy
planet	invent	exhort
avariciousness	Briton	wonder

PART II Using the **verb suffixes** change the following words to **verbs**.

EXAMPLE: height—height*en*

liquid	class	regular
integer	hearty	item
example	symbol	personal

Separate the **Greek prefix** from the **stem** of each of the following words. Give the meaning of the **prefix**, and then of the **entire word**.

EXAMPLE: anti/war   anti = against   anti-war = against war.

syllogism	diarrhoea	cataclysm
metaphor	euphemism	anachronism
hypercritical	euphoria	analogy
apathy	anarchic	symposium
paranoia	polyglot	synoptic
archaeology	metatarsal	neologism
epigraph	peripatetic	heterosexual
epilogue	catatonic	diagnosis
		periphery

Check answers with selected list.

Review Work on Roots, Prefixes, and Suffixes

For each of the following words, add appropriate prefixes and suffixes to create as many derivative words as possible. Keep the same **stem** throughout. Be certain of the meaning of each derivative word.

EXAMPLE: *compel* (*Lat.* pellere, pulsus, to drive)

Derivative words from *compel*

NOUNS	VERBS	ADJECTIVES	ADVERBS
compulsion	compel	compulsory compulsive	compulsorily
repulsion	repel dispel	repellent	repulsively
pulsation pulse pulsometer	pulsate	pulsatory	
propellor propulsion	propel		
impulse	impel	impulsive	impulsively

describe (*scribere*, write)
factor (*facere*, make, do)
pathos (*pathos*, suffering)
dependent (*pendere*, *-pensus*, to suspend)
graphic (*graphos*, writing)
spirit (*spirare*, to breathe)
vitalize (*vita*, life)
philology (*philos*, love)
chronology (*khronos*, time)

LEARNING THE ORIGIN OF WORDS

Knowing the root of a word sometimes fails to produce a logical meaning. The root of *salary*, for example, is *sal*, meaning 'salt', a far cry from our usage today. Yet if one thinks for a moment of a common expression such as 'he is not worth his salt', he must realize that somewhere in the history of that root, a connexion existed between money and salt. The connexion dates back to the days of the Roman Empire when Roman soldiers were often paid for their services with enough money to buy the salt they needed for personal use. Thus what they earned was literally 'salt money'.

The search for the historical origins of words is called **etymology** (*etymos*, the real, or true + *logos*, the study of). The realms of etymology may be fully explored only by the professional philologist (See Skeat's *Etymological Dictionary of the English Language*), but the amateur can have considerable and profitable fun tracing words as far back as he can.

Other examples:

CARTRIDGE—French, *cartouche*, Latin, *carta*. The Latin word, *carta*, means 'paper', and the later French *cartouche* likewise meant a paper scroll on which messages were written. The first cartridges used in guns were rolled cylinders made of heavy paper; their resemblance to the letter scroll earned them the name *cartouche*, whence modern English *cartridge*.

DANDELION—French, *dent de lion* (teeth of a lion). The petals of the flower resemble teeth.

RICKSHAW—Japanese. Here the roots provide the literal meaning of the original word (jinrikisha).

$$jin = \text{man}$$
$$riki = \text{power}$$
$$sha = \text{carriage}$$

EXCHEQUER—French, *eschequier*, chessboard. Accounts were originally made by counters arranged on a chequered board.

See what your dictionary tells about these words:

pastor	blitz	tawdry
congregation	daisy	grammar
eliminate	silly	hysteria
curfew	alphabet	taboo
assassin	hors d'oeuvre	nosegay
neighbour	phlegmatic	trivial

Words derived from Proper Names. Do you know these people?

Jean Nicot	J. A. Hansom
John Mercer	Vulcan
Amelia Bloomer	James Watt
Pierre Magnol	Thespis
Tantalus	Hector

Each of them has given a word to the English language.

Jean Nicot—introduced tobacco to France in 1560—*nicotine*.

John Mercer—discovered a way to make cotton stronger for use as thread—*mercerize*.

Amelia Bloomer—designed a gown to fit over ankle-length pantaloons—*bloomers*.

Pierre Magnol—French botanist—*magnolia*.

Tantalus—the king in Greek mythology condemned to reach for fruit ever beyond his grasp, and for water which receded when he sought to slake his thirst—*tantalize*.

J. A. Hansom—inventor of the *hansom cab*.

Vulcan—the Roman god of fire—*vulcanize*.

James Watt—scientist who worked in electrical measurements—*watt*.

Thespis—Greek poet responsible for the drama—*thespian*.

Hector—Trojan warrior, brave, but a bully—*hector* (to torment or bully).

Look up the following words:

boycott	quixotic	rodomontade
ampere	stentorian	simony
volt	dunce	Rosicrucian
wisteria	daguerreotype	maudlin
martial	herculean	

Portmanteau Words, or Blended Words—like the contents of a trunk sometimes get squeezed together to form a new word:

$$lunch + breakfast = brunch$$
$$chuckle + snort = chortle$$
$$dance + handle = dandle$$

Lewis Carroll's 'Jabberwocky' in *Alice Through the Looking Glass* is the finest example of the imaginative use of **blended words**:

slithy from *slimy* and *lithe*
mimsy from *flimsy* and *miserable*
nome from *far from* and *home*

Exercise No. 95

What are the components of the following 'blend'?

flurry　　riffle　　smog　　squelch

SUMMARY OF METHODS OF BUILDING VOCABULARY

1 Learn only those words that you intend to use.
2 Keep a notebook or file card collection of new words.
3 Use the dictionary.
4 Try to recognize the use of the word in context.
5 Learn roots, prefixes, and suffixes.
6 Convert each new word into other parts of speech.
7 Be curious about word origins and changes in word meaning.
8 Study your words daily and *use* them in writing and speaking.

Exercise No. 96

Each of the following numbered words is followed by five suggested words. Circle the word which is most nearly the same in meaning. (Choose the word most closely related to the given one, even if it is not a valid synonym.)

1 prorogue   (*a*) blackguard (*b*) request (*c*) postpone (*d*) convene (*e*) pretend
2 desultory   (*a*) changeable (*b*) careful (*c*) timely (*d*) descriptive (*e*) logical
3 traduce   (*a*) transfer (*b*) calumniate (*c*) betray (*d*) persecute (*e*) subdue
4 unconscionable   (*a*) unintelligible (*b*) unaware (*c*) inordinate (*d*) unreasonable (*e*) unconscious
5 requite   (*a*) reward (*b*) delay (*c*) regard (*d*) acquit (*e*) repeat
6 venal   (*a*) poisonous (*b*) mercenary (*c*) pardonable (*d*) sacred (*e*) incorruptible
7 desuetude   (*a*) unaccustomed (*b*) despair (*c*) disuse (*d*) demeanour (*e*) disinterest
8 assiduous   (*a*) annual (*b*) sour-tempered (*c*) anxious (*d*) careless (*e*) unremitting
9 captious   (*a*) naive (*b*) reactionary (*c*) captivating (*d*) cavilling (*e*) captive
10 jocular   (*a*) mirthful (*b*) sympathetic (*c*) careful (*d*) haphazard (*e*) morose
11 perspicuous   (*a*) conforming (*b*) lucid (*c*) perverse (*d*) captious (*e*) defiant
12 clandestine   (*a*) sticking together (*b*) faithful (*c*) woeful (*d*) open (*e*) closed
13 anomaly   (*a*) anonymous (*b*) upper (*c*) success (*d*) irregularity (*e*) prospect
14 polyglot   (*a*) many-husbanded (*b*) many-jewelled (*c*) much-married (*d*) many-languaged (*e*) much-feared
15 collusion   (*a*) contact (*b*) conspiracy (*c*) confinement (*d*) congregation (*e*) conjunction

Exercise No. 97

Same instructions as for Exercise No. 96.

1 plethoric   (*a*) lean (*b*) poor (*c*) corpulent (*d*) emaciated
2 ubiquitous   (*a*) omnipresent (*b*) obvious (*c*) fortuitous (*d*) ameliorate
3 pertinacious   (*a*) pertinent (*b*) servile (*c*) inflexible (*d*) rude
4 rancour   (*a*) obesity (*b*) chance (*c*) resentment (*d*) rot
5 gregarious   (*a*) dangerous (*b*) agricultural (*c*) communal (*d*) egregious
6 calumny   (*a*) applause (*b*) slander (*c*) celebration (*d*) eulogy
7 autonomous   (*a*) self-governing (*b*) automatic (*c*) synonymous (*d*) apparent
8 apathy   (*a*) emotion (*b*) attitude (*c*) fury (*d*) insensibility
9 condign   (*a*) deserved (*b*) condemn (*c*) belie (*d*) conduct
10 cataclysm   (*a*) catastrophe (*b*) comfort (*c*) pleasure (*d*) prosperity
11 complaisant   (*a*) complacent (*b*) friendly (*c*) unmoved (*d*) discouraged
12 denouement   (*a*) outcome (*b*) end (*c*) blessing (*d*) help
13 credulous   (*a*) ready to believe (*b*) diverse (*c*) oily (*d*) infamous
14 derogatory   (*a*) commendatory (*b*) praising (*c*) disparaging (*d*) heinous
15 diaphanous   (*a*) transparent (*b*) sylph-like (*c*) dim (*d*) turbid

SECTION SEVEN

STYLE

IMPROVING THE WORD PATTERN

Levels of Usage

Diction refers to the choice of words—precise or imprecise, forceful or weak—used to express thoughts and feelings.

Usage (what people say and write) **determines the correctness or incorrectness of diction.** Although diction varies according to the pressures of the society in which it functions, two general levels of usage may be distinguished:

Standard English—the level of language of most educated people in English-speaking nations.

INFORMAL ENGLISH—the level most commonly used in conversation and informal writing (personal notes, diaries, dialogue in fiction and drama, and the like).

FORMAL ENGLISH—the level most commonly used in official reports, text and reference books, lectures, and the like.

Substandard English—the level of language generally considered unacceptable in polite society. It seems unlikely that any intelligent person would consider expressing himself seriously in the following way—unless facetiously:

Dick got *sloshed* last night at our *do* and was still *crashed out* when we carted him home. This morning his *old woman beat him up*.

The italicized expressions are **substandard, illiterate,** or **vulgar** usages, and, when employed seriously, reflect unfavourably on the taste and education of the man who uses them.

On the other hand, pomposity characterizes the following passage, an absurdly pedantic attempt at formal usage, ill-suited both to the subject matter and to any conceivably interested audience:

Richard *underwent* extraordinary inebriation at last evening's *soirée,* and remained *comatose* even after we *transported* him to his *domicile.* This morning his *spouse submitted him to severe physical abuse.*

Most people, however, would accept either of the following **Standard English** versions:

INFORMAL: Dick got drunk at last night's party and was still out to it when we took him home. This morning his wife gave him a beating.

FORMAL: Richard Jones became intoxicated at a party held last night at a friend's home. The following morning his wife beat him severely.

In each of these passages, the language is appropriate to the subject and to the audience. The **informal** passage is addressed to an educated audience. Its level is standard; its mode is speech. Its diction is simpler than that in the

166

formal passage (*drunk*, *intoxicated*), and its tone more personalized. The formal version, more dignified and impersonal, resembles the kind of reporting found in better newspapers.

Thus, the first step towards improving word-patterns involves discriminating between levels of usage. Substandard and pompous English have no place in the diction of an effective writer or speaker. Good diction successfully meets the demands of both the subject and the audience.

STANDARD ENGLISH

FORMAL	INFORMAL
psychotic	insane
incarcerated	in jail
policeman	bobby
recline	lie
inebriated	drunk
May I have this dance?	What about a dance?

SUBSTANDARD ENGLISH

VULGAR	POMPOUS
loony	cerebral malfunctioning
inside	immured within the house of correction
have a blow-out	indulge in a repast
get hitched	make fast the nuptial knot
Let's get with it	Shall we emulate Terpsichore?
natter	verbal intercourse
bird	damsel

Exercise No. 98

Give the informal and formal usage for the following substandard expressions:

posh	kicked the bucket	up the spout
tart	cosh	loo
skint	square	ball and chain

INFORMAL ENGLISH. Today, the informal level of usage dominates both spoken and written English. Although it carefully avoids both the vulgar and the pompous, it possesses raciness and dignity. Study the diction in the passage below from 'The Talk of the Town' in the *New Yorker* magazine:

'Our cat, who for many years dozed on the hearthstone before our living-room fireplace, has changed her ways. Her favourite couch now is the top of our television set, where, basking in the warmth generated by the big tube, she naps contentedly, apparently unconscious of the racket the strange characters below are making. We've checked with a couple of other cat-and-television owners and find that her behaviour isn't exceptional; sleeping on top of television sets is the mode of the day for cats. They do it even when the set is turned off, either because they're victims of habit or because they can detect some lingering emanations of heat imperceptible to their masters. Pussycat's migration from the hearth to the console embarrasses some of our staple literature, but from a cat's point of view it would seem to make sense. No more lying on the floor, exposed mercilessly to nipping dogs, roistering children, and roaring vacuum cleaners. Instead, a clean, secure, elevated haven in the one blessed spot in the room from which those flickering images are invisible.'*

Words like *emanations*, *imperceptible*, *generated*, *migration*, and *roistering* keep the level of diction high, but the easy grace of cultivated conversation emerges in colloquialisms like *racket* and *checked with*. Note also the liveliness of phrases like *cat-and-television owners*, and *Pussy-cat's migration from the hearth to the console*.

No one should—or can—draw a clear-cut, final line of demarcation between the diction of formal and that of informal English. One's diction ought to be sufficiently flexible to meet the demands of formal or informal situations. Although informal English is the norm today, one may occasionally have to move to the formal level. And the transition ought to be made gracefully, not laboriously or pompously. Alert observation and unremittant practice help one to adjust to different levels. Specific instruction may accelerate the process.

Exercise No. 99

What kind of diction would you use in the following circumstances?

1 An article about community activities for your church magazine.
2 A letter to the editor of your local newspaper disagreeing with his stand on comprehensive schools.
3 An article (factual) discussing the increase in the number of polio victims in an area hitherto only lightly afflicted.
4 A letter to a friend serving in the army.
5 A talk about your trip round the world, to be delivered to a Darby and Joan Club.

THE DICTIONARY AND LABELLED WORDS. Good dictionaries label many words to indicate their appropriateness to formal and informal usage. When in doubt about using a word in a given context, check it in the dictionary.

Labels indicating that the word is **acceptable** for use in **informal** writing or speaking:

Colloq. (colloquial):

boyfriend meaning 'sweetheart'. Mary's *boyfriend* telephones her every day.
awful meaning 'unpleasant, extremely bad': Marge's début on television was simpy *awful*.

Labels indicating that the word is **acceptable** for **rare** use in **informal** writing or speaking to effect novelty or particular stress:

Slang:

kid meaning 'to hoax': The youngsters *kidded* their teacher that they had permission to stay away from school.
sack meaning to 'dismiss': Poor Bill was *sacked* when he forgot to punch the time clock.

Note: Slang invigorates diction because it is often imaginative and colourful. Used too often, however, it loses its effect and degenerates into sub-

---

* By permission of The New Yorker Magazine, Inc.

standard prose. Neither slang nor colloquialisms are suitable for formal diction.

Labels indicating that the word is **unacceptable** for **normal** use in either informal or formal writing or speaking:

Illit. (illiterate, substandard):
yourn   ain't

Obs. (obsolete). Obsolete words are those no longer in current use:

> *mint* meaning 'a coin'
> *nice* meaning 'foolish, silly'

Arch. (archaic). Archaic words are those no longer in current use, but still meaningful in certain contexts:

> *quoth* meaning 'said'
> *methinks* meaning 'I think'

But note that *ado*, although generally superseded by *to do*, *stir*, *fuss*, *tumult*, etc., still survives in expressions like *So much ado about nothing*.

Dial. (dialect, dialectal). Dialectal words are those typical of a specific geographic region and are not in common use elsewhere.

> *galasses* (braces in Scotland)
> *dicky* (donkey in Norfolk)

Note: Dialectal words are gradually disappearing because of standardization fostered by schools and by media of mass communication. Many people, however, advocate retaining colourful local expressions, particularly in informal usage. Probably one should take a middle road. Like slang, dialect is appropriate when used discreetly, not promiscuously.

Labels indicating **American usage** as distinct from **British:**

U.S. (Americanism). The words an American uses to describe an object often differ entirely from the words an Englishman would use:

BRITISH	AMERICAN
underground	subway
lorry	truck
ladder (in a stocking)	run
lift	elevator
napkin	diaper
pub	bar
ironmonger's	hardware store
chemist's	drug store
pavement	sidewalk

Most words in the dictionary are not labelled, indicating that they are in current use. Note, however, that many of these words are useful only in highly technical contexts and should not be indiscriminately used merely because they are not labelled.

hurter—a buffer piece used to check the forward motion of a gun carriage.

paludal—referring to marshes or fens.
thrombus—growth of blood cells.
tierce—a liquid measure.

Exercise No. 100

Use your dictionary to determine whether the italicized words used in the following sentences are **Colloquial, Slang, Archaic, Dialectical, Illiterate,** or **U.S.**:

1 *Certes*, my *sweeting* and I shall be wed at *Eastertide*.
2 Edgar keeps on *muscling in* where he's not wanted.
3 I *ken* what she wants from me.
4 I'll *lay* that *bird*.
5 I *never done* it.
6 I can't *enthuse* about her new dress.
7 The *travelling salesman* sold a number of *undershirts* to the *dry goods store*.
8 Uncle Albert is so *tight* that he won't give a penny to the children.
9 Angus will *lay it on* with grandfather in the hope that he will change his will.
10 Jimmy got *wild* when I took his cricket bat.

CLARITY, EXACTNESS, CORRECTNESS, AND ECONOMY IN DICTION. Jargon, the art of saying nothing at great length.

'Caution,' said Sir Arthur Quiller-Couch in his famous essay, *On Jargon*, 'is its father; its mother Indolence.' He was referring, of course, to the parentage of jargon, the enemy (often the mortal enemy) of clear, precise communication. Although most people want to be understood, they are frequently either afraid to say exactly what they mean, or just too lazy to say it. The results of their efforts to beat about the bush go by the name of **jargon**, or, more familiarly, **gobbledygook**, or **barnacular**. Jargon invades almost every realm of expression:

Government:

Such preparations shall be made as will completely obscure all Government buildings and non-Government buildings occupied by Government employees during an air-raid for any period of time from visibility by reason of internal or external illumination. Such obscuration may be obtained by blackout construction or by termination of the illumination:
TRANSLATED: During wartime, in buildings where work must continue after dark, windows must be completely covered, or lights turned out.

Economics:

A *textiles recession* resulted in *negative adjustments* being brought about in many lines.
TRANSLATED: Because the demand for textiles was less, manufacturers were forced to drop their prices.

Medicine:

He procured a week's vacation to recover from the effects of his *nasal coryza*.
TRANSLATED: He took a week's holiday to recover from a cold.
The fight was stopped because Jones suffered a *circumorbital haematoma*.
TRANSLATED: The fight was stopped because Jones had a black eye.

General:

Since the onset of salubrious weather has encouraged perambulation, and more particularly noctambulation, of the public greenswards, many complaints have been received concerning certain ostentatiously amorous behaviour carried far beyond consuetudinary lengths. Young persons of both sexes and in improper juxtaposition, apparently fail to realize that the traditional spring time licence to pursue erotically a nubile neighbour may not be interpreted equally concupiscently by observers.

TRANSLATED: Love-making in public disturbs not only those actively involved.

That such writing is a mockery of communication seems clear. Yet some misguided people might even defend it, insisting that many write and speak just that way. Jargon afflicts those who lack decisiveness and cannot think for themselves. Getting rid of jargon requires that a writer have the courage to *strike out* passages, however sharp the pain of parting. He must learn to eliminate irrelevancy and destroy deadwood.

Techniques for Eliminating Jargon. Use precise words instead of circumlocutions (words that *speak around: circum,* 'around' + *loqui,* '*speak*').

Circumlocution:

EXAMPLE: In the matter of deadwood, which resembles in nature jargon in that it exhibits a tendency towards circumlocution, the writer's prose suffers due to the fact that he occupies a lengthy period of time in the process of being explicit.

Substitute precise words for the circumlocutions:

In the matter of	Eliminate the phrase; it accomplishes nothing.
which resembles in nature	use *like*
exhibits a tendency towards circumlocution	Use *beats about the bush.*
due to the fact that	Use *because.*
occupies a lengthy period of time	Use *takes too long.*
in the process of being explicit	Use *to explain.*

Clear:

Deadwood, like jargon, beats about the bush, and the writer's prose suffers because it takes too long to explain a simple matter.

Thus, **clarity, exactness, correctness,** and **economy** may be gained with a few precise words. **The fewest exact words produce the strongest prose.**

Exercise No. 101

Substitute the exact word or words for the following circumlocutions:

1 in this day and age
2 I am of the opinion that
3 as regards
4 in regard to
5 necessary funds
6 in respect to
7 relative to
8 my field of endeavour is law
9 reach a decision
10 this meets with my approval
11 during the time that
12 it is the belief of
13 come in contact with
14 in connexion with
15 it is directed that
16 in view of the circumstances

Use the exact expression or word instead of a *redundant* one. **Redundancy** (or *tautology*) means needless repetition of the same idea.

Redundant: I asked her to *refer back* to her notes. *refer* (*re-*, 'back', *fer-*, 'carry') means send back. Thus, *back* is redundant in the sentence.

Right: I asked her to refer to her notes.

Redundant: Will you *repeat again* what you have said before I *continue on* with my typing? *repeat* means say again, and *continue* means go on.

Thus, *again* and *on* are redundant.

Right: Will you repeat what you said before I continue with my typing?

Exercise No. 102

Eliminate the redundant words from the following sentences:

1 His workmanship is absolutely unique and alone in the field of jewellery.
2 The consensus of opinion favours his retirement from office.
3 Her complexion is pink in colour.
4 The modern woman of today makes up her mind without assistance from anybody else.
5 Every genius of great talent needs a wealthy millionaire to further his career onwards.
6 The audience at Simon's lecture was few in number.
7 The vase I bought was elliptical in shape.
8 These basic fundamentals, combined together, will teach any student to write well.
9 William's clothes are invariably too large in size.
10 Brett and Maria, two of Hemingway's heroines, are diametrically opposite types of women.

Use concrete words (specific words), **particularly when explaining abstract ideas** (general ideas).

Concrete words name or describe persons, places, or things. Both concrete and abstract words are needed in communication, but concrete words help to avoid jargon:

Excessively abstract:

In a *case* of this kind, where the diagnosis is lung cancer, the doctor must examine carefully the *condition* of the patient to determine the *degree* to which the disease has spread.

case—one of several abstract nouns too vague to be effective, may easily be omitted.

condition—the doctor ought to examine the *lung*, not the *condition*.

degree—like *case*, is vague.

Clear:

When he has diagnosed lung cancer, the doctor must examine the patient's lung carefully to determine how large an area is morbid.

Note that *lung* is repeated in this sentence. It is better to repeat a concrete word than to write around it with abstract words.

Exercise No. 103

Rewrite the following paragraph, substituting concrete and specific words for the italicized abstractions. Note that some of the italicized words, although not abstract in themselves, are inadequately specific in context.

EXAMPLE: I was so angry that I threw *something* at him.
I was so angry that I threw the cake plate at him.

Bill Wilson has the *character traits* of a man who wants *things* that lead to success and does *something* about the fact. Not only does he read in his field, but also he talks to persons who know a lot about *different subjects. Knowledgeability* is what he is after because he knows it will lead to improvement in his *position* in the *legal field.* All these factors are *outstanding* in my *fundamental feeling* that Bill is going to be a *worthwhile force around here.*

Denotation and Connotation. The denotation of a word is its actual meaning; its connotation, that which it suggests or implies in addition to its actual meaning.

Concrete words may be connotative as, for example, *mother, soldier, skinny, fat, home.* Abstract words are more likely than concrete to have connotative meanings: *communism, Fascism, liberty, love, happiness.* Words carry emotional overtones, evoke associations pleasant or unpleasant, that the dictionary does not include. To improve his diction, a writer must be sensitive to distinctions between the literal and emotional content of the words he uses.

The *young boy's* face was *whitish*, his features *small* and *round*, almost *womanly.* But his *behaviour* was completely that of a boy who enjoyed rough play and who returned to his *house* after a *day of activity* with his clothes quite soiled.

Denotative words, clear but colourless, fail to evoke a vivid picture of the boy. Connotative words produce the desired effect:

The *youth's* face was *pale*, his features *delicate*, almost *feminine.* But his *mischievousness* proved him to be wholly a boy. He loved *boisterous games*, and invariably returned *home filthy* at the end of the afternoon.

'Every *American boy* knows—because his *mother* has taught it to him since the *cradle*—that *family love* brings *happiness* to the individual, the community, and the nation. The *American family* has been the *cornerstone* of *freedom* in our *democracy* since the time of *Washington*, and it will remain so for as long as our nation endures. In nations under *Red domination, bureaucracy* supersedes the family. Bureaucracy becomes a cornerstone too, not of freedom, but of *tyranny*.'

Here is the material of the propagandist. Note how the writer has combined concrete words (*American boy, mother, cradle, American family, Washington, cornerstone*) with abstract words (*family love, freedom, democracy, Red domination, bureaucracy, tyranny*) to obscure the basic technique— pure emotional appeal, connotation. Nowhere does he rely upon the literal meaning of any of the words he uses; always he proceeds by emotional suggestion. By the time he has finished, the reader knows little, but feels much. An intelligent reader must be alert to the devices involved; an intelligent writer will avoid such devices when he is trying to clarify an abstraction:

In America, young people are taught to respect the family as the principal foundation upon which democracy rests. They are urged to contrast this emphasis upon the family and its individual members with the totalitarian emphasis upon the supremacy of the state, as the basis and touchstone of individual morality.

Exercise No. 104

Read the following paragraph carefully. Underline the emotionally charged words which try to sway the reader by feeling rather than thought.

All truly responsible and Christian men cannot but give their all to ensure the triumphant advance of the Conservative Party, the intrepid custodian of our island heritage and staunch defender of our hard-won liberties. The creed of the Conservative Party comes direct from the teachings of Jesus and no honest Christian who studies his Bible can ignore its exhortations and support another party. Consider, for example, the parable of the talents: here Jesus shows that it is our duty to take the share of the world's goods allotted to us and to multiply it as freely as possible. The Conservative Party urges loyal and freedom-loving men everywhere to do their utmost to fulfil this behest and to cast all agitators and would-be oppressors from our midst so that the Lord can say to the Conservative Party: 'Well done, thou good and faithful servant: thou hast been faithful over a few things, I will make thee ruler over many things.'

Synonyms—are words which have the same or nearly the same meaning. Thus, word pairs like *gift-donation, woman-lady, intelligent-wise,* are essentially similar in denotative meaning.

Careful writers must note, however, that despite similarities, no two words are exactly alike. Usage, connotation, and idiom give to words special meanings which discriminate them from one another:

Average—mean: both words denote 'a middle point between extremes'. Nevertheless, whether in a specifically mathematical context or in more general usage, they differ slightly but significantly.

We swam, played tennis, and relaxed—in brief, we had an *average* holiday. Here *average* suggests what is typical or ordinary.

The ancient Greeks set the model behaviour pattern for pursuing the *golden mean.*

Here *mean* suggests a middle road, a moderate course between extremes. Neither word could be effectively substituted for the other in these contexts.

Scholar-pupil student: each word denotes 'one who studies under a teacher'.

He has written several books about Elizabethan England, each of which has proved him a true *scholar.*

Scholar suggests a learned, erudite person.

His outstanding academic record helped him to become a Rhodes *scholar.* Because they had not prepared their exercises, the teacher kept her *pupils* after school.

Pupil suggests more active supervision by a teacher, whether in the classroom or in private tutoring.

A *student* of semantics, Jones has been investigating responses to connotative words.

Student (which may also mean *one who attends school*) suggests one who loves study and is capable of doing some work independent of a teacher's guidance.

Thus, discriminating between synonyms is an important step towards achieving clarity and exactness in diction. Consult your dictionary whenever you are uncertain that two words are synonyms.

Exercise No. 105

In each of the following sentences choose the most suitable of the synonyms provided. Use the dictionary.

1 Nell Gwynn, the (celebrated, notorious, renowned, illustrious) courtesan and mistress of King Charles II, was illiterate but intelligent.

2 The head cashier (embezzled, purloined, stole, looted) the bank's funds and (decamped, fled, absconded, skipped).

3 He eliminates jargon from his prose and writes (concisely, tersely, compendiously, pithily).
4 Hemingway's descriptions of bullfights are so (graphic, colourful, vivid, pictorial) that one almost feels and smells the struggle between matador and bull.
5 His lively puns merely attest to his (intelligence, wit, brilliance, alertness) but in no way prove his (intelligence, wit, brilliance, alertness).
6 If he violates the law, he is (exposed, liable, susceptible, prone) to punishment.
7 I admire a man who, despite the honours heaped upon him, remains (humble, meek, modest).
8 The heavyweight wrestlers faced one another, two (colossal, big, monstrous, prodigious) specimens of living but unthinking animal matter.
9 Andersen's fairy tales abound in (sound, robust, wholesome, hale) charm.
10 The man who ridicules sincerity is a (misogynist, cynic, misanthrope, pessimist), and must be carefully distinguished from the (misogynist, cynic, misanthrope, pessimist) who is simply a woman-hater.

FRESHNESS AND VIVIDNESS IN DICTION. Scientists frequently write prose that is clear, exact, and economical, but rarely **vivid. To be vivid, diction must be concrete, but imaginative, capable of awakening the reader's sense impressions and arousing his feelings.**

Note how Mark Twain uses verbs, adjectives, and adverbs in the following passage to describe how it feels to be shaved by a Parisian barber:

'I sat *bolt upright, silent, sad,* and *solemn.* One of the *wig-making* villains lathered my face for ten *terrible* minutes and finished by *plastering* a mass of suds in my mouth.... Then this outlaw *stropped* his razor on his boot, *hovered* over me *ominously* for six *fearful* seconds, and then *swooped* down on me *like the genius of destruction.* The first rake of his razor *loosened* the very hide from my face and *lifted* me out of the chair. I *stormed* and *raved* and the other boys enjoyed it.'

Test the effectiveness of Twain's diction by substituting:

putting for *plastering*
stood for *hovered*
began to shave me for *swooped down on me like the genius of destruction*
cut my face for *loosened the very hide*
protested and argued for *stormed and raved*

The substitute words, although clear, lack the vividness of Twain's diction.

Making Verbs Vivid. Simple Anglo-Saxon verbs like *go, come, say, walk, run, think, know, get, fix,* and the like are indispensable. In some sentences, however, they fail to do the job as effectively as a more colourful (connotative) verb:

Weak: Toby *walked* into the room and *said,* 'I'm going to commit suicide.'
Improved: Toby *walked furiously* into the room and *said hysterically,* 'I'm going to commit suicide.'

The adverbs help slightly, but *walked furiously* is not a really sensible description.

Vivid: Toby *burst* into the room and *shrieked,* 'I'm going to commit suicide.'

The single verb, clear, accurate, and vivid, is more dynamic than the verb-adverb combination.

Linking verbs sometimes serve to make useful distinctions:

Angela *appears* innocent, but actually she *is* a dangerous paranoiac.

The difference in meaning between *appear* and *is* underscores the effect of the sentence.

Generally, however, linking verbs do not communicate as directly or vividly as verbs of action. Furthermore, linking verbs require additional clauses or phrases to clarify their meaning, and thus weaken the economy of the sentence.

Weak: Language is what we call the sounds by which man *is* able to communicate his ideas and observations to his fellow man. Animals *are* also able to communicate by means of sound, as *is* evident if we *are* willing to watch puppies, kittens, mice, and young lions. Man, however, *was* to take an extra and important step forward when he *was* able to invent a method which *was* to preserve his speech forever.

The passage suffers from an excess of linking verbs which deaden the impact of meaning.

Better: 'Man communicates his ideas and observations to his fellow man by means of sounds we call *language*. But animals too communicate through sound; witness puppies, kittens, mice, and young lions. Man, however, advanced significantly beyond animals by inventing printing, a method designed to preserve his speech forever.'   (Van Loon)

The linking verbs have been eliminated, and live, vigorous verbs substituted to shorten the passage, and vivify its content.

Exercise No. 106

Substitute for the verb in parentheses one that more appropriately suits the context of each of the following sentences:

EXAMPLE: He placed the mint julep on the cocktail table, and leisurely (*sat*) on the divan. (use *settled* instead of *sat*)

1 The young slattern in the bright red dress (walked) across the street.
2 Matthews (thought) that repairs on his barn would amount to two thousand pounds.
3 The cabin cruiser, its engine (making noise), (went laboriously) through the rough sea.
4 Rickie (sat) on top of the radiator, his eyes (moving) lightly from his aunt to his fiancée.
5 As Rose Ann (rested) on the window-sill, the scent of summer, borne by a southerly wind, (came) by her and into the house.

Exercise No. 107

Eliminate the linking verb by recasting the following sentences:

1 The subject of the Member of Parliament's address was the elimination of housing shortages.
2 Words which are taken out of context are not always likely to mean the same as they do when they are in context.
3 His answer was an evasion of the question which had been put to him.
4 Shortages of raw materials are the cause of increase in price.
5 It appeared to me that he was a philosopher who was in search of a universal truth that was applicable only to him.

Making Adjectives and Adverbs More Vivid. Adjectives and adverbs cannot take the place of well-chosen verbs, but when they are fresh and lively, they contribute to vigorous diction.

Sara was an *extraordinarily beautiful* girl and everyone watched her as she walked *casually* by. *Extraordinarily* and *casually*, the adverbs, and *beautiful*, the adjective, fail to convey the desired picture because the verbs, *was, watched,* and *walked* are dull.

Sara's *piquant* beauty *turned* heads whenever she *sauntered* by.
Two verbs, *turned* and *sauntered*, supplemented by an appropriate adjective, *piquant*, achieve the picture.

Avoid 'dead' adjectives like: *nice, pretty, awful, terrific, rotten, big, little,* etc. Avoid over-using adverbs like: *rather, quite, very, somewhat,* etc.

Colloquially acceptable, but dull and inaccurate: Jim has a *nice* wife, and we had a *good* time at their party.

Improved: Jim's wife is a *warm, generous* hostess, and she helped make our evening *delightful*.

Colloquially acceptable, but dull and inaccurate: The evening was *rather hot,* and so we walked along the shore beneath the *very tall* and *big poplars*.

Improved: The evening was so *sultry* that we sought fresh air near the shore beneath the *towering* poplars.

Avoid excessive use of adjectives and adverbs. Used indiscriminately, they lead to 'overfine writing', or 'purple prose'.

'Purple prose': Jeff wandered disconsolately, alone amidst the moon and star-brightened darkness. Vast western hills loomed purple and grey against the black sky, as if to reflect the melancholia seeping perniciously through Jeff's spirit. Through the impenetrable stillness that bore down upon his seething consciousness came the irritable chirp of a cricket and a mismated echo from a bullfrog. Jeff plodded wearily onwards, his nostrils filling with the barely perceptible sweetness of moist young grass. The blood began to pound wildly in his ears and every fibre of his tortured being shrieked ceaselessly for escape.

Symptoms of ability show through the thick, ornate diction. But the passage needs to be completely rewritten and simplified.

Exercise No. 108

Substitute for the adjective or adverb in parentheses one that more appropriately suits the context of the sentence.

1 Harry has a (big) heart, but he is (very slow) at following a (clever) conversation.
2 Stale butter has a (sour) taste and a (sour) smell.
3 I felt the (awful) heat of the blast furnace sear my face.
4 Winter makes the city (old) like the fur of winter bears; spring makes the city (new) like kissing on the stairs.
5 Before us stretched the (big) expanse of the Gobi desert.
6 He has an (awful) nerve daring to invite me out with his (dull) sister.
7 The actors gave a (terrific) performance, but the play was (rotten).
8 With skill she vibrates her (continuous) tongue, For ever most (pleasantly) in the wrong.
9 Elaine heard the (loud noise) of the (big) air-raid siren.
10 Enter the (big) Mrs. Fezziwig, one (big) smile decorating her (big) face.

Figures of Speech—vary expressions by using words to evoke images or to suggest relationships different from their usual meanings. The figures most common in current use are:

Metaphor: an implied comparison between two unlike objects or ideas sharing a single likeness.

The chambered nautilus is a *ship of pearl*.

Sweet day, so cool, so calm, so bright, the *bridal* of the earth and sky.

Simile: a stated comparison (using *like* or *as*) between two unlike objects or ideas sharing a single likeness.

> My delight and thy delight
> Walking, *like two angels white*,
> In the gardens of the night.

> *Like as the waves make towards the pebbled shore*,
> So do our minutes hasten to their end.

Figures of speech enliven both prose and poetry. They must, however, impress the reader with their originality if they are to evoke memorable pictures. Originality comes hard and writers face **two dangerous hazards**—the **cliché** and the **overwrought figure**.

The cliché (*trite*, *hackneyed*, or *stereotyped* expression) **is a word or phrase that has become stale from over-use.** It occurs in several forms:

1 *Quotations* like 'He who hesitates is lost', 'Footprints on the sands of time', 'The calm before the storm', 'Home, Sweet Home'.
2 *Figures of speech* like 'cold as ice', 'meek as a lamb', 'he is a rat (mouse, tiger, lion)', 'Mother Nature', 'Father Time', 'Old Man River', 'busy as a bee'.
3 *Catch phrases* like 'hit the nail on the head', 'burn the midnight oil', 'it stands to reason', 'crack of dawn', 'shadow of a doubt', 'little by little'.

Although it is difficult to avoid clichés entirely, a careful writer will try to keep them at a minimum. He will, moreover, try to create the appropriate figure of speech—the one that suits his need—and he will search for the fresh and natural phrase—the one that energizes his writing.

The overwrought figure bungles the effect it strives for because it strives too hard. If an original figure of speech eludes a writer's grasp, he is wiser to depend upon clear, exact words than to destroy clarity and precision with a far-fetched, confused, or unconvincing analogy.

Overwrought: The age of the atom has transfigured man, but the transfiguration has been from spirituality to materialism, exactly the reverse of the counsel of the ancient prophets. Today, man surges forward in his march of mind, but his soul is mired in an abyss of false yearnings. In splitting the atom, man has split his own being and lost the unity of his molecular whole.

The writer begins with an interesting image—transfiguration—but shortly afterwards loses it in an unrelated figure about a *march of mind*. Furthermore, he gets his metaphors tangled when he gets a soul *mired* in an *abyss*. Finally, he returns to the atom, but the original image of transfiguration has now entirely disappeared, and the reader wallows in the murky depths of a *molecular whole*. A simple, unadorned statement of facts would be better:

The atomic age has halted man's spiritual development. Intellectually, he has surged forward, but his ideals and his values have stood still. If man's moral being regresses, atom splitting may prove an illusory advance.

Exercise No. 109

Revise the following sentences. Provide fresh images for the clichés and simplify the overwrought figures.

1 To borrow a leaf from olden days, I promise to don the shining armour of a crusading knight and struggle onwards for enduring peace and freedom.
2 Sadder but wiser, the shivering mongrel crawled out of the icy pond.
3 Luke favoured his company with a rendition of songs redolent of the good old days.
4 Hay fever spreads like wildfire during the summer months, but scientists keep searching for new methods to iron out the problem.
5 Jones is the one man in a hundred who can lead us out of the morass of corrupt politics without beating about the bush.
6 It stands to reason that Mother Nature must protect the denizens of the deep lest the devotees of the hook and rod uproot them from their watery homes.
7 We watched with bated breath as the blushing bride, her eyes starry, her dress white as snow, approached the altar of matrimonial bliss.
8 Hector's jokes are too funny for words. They make the other comedians green with envy.
9 He's a dead duck now that these disclosures of his taking of bribes have been put on the record.
10 Little by little, a fool and his filthy lucre come to the parting of the ways.

SUMMARY OF WAYS TO IMPROVE WORD PATTERNS

Clarity, Exactness, Correctness, and Economy

Choose the **level of usage** appropriate to the subject and the audience.
Choose **concrete words** wherever possible, and especially when explaining abstractions.
Choose **denotative** and **connotative** words discriminatingly.
Choose the **precise**, not the approximate synonym.

Freshness and Vividness

Choose 'live' parts of speech, paying especial attention to verbs.
Choose vigorous and original figures of speech.

The Pitfalls

Avoid the **vulgar** and the **pompous.**
Avoid the **trite** and the **overwrought.**

IMPROVING THE SENTENCE PATTERN

The Purpose of a Sentence

Words, phrases, and clauses—the structural elements of communication— derive their import from sentence context. The sentence is the basic unit of communication. Its function, then, is to communicate: with force and grace if possible, but with clarity and precision at least. Whatever blocks or distorts the meaning of the sentence, whatever obscures its point or impedes its readability, whatever, in short, detracts from its effectiveness as a vehicle of communication, must be corrected—no matter what temporary surgical pain it may cause the author.

Clarity and precision, of course, do not necessarily equal simplicity. Some ideas will not yield to simple expression: to explain the theory of relativity or the philosophy of existentialism, the writer needs sentences different from those he would need to describe the right way of baking a cake, different and more complex. Nevertheless, any idea may be rendered excessively difficult by a writer who rejécts the first principle of style, to get his idea across to his reader.

But isolating lucidity from the other prose virtues is ultimately an artificial procedure. To get his idea across as he experienced it, with all its force and all its immediacy, the writer must emphasize what is important, subordinate what is minor, and eliminate what is inconsequential. He must call on all the resources of style to tell the truth as he felt the truth. For the writer, therefore, morality has its centre in the integrity of his sentences.

CLARITY AND COHERENCE

ECONOMY. You should write sentences that the reader can understand with a minimum expenditure of energy. The great law of style, a philosopher observes, is to economize your reader's attention. In order to practice this kind of economy, marshal your words so that they proceed in firm, close array to the objective you have set for them. Make your sentences hang together: make them coherent and unified. Compare:

Incoherent: I like herring, and it is a fish which to the poor man is what sturgeon is to the rich man.

Coherent: I like herring, the poor man's sturgeon.

Coherent: When I realized that I would remain poor, I determined to develop a taste for herring, the poor man's sturgeon.

Note the variety of other faults in the first sentence, faults which issue from its incoherence and disunity (the two are inseparable): the three linking verbs which impair force; the wordiness which blurs lucidity; the clumsy rhythm which undermines euphony. The reader has to work too hard for too little, and justly blames the writer. His pen or typewriter initiated his thought. Had he performed his duty—planned before writing—he could have conformed to the 'law of economy'.

Exercise No. 110

The following sentences are uneconomically phrased. Improve them.

1 I am fond of ice-cream, and it is a high-caloric food.
2 Emma Lazarus was born in 1848. It was a year of revolutions.
3 I rarely eat oysters, but they are shellfish.
4 By repeatedly performing an action, one acquires a habit; it denotes a fixed response to a given stimulus.
5 In a battle you should trust in God and it is also important to take good care of your ammunition.

CONSISTENCY. You should never leave the reader in doubt as to who is speaking to whom and about what.

Inconsistent: We have utterly forgotten the slang of the generation before ours. We never, for example. hear of a *lounge-lizard* nowadays. He is with the *flapper*. Yet we can remember when it was on everybody's tongue.

Who is *we*? In the first and second sentences *we* seems to mean 'people in general'. In the last sentence, however, *we* seems to refer to the author; for if people in general have 'utterly' forgotten the slang of a past generation, they can hardly recall the particular slang term referred to, though perhaps the author can. But what slang term does he refer to—*lounge-lizard* or *flapper? Lounge-lizard* seems the likelier antecedent of the pronoun *it* in the last sentence (in spite of the fact that *flapper*) is nearer and ought logically to be the antecedent. But in the third sentence the author has referred to the *lounge-lizard* as *he*. And if *lounge-lizard*, like the other slang of its generation, has been utterly forgotten (a dubious contention, by the way), should not the author define it? Finally, which is 'the generation before ours'? One could perhaps answer—if he knew, as he does not, whom *we* represented.

Consistent: People forget the slang of the generation before the one in which they came of age. Nowadays, for example, no one ever hears of the *lounge-lizard*. That effeminate trifler has joined the *flapper*. And yet I [or *we*, if it is consistently used to mean 'the author' or 'the authors'] can remember when he [or *lounge-lizard*] was on everybody's tongue.

Exercise No. 111

Rewrite each of the sentences below, removing the inconsistencies they contain.

1 We often get into difficulty by not defining technical terms precisely; in order to avert the difficulty, we shall begin by defining as precisely as we can all the technical terms employed in the ensuing pages.
2 We seldom care about the history contained in a historical novel. Nevertheless, we have been careful to include in ours no incidents which have not a sound basis in fact. If any of them appear dubious to you, I suggest that you refer to the notes at the end of each chapter.
3 The reader will think the present writer conceited, perhaps; but I ask you to consider my great and enduring achievements.
4 People climb mountains because they are there.
5 Men who live in our industrial society are different in some ways.

LOGIC. Your sentences must be structured logically, internally consistent. Avoiding the loose and illogical thinking which breeds muddled writing is a more difficult matter than a few paragraphs can successfully demonstrate. Be wary of these pitfalls.

Equivocation or Double Meaning. Maintaining a nuisance is a crime; wives are generally nuisances; therefore maintaining a wife is generally a crime. (Here *nuisance* has been given its legal meaning in the first premise, its common meaning in the second.)

Begging the Question (circular reasoning). God exists because the Bible says He does. (Here the premise assumes as true the proposition to be proved, since the word of the Bible is valid only if God exists.)

Facile Assumption. Everybody loves a lover. Since I love you, I am a lover. Consequently, you love me. (The proverb uncritically accepted often leads to error.)

Non sequitur (a conclusion that does not follow from the premises). All blackbirds are black. Some hawks are black. Therefore, some hawks are blackbirds. (Here the writer affirms solely that blackbirds are black. He does not maintain that they are the only black birds.)

John will one day be a great singer: he has absolute pitch. (Here the easy generalization operates: John may possess a frog-like voice or he may hate music.)

Ignoring the Question (arguing off the point).

(1) Arguing against the man.

No wonder you believe in evolution—you look like an ape. (Here the argument attacks the man, not the idea he advocates.)

(2) Referring to authorities.

Students of the theatre, from Nahum Tait to Henry Irving, have agreed that Shakespeare's plays should be freely cut and adapted for the time in which they are being played. (Here the force of authority substitutes for the force of ideas and facts. But an equally impressive group of counter-authorities ['from William Poel to Granville Barker'] may be cited for a different view of the theatre.)

(3) Appealing to prejudice.

He must be a good cabinet minister because the ignoramuses hate him. (Here the argument ignores the non-ignoramuses who may hate him—and also the possibility that the ignoramuses, though generally without understanding of political matters, might be right about this one.)

Misuse of Statistics. He earned ten pounds a week in 1939, twenty pounds a week in 1959. Thus, his purchasing power doubled in twenty years. (Here the fallacy consists of ignoring the possible decrease in the purchasing power of the pound in twenty years.)

False Cause. Brandy is good for colds: I drank a half bottle of cognac and my cold disappeared. (Here the supposition that the earlier act is the causative act—as if day were the cause of night because it inevitably precedes night.)

Exercise No. 112

Point out the logical fallacy in each of the first seven sentences; correct the errors in linkage in the others.

1 Albert Smith, a great thinker, has backed Jones for Conservative candidate; consequently Jones must be a better candidate than his opponent.
2 Five out of six people interviewed say that cigarette *A* tastes better than any other cigarette. Most people, therefore, will prefer the taste of cigarette *A* to that of any other cigarette.
3 All dogs are animals; a man is an animal; therefore, men are dogs.
4 Some women have read Toynbee; my wife has read Toynbee; hence my wife is *some* woman.
5 *A.* Our leader is a holy man: he speaks with God every day.
  B. How do you know he does?
  A. He says so.
  B. He may be lying.
  A. Ridiculous! Would a man who speaks with God every day lie?
6 Oysters ought to be eaten only in months spelled with an *r*. It follows that oysters ought not to be eaten in May, June, July, and August.
7 I cough each morning until I smoke a cigarette. From that fact I deduce that smoking cigarettes is an anti-cough measure.
8 Jack Spratt could eat no fat, while his wife could eat no lean.
9 Although he married, he came of a long line of bachelors.
10 Look when you leap.

LEVEL OF LANGUAGE. Unless you calculate a special effect, you should employ the same level of language throughout. Inconsistency in tone—formal phrases alternating with colloquial and slang phrases—distracts the reader and generally entangles the writer.

Faulty: She was trained at the Cacophonic School of Music, which turns out lots of hep cats each year.

The formal *was trained at* jangles with the informal *turns out*, the colloquial *lots of*, and the slang *hep cats*.

Informal: She studied at the Cacophonic School of Music, which produces many jazz musicians each year.

Here the words and phrases are appropriate to their informal context.

Exercise No. 113

Rewrite informally or formally:

1 One cannot always be on the look-out for con-men, however aggravating such characters may be.
2 A really delectable dish, she unfortunately possessed several grave intellectual deficiencies.
3 When the auditor asked for the phone number of the Fraud Squad, Mr. Dobben seemed to be in a pretty fix.
4 Madge is up against it with five kids to see to.
5 As you suggest, I am going to give it to you straight.

LENGTH. You should keep long winding sentences to a minimum. The reader tends to lose his way in them. At least the modern reader does. The sentences he reads in popular magazines and newspapers average from ten to twenty words, in 'quality' magazines and serious books from twenty to thirty words. (One authority declares that twenty-one words is the average length of sentences written by professional authors.) The nineteenth-century reader faced longer sentences as a rule—probably between five and ten words longer, and the eighteenth century reader had to cope with sentences averaging between thirty-five and forty words.

Consider how difficult the following sentence is to comprehend, how the author gets caught in its coils towards its end; yet it was written by a great Victorian stylist, John Ruskin.

Excessively long: If there be—we do not say there is—but if there be in painting anything which operates as words do, not by resembling anything, but by being taken as a symbol and substitute for it, and thus inducing the effect of it, then this channel of communication can convey uncorrupted truth, though it does not in any degree resemble the facts whose conception it induces.

Most modern writers would break this tortuous sentence into three or four smaller ones:

Simpler: Words induce the effect of things by being taken as symbol and substitute for them. If there be anything in painting—we do not say there is—which operates as words do, then this channel of communication can convey the uncorrupted truth. For then paintings can induce in us a conception of facts, though not in any degree resembling them.

Note that *painting* has been changed to *paintings:* 'painting' corresponds to 'writing'; 'paintings' seems better because it corresponds to 'words'. But perhaps the original sentence needs more extensive repairs—perhaps a total reconstruction.

Exercise No. 114

Break up the long and cumbersome sentences below, making whatever revisions you consider necessary.

If we endeavour to form our conceptions upon history and life, we remark three classes of men, the first consisting of those for whom the chief thing is the qualities of feelings and who create art; the second of the practical men, who respect nothing but power and respect power only so far as it is exercised; and a third class consisting of men to whom nothing seems great but reason and who, if force interests them, it is not in its exertion, but in that it has a reason and a law. For men of the first class, nature is a picture; for men of the second class, it is an opportunity; for men of the third class it is a cosmos so admirable that to penetrate to its ways seems to them the only thing that makes life worth living, and these are the men whom we see possessed by a passion to learn, just as other men have a passion to teach and to disseminate their influence; who, if they do not give themselves over completely to their passion to learn, do not because they exercise self-control; who are the natural scientific men, and who are the only men that have any real success in scientific research.

CO-ORDINATION AND SUBORDINATION. You should avoid the 'primer sentence'. It is as bad, in a different way, as the overlong sentence.

Primer sentence: Modern English is full of bad habits. This is especially true of written English. The bad habits spread by imitation. They can be avoided. But one must take the necessary trouble.

Improved: Modern English, especially written English, is full of bad habits which spread by imitation and which can be avoided if one is willing to take the necessary trouble.   (Orwell)

Not only does the primer style become dreadfully monotonous after a few paragraphs, but also it inhibits any sustained and thoughtful treatment of a subject. To fathom, to explore, to distinguish—to write accurately and subtly—you must co-ordinate thoughts of equal importance, subordinate those of lesser importance.

From improperly attributing equality to ideas that are not equal stem most errors of co-ordination.

Excessive Co-ordination. I was a private in the army once and then I discovered that sergeants were often impolite and they were generally most impolite when they had least cause to be.

The structural likeness of the clauses joined by *and* leads the reader to suppose that they are all of equal importance.

Improved: As a private in the army, I discovered that sergeants were often impolite, generally most impolite when they had least cause to be.

Excessive co-ordination: I want to go to the Continent next summer, and so I am hoarding my money.

Improved: I am hoarding my money because I want to go to the Continent next summer.

Unnatural Co-ordination—(joining clauses apparently unrelated).

Unnatural co-ordination: Robert Frost was born in California and he wrote about the New England landscape and New Englanders.

There seems to be no connexion between the two clauses.

Improved: Although Robert Frost was born in California, he wrote chiefly about the New England landscape and New Englanders.

Improved: Robert Frost was born in California, but having lived for many years in New England he wrote chiefly about its landscapes and its people.

Unnatural co-ordination: He lived in an attic and he could see only a blank wall.

Improved: He lived in an attic, his only vista a blank wall.

From improper analysis of the relation between ideas stem most errors of subordination.

Upside-down Subordination—(illogical subordination).

Upside-down subordination: When I gave her custody of our Asiatic ibexes, she asked for it.

Right-side-up subordination: When she asked for custody of our Asiatic ibexes, I gave it to her.

Upside-down subordination: He besought her hand daily for twenty years, finally seeking elsewhere.

Right-side-up subordination: After beseeching her hand daily for twenty years, he finally sought elsewhere.

Thwarted Subordination. Andrew Jackson courted a wealthy lady named Rachel Donelson, and whose family helped him in getting on.

The *and* before the subordinate clause thwarts subordination.

Proper subordination: Andrew Jackson courted a wealthy lady named Rachel Donelson, whose family helped him in getting on.

Proper subordination: Andrew Jackson courted Rachel Donelson, who was a wealthy lady and whose family helped him in getting on.

Exercise No. 115

By subordination and co-ordination, convert the primer sentences below into mature prose.

Almost every child, as soon as he is old enough, wants to kill flies and other insects. This leads on to the killing of larger animals and ultimately of men. In the ordinary English upper-class family, the killing of birds is considered highly creditable. The killing of men in war is regarded as the noblest of professions. This attitude is in accordance with untrained instinct. It is that of men who possess no form of constructive skill. They are therefore unable to find any innocent embodiment of their will to power. They can make pheasants die and tenants suffer. When occasion arises, they can shoot a rhinoceros or a German. But in more useful arts they are entirely deficient. Their parents and teachers thought it sufficient to make them into English gentlemen.

FORCE AND VIGOUR

PERIODIC AND LOOSE SENTENCES. You can achieve a more emphatic utterance by the strategic employment of suspense. Normally, the English sentence has **loose structure**: it discloses its meaning near its inception; that is, it declares its subject and verb early. **Periodic structure** may constitute an effective variation from the normal pattern. The periodic sentence suspends its meaning until it nears its end; that is, it withholds its subject and verb to the last.

Loose: 'It [snow] was falling on every part of the dark central plain, on the treeless hills, falling softly on the bog of Allen and, farther westward, softly falling into the dark mutinous Shannon waves.' (James Joyce)

Periodic: 'Yet if the only form of tradition, of handing down, consisted in following the ways of the generation before us in a blind or timid adherence to its successes, "tradition" should positively be discouraged.'   (T. S. Eliot)

The first three words in the loose sentence quoted disclose the subject and the verb. Though the sense unfolds progressively, each phrase reveals a segment of meaning. The loose sentence approximates speech rhythm; its movement seems natural, spontaneous. For that reason, it is the sentence norm: more than ninety per cent of English sentences are loose in structure.

The periodic sentence quoted above attains suspense by withholding its verb to the end of the sentence. It builds to a climax; satisfying the curiosity it arouses by the *if-clause* after a purposeful delay. Since climax connotes delayed effect, periodice sentences are generally longer than loose sentences. Somewhat unnatural, the periodic sentence should be sparingly employed: orators (who often over-use it) find it valuable for emphatic statement and writers of fiction for dramatic revelation.

Exercise No. 116

Convert the loose into periodic sentences and the periodic into loose sentences.

1 The boxer acknowledged defeat after ten rounds, during which he lost precisely four teeth and about two quarts of blood.
2 Having penetrated the enemy's flank and reassembled our forces, we struck hard.
3 Not by force only but by fraud also are men enslaved.
4 He despised children although he liked dogs and tolerated cats.
5 He faltered when he saw, a bit foggily, the vague luminous form approach with slow deliberate steps.

PARALLELISM. **You should employ parallelism when it is appropriate to your thought.** Parallelism achieves its effects by balancing like grammatical units against each other—similar parts of speech (noun against noun, verb against verb, and so on), phrases, clauses, sentences. Sometimes one element echoes the other.

How shall I curse, whom God hath not cursed?
And how shall I defy, whom the Lord hath not defied?

Here the second line repeats the idea of the first. But parallelism may embrace contrasting statements as well:

For the Lord knoweth the way of the righteous;
But the way of the wicked shall perish.

Here the second line opposes the first.

Balanced sentence structure gives discourse neatness and precision; it allows no part of a thought to get lost. However, when the elements of a sentence have no mutual correspondences, when they neither echo nor contrast with each other, forcing them into a sham parallelism of structure distorts meaning. The writer who balances his sentences relentlessly often finds himself unable to tell the truth. An important technique for securing structural form and precision when used temperately, parallelism can become a pernicious device when used promiscuously. Here is parallelism employed with consummate skill:

But in a larger sense, we cannot dedicate, we cannot consecrate, we cannot hallow this ground. The brave men, living and dead, who struggled here, have consecrated it far above our poor power to add or detract. The world will little note nor long remember what we say here, but it can never forget what they did here.   (A. Lincoln)

Exercise No. 117

Restore the parallelism to these famous sentences:

1 Out of his (Nicholas Machiavelli's) surname people have coined an epithet for a knave; they use 'Nick' as a synonym for the Devil.
2 [Boswell was] regarded in his own age as a classic; today it is as a companion that we think of him.
3 I come to bury Caesar; praising him forms no part of my intention.
4 The evil that men do lives after them, and, with their bones, whatever good they have done is oft interred.
5 The Puritan hated bear-baiting, not because it gave pain to the bear, but for the reason that the spectators received pleasure from it.

EMPHASIS. You should give emphatic expression to the ideas you regard as important. Perhaps the most obvious way of gaining emphasis is italicization (underlining).

We *never* liked puns or pundits.

That way, however, is mechanical, artificial—easily abused.

There are more telling ways of securing emphasis, ways less liable to misapplication. To the writer who wants to be emphatic without being mannered, psychology offers an important clue. One psychological law says that, other things being equal, the stimulus which comes first, last, or most often, is the stimulus that impresses us most forcefully, the one most easily recalled.

To gain emphasis, then, place the important words at the beginning of the sentence or at the end of the sentence or repeat them during the course of the sentence.

Weak: Of late, Romanticism has appealed to many poets who seemed to have taken up residence in the Wasteland.

Stronger: 'Romanticism has of late appealed to many poets who seemed to have taken up residence in the Wasteland.' (John Henry)

Weak: . . . closed fists beat against breasts which were contrite all of a sudden.

Stronger: ' . . . closed fists beat against suddenly contrite breasts.'

(James T. Farrell)

Weak: . . . that government of, by, and for the people shall not perish from the earth.

Stronger: ' . . . that government of the people, by the people, for the people, shall not perish from the earth.' (A. Lincoln)

Repetition carried to excess may, however, become an irritating device. Used rarely and discreetly, it can compel attention. Matthew Arnold, many people may be inclined to think, rather overdoes the repetition of (especially) *truth and seriousness* and *diction and movement*, pairs that act in the following passage almost as refrains.

' . . . the superiority of poetry over history consists in its possessing a higher truth and a higher seriousness. Let us add . . . that the substance and matter of the best poetry acquire their special character from possessing, in an eminent degree, truth and seriousness. We may add yet further what is in itself evident, that to the style and manner of the best poetry their special character, their accent, is given by their diction, and, even yet more, by their movement. And though we distinguish between the two characters, the two accents, of superiority, yet they are nevertheless vitally connected one with the other. The

English Made Simple

superior character of truth and seriousness, in the matter of the best poetry, is inseparable from the superiority of diction and movement marking its style and manner. . . .'

There are several other repetitions in the course of the paragraph; it is easier to be emphatically repetitious than to be emphatic through repetition.

Exercise No. 118

Rephrase the following sentences more emphatically.

1 Science answers many questions, but never 'Why?' the ultimate one.
2 The ultimate question, 'Why?' science never pretends to answer.
3 As every intelligent observer knows, dictatorship means the triumph of the inferior man, not of the superior one.
4 To be sure, the Psalms are a passionate criticism of life.
5 Though I speak with the tongues of men and of angels and have not charity, I am become as sounding brass or a tinkling cymbal. Grant, furthermore, that I possess the gift of prophecy and understand all mysteries and all knowledge; assume additionally that I enjoy comprehensive faith, enough to move mountains; yet devoid of charity I am nothing. Even should I bestow my goods to feed the poor and give my body to be burned, if I am without charity it profits me nothing.

VARIETY AND EUPHONY

You should vary the length and structure of your sentences, always striving, moreover, to form sentences pleasing to the ear.

VARIETY. Vary the length of your sentences. Too many long sentences strain the reader's attention. Sameness, in sentence length as in other matters, produces monotony. Changing pace by introducing an occasional terse sentence, particularly at the end of a paragraph, helps prevent monotony. Thoreau here speaks of John Brown:

'Literary gentlemen, editors, and critics think that they know how to write, because they have studied grammar and rhetoric; but they are egregiously mistaken. The *art* of composition is as simple as the discharge of a bullet from a rifle, and its masterpieces imply an infinitely greater force behind them. This unlettered man's speaking and writing are standard English. . . . It suggests that the one great rule of composition—and if I were a professor of rhetoric I should insist on this—is, *to speak the truth*. This first, this second, this third; pebbles in your mouth or not. This demands earnestness and manhood chiefly.'

Vary the openings of your sentences. Sentences all cut to the same pattern, all wearing the same uniform, move woodenly—or the reader after a while thinks they do, which amounts to the same thing. Inevitably, monotype sentences become monotonous sentences.

Since the beginning often determines the form of the sentence, become aware of the different kinds of beginnings. Delay introducing the subject by beginning with a phrase, clause, participle, absolute, or other subordinate construction.

TYPICAL: He followed truth too closely at the heels and had his teeth kicked out.

CLAUSE: Because he followed truth too closely at the heels, he had his teeth kicked out.

PHRASE: By following too closely at truth's heels, he had his teeth kicked out.

PARTICIPLE: Having followed [or, Following] truth too closely at the heels, he had his teeth kicked out.

Vary the pattern of your sentences. The subject, the verb, and the object or complement (if any)—that constitutes the pattern of the English sentence. But for both variety and emphasis, sometimes reverse the sequence: sometimes, not too many times; else your sentences will appear artificial, unidiomatic, un-English.

Normal pattern: Emerson said, 'Speak with the vulgar, think with the wise.'

Reversed pattern: 'Speak with the vulgar, think with the wise,' said Emerson. (Object-verb-subject)

Normal pattern: The theory of divine right and the head of Charles I fall together.

Reversed pattern: Together fell the theory of divine right and the head of Charles I. (Verb-subject)

Normal pattern: I hate Croker and cold mutton equally.

Reversed pattern: Croker and cold mutton, I hate equally.
(Object-subject-verb)

Normal pattern: The days of our glory are vanished.

Reversed pattern: Vanished are the days of our glory.
(Complement-verb-subject)

Vary the kinds of sentences. An occasional question or exclamation or command may relieve the monotony of the declarative. Be wary, though: over-use (of the question particularly) may become an obnoxious mannerism. In the paragraph quoted below, Emerson resorts naturally and skilfully to the exhortation and question, enforcing his point and varying his mode.

'A foolish consistency is the hobgoblin of little minds, adored by little statesmen and philosophers and divines. With consistency a great soul has simply nothing to do. He may as well concern himself with his shadow on the wall. Speak what you think now in hard words and tomorrow speak what tomorrow thinks in hard words again, though it contradict everything you said today—"Ah, no you shall be sure to be misunderstood."—Is it so bad then to be misunderstood? Pythagoras was misunderstood, and Socrates, and Jesus, and Copernicus, and Galileo, and Newton, and every wise and pure spirit that ever took flesh. To be great is to be misunderstood.'

The paragraph might stand as a mode of supple, varied expression.

Vary the complete-sentence norm. Though the use of sentence fragments—elements containing neither subject nor predicate—demands sober control, abstention may deprive the writer of an excellent (occasional) resource, one that modern writers avail themselves of increasingly. The danger, of course, is that intemperate use of incomplete sentences will fragment communication, make it sporadic, discontinuous, wearisome. Nevertheless, advantages worth the risk accrue from intelligent usage.

'The tractors came over the roads and into the fields, great crawlers moving like insects, having the incredible strength of insects. They crawled over the ground, laying the track and rolling on it and picking it up. Diesel tractors, puttering while they stood idle; they thundered when they moved, and then settled down to a droning roar. Snub-nosed monsters, raising the dust and sticking their snouts into it, straight down the country, across the country, through fences, through dooryards, in and out of gullies in straight lines. They did not run on the ground, but on their own roadbeds.'

(John Steinbeck)

Here the prose gives the direct impression of a man's thinking, of the movement of his mind. The parting sentences seem to require neither subject nor verb: the reader feels their absence not at all.

Exercise No. 119

Rewrite the passages below, varying the length and structure of the individual sentences.

1 The art of conversation is the art of hearing as well as of being heard and authors in general are not good listeners and some of the best talkers are, on this account, the worst company. Some who are very indifferent, but very great talkers, are as bad and it is sometimes wonderful to see how a person, who has been entertaining or tiring a company by the hour together, drops his countenance. It is as if he had been shot, or had been seized with a sudden lockjaw, the moment anyone interposes a single observation but the best converser I know is, however, the best listener.

2 It is profoundly characteristic of the art of Virginia Woolf that when I decided to write about it and had planned a suitable opening paragraph, my fountain pen should disappear, tiresome creature, it slipped through a pocket into a seam. I could pinch it, chivy it about, make holes in the coat lining, but a layer of tailor's stuffing prevented recovery—so near, and yet so far—which is what one feels about her art. The pen is extricated in time, but during the struggle the opening paragraph has escaped; the words are here but the birds have flown; 'opals and emeralds, they lie about the roots of turnips,' it is far more difficult to catch her than it is for her to catch what she calls life—'life; London; this moment in June.'

3 The age we live in is a most dangerous one. It is an age of supersonic airspeeds, of biological warfare, of atomic and hydrogen bombs. Nobody knows what is next. We all exist on borrowed time today; that is no exaggeration. We of this generation may deserve no better fate. We are sure our children do, however.

LANGUAGE. You should, as a rule, phrase your sentences directly, employing the passive and other indirect constructions only for specific reasons. If the agent is unknown, or (for some reason) better left unidentified, or less important than his act, the passive is a legitimate construction.

> Black masses are conducted nightly.
> He was called Oedipus.
> French is spoken here.

However, the passive breeds circumlocution. It has not the pulse of normal speech. It shortly waxes boring. Compare:

Indirect: A style consistently laconic, excessively terse, is defeated by itself.
Direct: A style consistently laconic, excessively terse, defeats itself.
Indirect: False words ought to be hated and true ones sought by you.
Direct: Hate false words and seek true ones.

You should use fresh, vivid, imaginative language. It enlivens writing, adds reality to it. Compare:

Dull: In Trollope's novels, right and wrong are very plain.
Better: In Trollope's novels right and wrong are as palpable as a clergyman's gown or a barrister's wig.

Note that the language ought to be appropriate to the context: 'as a tractor', for example, would not fit the context in the sentence quoted.

Imaginative: 'Often, if the emergency brake [of the Model T Ford] hadn't been pulled all the way back, the car advanced on you the instant the first explosion occurred and you would hold back by leaning your weight against it. I can still feel my old Ford nuzzling me at the curb, as though looking for an apple in my pocket.' (Lee Strout White)

'Welcher was a rich lawyer, with a face like a bad orange. Yellow and blue. A little grasshopper of a man. Five feet of shiny broadcloth and three inches of collar. Always on the jump. Inside or out. In his fifties. The hopping fifties. And fierce as a mad mouse.' (Joyce Cary)

Exercise No. 120

Rephrase the following sentences, substituting active for awkward passive constructions and vivid for dull language.

1 Lots were drawn by the three conspirators to determine the one by whom the assassination would be undertaken.
2 The sleeves of the shirt were stretched out on the drying line.
3 Pope made an odd impression on people: his back was humped and so weak that he could not stand erect.
4 Julia's dainty leg is white and has no hair.
5 What awaits him when a door is opened by him is known by no man. Surprises may be harboured in even the most familiar room.

EUPHONY. You should construct sentences that are pleasing to the ear. Avoid the jingling recurrence of the same sound:

I bathed, made my bed, and ate a breakfast of bread and butter.

Here the alliteration of *b*'s, the assonance of long *a*'s, and the rhyme of *bed* and *bread* distract the reader from the sense, focus his attention on the sound. The example given is extreme, of course; but more moderate recurrences of sound, because they are more moderate, often escape the notice of the writer. Yet they may be irritating to the reader. Read your sentences aloud; your ear will usually inform you of jingles that your eye misses.

Avoid the needless repetition of the same word. 'Elegant variation'—the piling up of synonyms—does not constitute the alternative: if only one word meets your need precisely, repeat it. But a sentence like this demands rewriting:

Repetitive: The woman whom I marry must be a woman who does not regard me as someone whose chief function is to convert her into a woman who has twelve children.

Improved: The woman whom I marry must not regard me chiefly as the father of her twelve potential children.

Avoid heaping phrase on phrase in your sentences. A succession of phrases (especially prepositional phrases) imparts a jerky rhythm to your sentences.

The dog refused to come out of the pool on to the tiles.

Avoid a too marked rhythm in your sentences. Prose has a harmony other than verse, a great critic noted. Some great writers offend—but not in their great passages. This passage is from Dickens: it has been set as verse, though originally written as prose.

I think in every quiet season now,
Still do those waters roll, and leap, and roar,
And tumble all day long;
Still are the rainbows spanning them
A hundred feet below.
Still when the sun is on them, do they shine
And glow like molten gold.
Still when the day is gloomy do they fall
Like snow, or seem to crumble away,
Like the front of a great chalk cliff,
Or roll adown the rock like dense white smoke.

Either as prose or poetry the writing fails. This, from Disraeli, is even worse:

'Why am I here? are you not here? and need I urge a stronger plea? Oh, brother dear, I pray you come and mingle in our festival. Our walls are hung with flowers you love; I culled them by the fountain's side; the holy lamps are trimmed and set, and you must raise their earliest flame. Without the gate my maidens wait to offer you a robe of state. Then, brother dear, I pray you come and mingle in our festival.'

To read this paragraph without intoning it seems only less difficult than to read it without ridiculing it.

All good prose has rhythm, a rhythm which bears the imprint of the man who writes it, which rises and falls in response to the demands of his theme. Here is a passage that might easily have fallen into a te-dum-te-dum-te-dum rhythm, had not the author skilfully varied his stresses:

'Fair today and warmer. A hot sun ballooned on high, held to the sweltering earth by the thin line of a well-ordered universe. The hovering clouds, like cream turned sour by the heat, curdled into spoondrift.'   (Ellis St. Joseph)

Exercise No. 121

The sentences below contain harsh or unpleasing combinations of sound. Eliminate them.

1 Why did you bring these two books to me to read out of?
2 The man who tries to live and die in peace is often grieved.
3 The boy's toys are noisy.
4 Since she is not of a suspicious nature, she seldom searches her spouse's trousers.
5 His mother thought that his adolescent ambition to fly was flighty.

FAULTY DICTION:
A GLOSSARY OF WORDS FREQUENTLY MISUSED

Accept, except

Though frequently confused, these words are nearly antonyms.
Accept means 'to take what is offered'.
Except (as a verb) means 'to exclude'.
Right: Jean was willing to accept all invitations, but all excepted Jean from their invitations.

Adapt, adopt

Adapt means 'to adjust or fit'.
Adopt means 'to take, receive, or assume as one's own'.
Dr. Hyde adopted a child who quickly adapted himself to his new environment.

Affect, effect

As a verb, *affect* means 'to act upon or influence'. As a verb, *effect* means 'to bring about or accomplish'.
Intemperate living will affect his health.
Temperate living will effect his cure.
As a noun, *affect* has a psychological connotation: 'feeling, emotion, desire'. As a noun, *effect* means 'result or consequence'.
Right: The effect of an affect is to influence behaviour or consciousness.

Aggravate

In standard English it means 'to make worse or less endurable'. Avoid the colloquial sense of 'irritate or annoy'.
Right: He aggravated injury by insult.

Agree to, agree with

English idiom demands that one *agrees to* a scheme, plan or project and *agrees with* a person. Additionally, a thing may *agree with* a person, and two things may *agree with* each other.
I agree to a quarrel.
I am happy to disagree with you.
Brandy agrees with me.
The verb agrees with the noun in person and number.

Ain't

Originally a contraction of *am not*, by extension *ain't* became a contraction of *is not* and *are not*, even of *has not* and *have not*. Dictionaries agree in labelling *ain't* 'dialectal or illiterate'.

No contraction of *am not* has proved generally acceptable, and so the rejection of *ain't* by educated speakers and writers may legitimately be cause for regret.

Some liberal grammarians call *ain't* 'colloquial' as a contraction of 'am not', substandard as a contraction of *is not*, *are not*, *has not*, *have not*. But educated colloquial usage seems to be increasingly against them.

Alibi

Alibi means 'a plea of having been, at the time of an act, at a place other than the place of the act'.

Sutton's alibi, that he was in jail when Arnold Shuster was murdered, seemed flawless.

Avoid the colloquial sense of 'excuse'.

Allude, refer

Allude means 'to touch on lightly and indirectly'. *Refer* means 'to mention distinctly and directly'.

Wrong: He alluded at great length to General Blenkinsop.

Right: In passing, he alluded to a certain general who had commanded the British armies in Europe.

Right: I refer to General Blenkinsop, commander of the British armies in Europe.

Alright

Alright, a simplified spelling of *all right*, has not yet won its way to dictionary approval. But it is a popular spelling, probably because of its likeness to *always* and *altogether*, and eventually will gain dictionary acceptance. (Don't pioneer, however.)

Alternative

Alternative derives from Latin *alter*, 'the second of two', a fact that people who esteem origins regard as decisive. To them, alternative means only 'a choice between two courses':

This is your alternative: believe either his report or your own eyes.

But educated usage and most dictionaries define *alternative* as signifying not only 'choice between two courses', but also 'choice'—though commonly they label the latter meaning 'loose' or 'less strict'.

Acceptable: It was his only possible alternative.

Acceptable: We had three alternatives.

Alternative must only be used, however, when there is a genuine choice. Not when meaning 'other'. (*Not*, for example: Mrs. Smith has found alternative help to replace her charwoman who dropped dead last Tuesday.)

Among, between

Between is used when speaking of two things or persons; *among*, when speaking of more than two.

He had a pumpkin between his ears.

He had a nose carelessly located among his features.

However, when used to denote contrast, or to express interrelation, *between* sometimes refers to more than two.

Right: Though *Sanctuary, This Side of Paradise,* and *The Masters* all deal with university life, there is a great difference between them.

Right: The treaty between the three governments lacked three signatures.

Amount, number

Amount applies to mass or bulk, *number* to separate units.

They had a large number of children and a small amount of money.

Apt, liable, likely

Apt means 'suited, pertinent'; or 'inclined, disposed'; or 'ready, prompt to learn'.

An apt student of the classics, Mr. Coolidge was apt to disregard 'the illusion of reality'; but now and then he would emerge from his studies with apt comments on men and affairs.

Likely means 'probable' and *liable* means 'responsible for consequences', or 'in danger of incurring something disagreeable'.

He is not likely to write love letters to Miss Becky Sharp, but all men are liable to make mistakes—and liable for them.

As, like

As introduces a clause, *like* a phrase.

Like Jane, Mary was tall as a giraffe.

Note: When *as* means 'in the role of' it may be used as a preposition.

She has a new job as secretary to the director.

Awful

Awful, as a loose substitute for 'very, excessively' or for 'ugly, extremely bad, shocking, ludicrous', is a colloquial usage—perhaps a low colloquial usage. In Standard English it means 'awe-inspiring, appalling'.

> The awful shadow of some unseen Power
> Floats though unseen among us.   (Shelley)

Because of, owing to, due to

Because of and *owing to* introduce an adverbial phrase, *due to* an adjective phrase.

Right: Because of Adam and Eve, we have been excluded from Eden. (The phrase modifies *have been excluded.*)

Right: Our exclusion from Eden is due to Adam and Eve. (Phrase modifies *exclusion.* What is due? *Our exclusion.*)

Besides, besides

Beside means 'at the side of', *besides* 'additionally'.

Right: No one sat beside me. (That is, the adjacent chairs were vacant.)

Right: No one sat besides me. (That is, everyone else stood.)

Between, among. *See* Among, between

Cannot help but

There are three acceptable idioms, each having a meaning slightly different from the others:

I can but hope means 'I can only hope'.

I cannot but hope means 'I cannot do anything except hope'.

I cannot help hoping means 'I cannot keep away from hope'.

The differences, though, have been obscured, the variant meanings being generally confounded.

Cannot help but, deriving from the popular confusion of *cannot but* and *cannot help*, has gained reluctant acceptance as a colloquial usage.

Circumstances

In the circumstances. Never use *under the circumstances.*

Contact

Contact is the sense of 'get in touch with' is a colloquial usage—one that many people abominate because it is greatly over-used. It functions as a loose substitute for *communicate with, write to, talk to, meet, telephone, call upon, inform,* and *ask about.*

Continual, continuous

Continual implies a regular but interrupted succession; *continuous* a constant and uninterrupted succession.

The continual rain in Wales keeps the countryside lush and green.

The continuous roar of Niagara depressed the honeymooners.

Could of

Avoid writing *could of*, a corruption of could've (*could have*).

Different from, different to

The standard idiom is *different from.* Some grammarians rank *different to* as 'standard' likewise, whereas others insist that it is 'colloquial'.

Right: Man, said a French savant, is different from woman.

Different than is accepted by some authorities but is not recommended.

Disinterested, uninterested

Disinterested means 'impartial', *uninterested* 'not interested'. An uninterested judge, it has been pointed out, might fall asleep on the bench; a disinterested one might be passionately interested in the progress of a trial, but he presides over it without bias, nevertheless.

Done, did

Did, not *done*, is the past tense of do.

Wrong: I *done* the washing on Monday.

Right: I *did* the washing on Monday.

Doubt that, doubt whether

Doubt that implies little uncertainty, *doubt whether* much.
I'm no weather prophet, but I doubt that it will rain cats and dogs.
He doubted whether he could become a weather prophet—a foolish doubt.

Due to, because of. *See* Because of, due to

Each other, one another

Each other and *one another* may be used interchangeably in Standard English. But some formalists still distinguish between them, holding that *each other* implies two only and that *one another* implies more than two:
Let us love, be true to each other.
Poets often write for one another.

Effect, affect. *See* Affect, effect

Emigrant, immigrant

An *emigrant* leaves one country to enter another. An *immigrant* enters one country from another.
The French emigrants sailed from Le Havre.
The French immigrants arrived in New York. Note that an emigrant must subsequently be an immigrant.

Enthuse

Many writers detest *enthuse*, a colloquialism meaning 'enthusiastic' or 'make enthusiastic'.

Equally as good

Equally as good mixes two good idioms, *as good as* and *equally good*, to produce a bad blend.
Wrong: A picture is equally as good as a thousand words.
Right: A picture is as good as a thousand words.
Right: A picture and a thousand words are equally good.

Etc.

Etc. is the abbreviation of *et cetera*, Latin for 'and so forth' (*et* 'and' plus *cetera* 'other things').
Use *etc.* sparingly.
Do not use *and etc.* at all: it equals 'and and so forth'.

Except, accept. *See* Accept, except

Farther, further

Farther and *further* may be used interchangeably in Standard English, though many careful writers prefer *further* when they intend 'more' or 'more extended' and *farther* when they refer to distance.
Right: John has moved farther north.
Right: I have nothing further to say.

Fewer, less

Fewer applies to number—to things countable. *Less* applies to quantity—to things that are measured.

The Mormons made an interesting discovery: the fewer wives, the less trouble.

Colloquially, *less* functions as a synonym for *fewer*.

Good, well

Good functions only as an adjective, *well* as both an adverb and an adjective.

Wrong: She dances good.

Right: She dances well.

Had ought, hadn't ought, didn't ought

Had ought, *hadn't ought*, and *didn't ought* are non-standard. Use *ought* (or *ought not*) alone: it says all that *had ought* says—without redundancy.

Human, humans

Human is an adjective. It is colloquial as a noun.

Colloquial: A multitude of humans gathered at White City.

Standard: A multitude of human beings gathered at White City.

Hang, hung

If a man is suspended by the neck until he is dead, he is preferably *hanged*. However, pictures, draperies, trophies, and the like are *hung*.

Hardly, scarcely, barely

Hardly, *scarcely*, and *barely* are negatives implying 'not quite'. Avoid using any of them with another negative.

Wrong: He admitted that he scarcely didn't escape death by drowning.

Right: He admitted that he scarcely escaped death by drowning.

If, whether

Standard usage prefers *if* to introduce a condition, *whether* to introduce an indirect question, an expression of doubt or uncertainty, or an alternative.

Condition: If we strike, the enemy will scatter.

Indirect question: He asked whether lightning had struck once.

Doubt: She wondered whether he was guilt stricken.

Alternative: They often strike their sails, whether the fish are striking or not.

Immigrant, emigrant. *See* Emigrant, Immigrant

Imply, infer

Imply means 'to suggest or hint'. (A writer or speaker *implies* to his audience.)

Infer means 'to conclude or derive from'. (An audience *infers* from a writer or speaker.)

The School Council implied that larger classes might result in reduced expenses. Many parents inferred from this statement that fees might be lower in future.

In, into

In implies 'location, situation, or position'.
Into implies 'direction, or motion towards a location'.
I sat in the darkened room watching moths fly into the candle flame.

Incredible, incredulous

Incredible means 'unbelievable or too far-fetched to believe'.
Incredulous means 'sceptical or disinclined to believe'.
The children recounted an incredible tale about killing a talking snake. Their parents listened; then smiled incredulously.

Is because. *See* Reason is because

Is when, is where

Do not use *is when* and *is where* in definitions. However, *when* and *where* may properly be used after *to be* to introduce a noun clause of time or place.
Right: This house is where Edgar Allan Poe lived.
Right: The time to attack is when the enemy retreats.
Wrong: Fascism is when one person may impose his will on all minority groups.
Right: In Fascism, one person may impose his will on all minority groups.
Right: Fascism is a system in which one person may impose his will on all minority groups.
Wrong: Heredity is where parents transmit their traits to their children.
Right: Heredity is the transmission of traits from parents to children.

Later, latter

Later, the comparative form of *late*, means 'more late'.
Latter means 'the second mentioned of two things'.
Hurry! It's later than you think.
He ate mussels and snails. The latter gave him ptomaine poisoning.
Note: To designate more than two, use *last, last-named*, or *last-mentioned*.

Learn, teach

Often confused, *learn* and *teach* are nearly antonyms. *Learn* means 'to gain knowledge or acquire skills'. *Teach* means 'to impart knowledge or to show how'.
Students learn most when they have been taught how to study.

Less, fewer. *See* Fewer, less

Liable, likely, apt. *See* Apt, liable, likely

Lie, lay

The irregular verbs *lie* and *lay* cause much confusion because certain of their forms are identical.
Lie, an intransitive verb, means:
1 To recline.
2 To utter a falsehood.

Lay, a transitive verb, means 'to put or place'. Note the trouble spots:
Lie (to recline) PRESENT
Lie (to deceive) PRESENT
Lay (to recline) PAST
Lay (to put) PRESENT

Right:

Lie (to recline):	I lie down when I'm tired. (*Present*)
	I lay down last evening. (*Past*)
	Often, when exhausted, I *have* (or had) *lain* down. (*Past Part.*)
Lie (to deceive):	Why do you lie when you know I'll learn the truth? (*Present*)
	He lied to the police to protect his aunt. (*Past*)
	He has (or had) lied too often to be trusted. (*Past Part.*)
Lay (to put):	Lay that revolver on the table. (*Present*)
	We laid our money on the counter. (*Past*)
	We have (or had) laid our ploughshares beside our scythes. (*Past Part.*)

Loan, lend

Prefer **lend** as the verb.
Standard: Will you lend me your pen?

Mutual

Strictly, *mutual* implies a reciprocal relationship—John is to Jack as Jack is to John.

Right: John and Jack are mutually dependent. (That is, John depends on Jack and Jack depends on John.)

Common, in the sense of 'that which is shared equally by two or more people', should be preferred to *mutual* in such phrases as 'our mutual friend', 'their mutual fondness for oysters', 'your mutual astonishment'.

Phrases like 'mutual co-operation' are redundant and ought to be avoided.

Never, not

Do not use *never* instead of *not*.
Wrong: I never heard her when she spoke to me.
Right: I did not hear her when she spoke to me.

Nice

Nice, as a colloquial word indicating vague approval should be avoided; over-use has made it trite. Use words that precisely meet your meaning.
Colloquial: Your furniture has a nice finish and should wear nicely.
Better: Your furniture has a rich, glossy lustre, one that will last.
Note: *Nice* used to mean 'precise, discriminating', makes an effective adjective.
Right: Good diction aims at nice distinction between words.

Number, amount. *See* Amount, number

Off of

Although frequently used as a colloquialism, *off of* is an uncultivated usage. *Of* is unnecessary.
Poor: Keep off of my property.
Right: Keep off my property.

One another, each other. *See* Each other, one another

Oral, verbal

Oral means 'spoken, by word of mouth'.

Verbal means 'of, or concerned with words'.

Right: In his *oral* examination he made *verbal* distinctions between such differentiated words as adulteration and adultery.

Right: When I put it to him *orally*, he made no *verbal* reply but heaved a sigh.

Party, person

Person means 'a single human being'. Standard usage prefers this reference to *humans*.

Party means 'a group of people'. It may be used to refer to *one person* only in the legal sense of 'one involved in a transaction'. Used to denote 'a person' it is substandard.

Right: He is the person to whom I gave the book.

Right: If the party to the deed signed the affidavit he will be released from further responsibilities.

Practical, practicable

Easily and often confused, *practical* and *practicable* are not synonyms.

Practical means 'useful or workable, as opposed to theoretical'. It may apply to persons or things.

Practicable means 'possible or feasible, particularly in reference to projects, schemes, or plans'. It applies only to things, never to persons.

Right: Fifty years ago practical businessmen showed no desire to invest in practicable schemes for jet-propulsion. Today jet-engines are as practical as the old petrol engines.

Prefer to, rather than

Prefer to is standard usage when the rejected alternative is expressed.

I *prefer* idling *to* working.

However, the object of *prefer* is often an infinitive which makes the use of *to* very awkward.

In this case, *rather than* should be used.

I *prefer to* idle *rather than* work.

It is also possible to use *rather than* as an independent construction.

I would *rather* idle *than* work.

Principal, principle

Principal means 'first in rank or importance'.

Principle means 'fundamental truth as basis of reasoning'.

Right: The *principal* feature of the *principle* of moral re-armament is the desire to establish God as the *principal* influence on the formation of our *principles*.

Mnemonic: The *principal* with the *a* is the adjective.

Raise, rise

Do not confuse *raise*, a transitive verb, requiring an object, with *rise*, an intransitive verb that does not require an object.

Right: I rise early because I keep chickens.

Right: When the conductor raised his baton to begin the national anthem, the audience rose.

Rarely ever

Substandard for *rarely*, or *hardly ever*.

Vulgar: I rarely ever get to the theatre.

Right: I rarely (hardly ever) get to the theatre.

Rather than. *See* Prefer to, rather than

Reason is because

Reason is because is incorrect; *reason is that* is standard. One objects to the redundancy of *reason is because*, since *because* means 'for this reason'.

Wrong: The reason I am late is because the drawbridge jammed.

Standard: The reason I am late is that the drawbridge jammed.

Reason why

Reason why is accepted by most linguists as standard.

The reason why he collects books is that he enjoys reading them.

Refer, allude. *See* Allude, refer

Said

As an adjective, *said* means 'previously mentioned' and should be used only in legal documents. In Standard English substitute a noun or pronoun.

Legal: The said parties are under subpoena to appear in court on June 15, 1972.

Standard: These persons are to appear in court on June 15, 1972.

Set, sit

Set, a weak transitive verb, means 'to place or put'. Its intransitive uses, when it means 'to decline or wane', are limited: *the sun sets*.

Sit, a strong intransitive verb, means 'to be seated'.

Right: I set the dog on his box and he sits there.—PRESENT

I set the dog on his box and he sat there.—PAST

I have set the dog on his box and he has sat there.—PERFECT

Teach, learn. *See* Learn, teach

Their, there, they're

Do not confuse these homonyms.

Their is the possessive form of they.—Pronoun

There means 'at that place or at that point'.—Adverb

They're is the contraction for *they are*.—Pronoun and Verb

If they're willing, we'll drive their car. Otherwise we'll take our car and leave theirs there.

Them, those

Do not confuse the personal pronoun with the demonstrative pronoun and, even if you do, do not use it in the objective case when it longs to be nominative.

Wrong: Them girls kept us boys waiting.

Right: Those girls kept us boys waiting.

Uninterested, disinterested. *See* Disinterested, uninterested.

Unique

Unique means 'the only one of its kind'. Thus, it should not be confused with *unusual*, *rare*, or *outstanding*, which can be compared, as *unique* cannot.

The unique manuscript of *Beowulf* is in the British Museum.

Verbal, oral. *See* Oral, verbal

Well, good

Good, an adjective meaning 'satisfactory or excellent', is often confused with *well*, an adverb meaning 'in a satisfactory or excellent manner'. *Good* cannot be used as an adverb.

Wrong: If her voice is well, she'll sing good.

Right: If her voice is good, she'll sing well.

Note: *Well* used as an adjective means 'good health'.

He looked well after his ulcer healed.

Whether, if. *See* If, whether

LETTER WRITING

THE LETTER IN MODERN SOCIETY

Though few people depend upon writing as their chief source of income, most have often found it necessary to compose a personal or business letter. Almost everyone needs to know the principles of effective letter writing.

More than two hundred years ago, the Earl of Chesterfield, one of the most famous of letter writers, gave his son excellent advice about both the personal and business letter. For **personal letters** he urged the **charm and wit of extemporaneous conversation;** for **business letters clarity and directness:** 'Every paragraph should be so clear and unambiguous that the dullest fellow in the world may not be able to mistake it, nor obliged to read it twice in order to understand it.'

One wonders what the Earl would say about a business letter of today which reads like this:

Dear Sir:

Yours of the 5th inst. at hand. We beg to state in re your enquiry concerning your purchase order X-2930-C, that the above order went forward from our warehouse in Greenwich via Smith collect.

We regret most sincerely any delay you have been caused, but feel assured that the order is en route to you now. If any further delay is encountered, an immediate reply from you will be appreciated. We trust that we may continue to be of service and remain

Very truly yours,

Or how the Earl might react to the 'charm' and 'wit' of this personal note:

Dear Jim,

Well, you sent me a letter, and now I suppose I owe you one. God, how I hate writing letters, specially because there's never really anything around here to write about. We did go to the cinema last night but I can't remember what the picture was about.

Mum and Dad are all right, and we saw your Aunt Mary last week. She's all right too and sends her regards.

Well, that's all I can think of for the moment. Write again soon and let me know how life's treating you. I'd be rather interested to know.

Regards to everybody.

Yours,

Figure 1. THE LETTER PICTURE

AVOID THIS

```
                                    36 Chester Road,
                                    London, SW4 2BJ.
                                    28th March, 1976.
      Box M 521,
        The Times,
            New Printing House Square,
                London, WC1X 8EZ.

      Dear Sir,
                  I wish to apply for the position of matron
      as advertised in this morning's Times.
                  I enclose a list of my particulars with
      details of my nursing qualifications and of experience
      I have had with children.
                  I should be very interested to meet you and
      see the school and I hope that you will grant me an
      interview.
                                    Yours faithfully,
```

```
                                    36 Chester Road,

                                    London, SW4 2BJ.


                                    28th March 1976.


            Box M 521,
            The Times,
            New Printing House Square,
            London, WC1X 8EZ.


            Dear Sir,
                        I wish to apply for the position of matron as
            advertised in this morning's Times.

                        I enclose a list of my particulars with details
            of my nursing qualifications and of experience I have had
            with children.

                        I should be very interested to meet you and see
            the school and I hope that you will grant me an interview.

                        Yours faithfully,
```

DO THIS

In the modern world, crammed as it is with excitement and movement, only laziness or ignorance explains letters like those on page 204. The sections below attempt to direct the modern letter writer to effective communication that is **correct, precise,** and **vigorous.**

ESTABLISHED CONVENTIONS IN LETTER WRITING

In communication, as in clothing, good taste is influenced by custom and convention. Therefore it is safer to follow certain rules in both personal and business correspondence.

STATIONERY AND GENERAL APPEARANCE

Business Letters. *Choose writing paper and envelopes of appropriate quality, colour, and size.*

Use good quality, plain paper. Standard sizes for commercial stationery are A4 (210 by 297 millimetres or $8\frac{1}{4}$ by $11\frac{3}{4}$ inches), and less commonly, A5 (148 by 210 millimetres or $8\frac{1}{4}$ by $5\frac{3}{4}$ inches).

Use envelopes of the standard size for the paper: 110 by 220 millimetres or $4\frac{1}{4}$ by $8\frac{1}{2}$ inches for A4 and 89 by 152 millimetres or $3\frac{1}{2}$ by 6 inches for A5.

The Post Office prefers the standard small envelopes and does not like any to be larger than 120 by 235 millimetres or $4\frac{3}{4}$ by $9\frac{1}{4}$ inches.

Use a typewriter.

Almost all business letters written today are typed. Only when specifically requested to do so ought one to write by hand, and then only in blue or black ink. Never use pencil.

In some business organizations, no corrections or erasures are permitted in correspondence. The typescript must be mechanically perfect.

Use one side of the paper only, whether the letter is typewritten or hand-written.

Arrange the letter on the page so that the writing becomes a picture, the white space a frame. (See Figure 1.)

Keep margins of at least one inch on all sides of the paper.

Be particularly careful not to crowd the right-hand margin or the bottom of the page.

Estimate the length of the letter and frame it to make the most attractive arrangement.

Fold letters properly. (See Figure 2.)

To prepare an A4 letter for a standard **small commercial envelope** (89 by 152 millimetres or $3\frac{1}{2}$ by 6 inches):

Step 1. Starting from the bottom, fold the sheet upward to within one-eighth inch of the top. The slight margin makes it easier to separate the ends when opening the letter.

Step 2. Now, starting from the left of the creased sheet, fold once from the left and once from the right to divide the width of the sheet into three equal sections.

Step 3. Place the letter in the envelope so that the left fold is down, the right fold up, and so that the right flap of the letter faces the back of the envelope.

To prepare an A4 letter for a standard **long commercial envelope** (110 by 220 millimetres or $4\frac{1}{4}$ by $8\frac{1}{2}$ inches):

Step 1. Starting from the bottom, fold the sheet upward to slightly more than one-third the length of the sheet.

Step 2. Now, starting from the top, make the second fold at the edge of the bottom of the page as it lies folded.

Step 3. Place the letter in the envelope so that the two flaps face the back of the envelope, and the top edge of the letter rests on the bottom of the envelope.

Make certain that the folded letter fits the envelope perfectly. If the fit is wrong, the fold has been made incorrectly.

Figure 2. FOLDING THE LETTER

a. A4 LETTER IN SMALL COMMERCIAL ENVELOPE

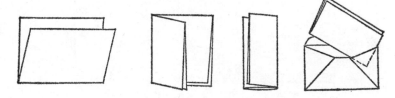

b. A4 LETTER IN LONG COMMERCIAL ENVELOPE

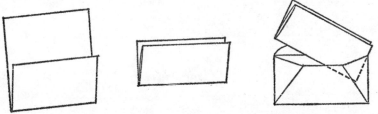

Personal Letters. The writer has a completely free choice in selecting paper for personal correspondence. What is used is entirely a matter of individual taste and there is a very large variety of styles, colours and sizes available. Envelopes should match the page in size and colour and lined paper should only be used if the writer finds it difficult to write in parallel lines.

Most personal correspondence is handwritten, especially when the content is intimate. Nevertheless, typewritten personal letters are now generally acceptable.

Make the letter legible and neat. Avoid crowding margins at the right and bottom. Avoid garish contrasts between ink and paper.

Paper is designed to fit the envelopes and it is normally quite clear how it should be folded. The larger standard sheet (180 by 230 millimetres or 7 by 9 inches) should be folded for its long envelope in the same way as the A4 letter above. The small standard sheet (180 by 140 millimetres or 5½ by 7 inches) should be folded once, in half, and placed in its envelope with the crease at the bottom. Some cards for short notes are made so that they fit their envelopes exactly and no folding is necessary and, of course, it is possible to write on a Post Office Air Letter or on a postcard and not use an envelope at all.

HEADING AND INSIDE ADDRESS FOR TYPED BUSINESS LETTERS

The heading and inside address must be consistent in form (*block* or *indented*) and punctuation. (See Figure 3 and Figure 4.)

Figure 3. BLOCK FORM

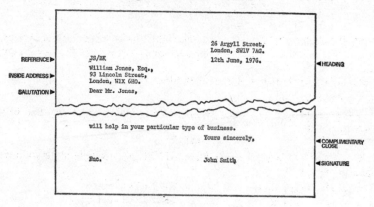

Figure 4. INDENTED FORM

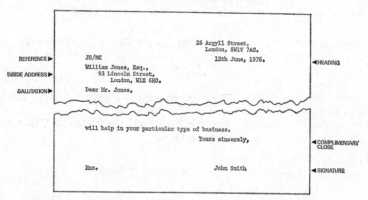

Block form is generally preferred in both heading and inside address.

The heading and inside address are single-spaced and separated from one another by a double space.

The **heading** provides the address of the writer and the date. It is placed in the **upper right side of the first page.**

Note: Many firms use printed headings and type only the date.

Use no abbreviations such as Ave., St., Gdns., Rd.

The only abbreviations generally approved are for counties: Bucks., Beds., Yorks.

Do not abbreviate the names of the months. Do not write Dec. 7; write December 7th or 7th December. Do not use figures for months: 7/12/76. Do not write June 15, '76.

The **inside address** gives the exact name of the person, firm, or organization written to. It is placed **flush with the left-hand margin**, and separated from the last line of the heading by a double space.

Observe the same rules for abbreviations as discussed under **heading.**

THE SALUTATION—is placed **flush with the left-hand margin.** It is separated from the last line of the inside address by a double space. (See Figure 3 and Figure 4.)

In all letters, the salutation is followed by a comma,

Dear Mr. Smith,

When the letter is addressed to a firm or organization rather than to an individual, use:

Dear Sirs,

When the letter is addressed to an individual, use any copy of the following salutations:

Dear Mr. Lump,   Dear Miss Jones,
Dear Mrs. Eichen,   Dear Dr. Pangloss,
Dear Professor Middlebrook,
Dear Lieutenant Dreyfus,

Note that abbreviations are permissible only with Mr., Mrs., Ms., and Dr. (The discarding of the full stop after these is now acceptable.)

THE COMPLIMENTARY CLOSE—(*see Figure* 3 *and Figure* 4)—should be placed on a **separate line and in the middle** or to the **right of the middle of the page.** It should be separated from the last line of the body of the letter by double spacing.

Capitals only to the first letter of the complimentary close. A comma should be used after it.

Keep the complimentary close in harmony with the salutation. If the salutation is formal, the close ought to be formal.

Formal close
  Yours faithfully,
  Yours truly,
  Yours very truly,

Increased formality
  I am (*or* I remain),
  Yours faithfully,

Personal close
>   Yours sincerely,
>   Yours very sincerely,

Intimate close (to be signed by Christian name only)
>   Yours,
>   Yours ever,
>   With love from

Note: Avoid oldfashioned phrases like 'Your obedient servant'; 'I am, dear sir, expectantly yours'; 'Your humble servant'—except for special effects.

THE SIGNATURE—(*see Figure* 3 *and Figure* 4). The writer's name should be in his own handwriting and should be placed two spaces below the complimentary close. In a business letter, a typewritten name should be added and should be placed two spaces below the handwritten signature.

Note: Letters from business organizations are usually signed with the name of the firm, typewritten, and the signature of the letterwriter, handwritten:

>   Mills Bottling Company
>
>   *John Smith*

If a woman gives no specific marital identification, she is assumed to be single and is addressed as *Miss*. Some women prefer that there should be no distinction made and like to be addressed as *Ms.* whatever their marital status. If a woman wishes to be addressed as one who is married, she should sign her own name (*not* her husband's) and follow it with *Mrs.* in brackets or write her husband's name preceded by *Mrs.*, enclose it in brackets, and write it on the line below her signature.

>   Single woman: Mary Robinson
>   Single woman: Mary Robinson (Ms.)
>   Married woman: Daphne Wallace (Mrs.)
>   Married woman: Daphne Wallace (Mrs. William Wallace)
>   Married woman: Daphne Wallace (Ms.)

Reference data are placed flush with the left margin, usually level with the date. (See Figure 3 and Figure 4.)

The writer who dictates a letter usually places his initials first, followed by a stroke and his secretary's initials. When errors or problems occur, identifying the writer is thus simplified.

When enclosures are added, the fact should be noted on the left margin, level with the signature.

ADDRESSING THE ENVELOPE—(*see Figure* 5)

The Address

Write the address legibly. Use pen or typewriter.

Place the address in the middle part of the envelope or postcard.

Indent each succeeding line after the first line of the address, and leave a space between lines.

Do not abbreviate names of cities, towns, streets or avenues.

Include postal codes in addresses.

Indicate clearly requests for special handling: air mail, registered, recorded delivery, and the like.

Affix the stamp in the upper right corner.

Esq. may be used after the name of any man but, then, do not use Mr., Dr., Rev., or any other title:

John Evans, Esq., M.P.

Arthur Brent, Esq., Ph.D. *or*

Dr. Arthur Brent

Figure 5. THE ENVELOPE

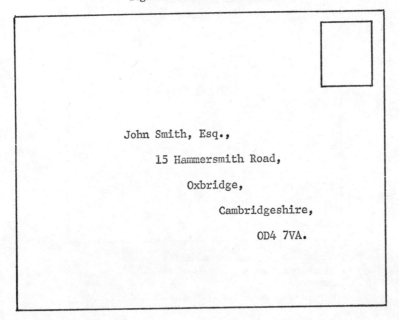

Give a married woman her husband's name or initials unless she is a widow:

Mrs. Douglas Mackay *or*

Mrs. D. B. Mackay (wife)

Mrs. Alice Mackay (widow)

Ms. Alice Mackay (unspecified)

The Return Address

The return address of the sender of a personal letter does not usually appear on the envelope but that of the sender of a business letter is normally printed either in the extreme upper left corner of the face of the envelope or on the back.

Exercise No. 122

Make any necessary corrections in the mechanical details of the following letter:

```
                                                  15 York St.
                                                  London W2B, 4LP.
                                                  Sept.,5,76.

        Mr. George Smith,
             Venus Foundation Garments Co.Ltd.,
                29 St. John's Square,
                    London WC2B, 5LJ

        Dear Mr. Smith;

             _____

             _____
             _____

             _____
             _____
          _____
          _____

                        Sincerely yours,
```

Exercise No. 123

Make any necessary corrections in the form of the address and return address on the following envelope:

```
                                          ┌──────────┐
                                          │          │
                                          └──────────┘


        Dr.P.Edwards,Ph.D.,
        Success Coaching Academy,
        The Headmaster,
        Dead Man's Lane,
        Camberley,
        Surrey GU1 2TB
```

THE METHOD OF WRITING BUSINESS LETTERS

Business letters deal with practical matters and in that sense may be thought of as impersonal in contrast to personal letters which are concerned with more subtle human relationships. In practice, though, the two categories constantly overlap and it is impossible to make a rigid distinction between them. Generally, business letters may be defined as those written in the course of commercial transactions. There are more of them than personal letters because in business dealings as much as possible is put on paper in order to provide a record of what has been agreed. They are also easier to write than personal letters because they have something definite to say and the only vital requirement is that they are absolutely clear and direct. No special language or style is necessary, just the writer's best and simplest expression and an exact attention to accuracy of detail. There is no reason why they should not be, in addition, pleasant in tone but the writer does not need to reveal himself in the way that is necessary to bring personal letters to life. It is just a matter of applying the same standards of good taste and good sense to business letters as to any other form of communication.

Be Clear and Correct

Vague: Have you anything about teaching deaf children or how to start a course of that kind? Any books, pamphlets, or references?

The reader probably will be able to work out what this letter means, but he must first untangle the bad prose, and then try to determine what the writer wants.

Clear: We are planning to begin courses for teachers of deaf children. Because we know that you have conducted excellent training programmes, we should like your assistance. Can you recommend any course syllabuses, reading references, film-strips, or other audio-visual aids?

Be Direct and Natural

Artificial:

This will acknowledge receipt of your letter in regard to the error you claimed we made in invoicing the batch of toothpicks, your order 18L14, invoice 1287A.

This is to advise you that we have located the error in the invoice, which was due to a transfer of our files. With reference to this error, a new invoice, 1398A, will be sent you in due course, which same should reach you soon.

We regret any inconvenience caused you and trust that our action as stated above will prove satisfactory.

What the letter really has to communicate appears—and then only vaguely —in the second paragraph. The first paragraph merely repeats what the reader already knows; the third paragraph doesn't convince because it is too wordy and too trite.

Direct and Natural:

Your claim is wholly justified. Our invoice is wrong and we are sorry about our error.

We are sending to you corrected invoice number 1398A.

This letter gets directly to the point, clearly explains the facts, and stops. Most of the trouble with business letters derives from roundabout language. If jargon were cut out, letters would communicate the sprightliness their writers display in talking, but not in writing.

Use Familiar Words

PRETENTIOUS	NATURAL
communication	letter, telegram
the writer	I or me
discrepancy	difference
assistance	help
unable to effect cancellation	cannot cancel
We regret most sincerely	I'm very sorry

Use Active Voice

PASSIVE	ACTIVE
No invoice has been received	We haven't had an invoice
It is desired that we receive	We want, We'd appreciate
An immediate reply will be appreciated	Please answer promptly, We'll appreciate a prompt reply.
The question was raised by you	You raised the question (or You asked)
Your letter of July 15th has been received and the contents of same carefully noted	(Just don't say it at all)

Use Straightforward Language

CIRCUITOUS	STRAIGHTFORWARD
We are in receipt of	We received
Please arrange to return	Please return
We are not in a position to	We cannot
May we suggest that you	Please
We will take steps to	We will
Please see that an investigation is made to determine	Please find out

Why use a Phrase . . . When a Word is Enough

inasmuch as	because
in order to	to
along the lines of	like
in the event of	if
at the present time	now
in regard to	about
with reference to	about
pertaining to	about
in the nature of	like
for the reason that	because
in the amount of	for

Avoid Hackneyed or Unnecessary Phrases

DEAD	STILL WITH US
attached please find	here is *or* I am attaching
enclosed please find	here is *or* I enclose
this will acknowledge receipt of— replying to your letter of— with reference to your letter of— we wish to advise that— please be advised that— contents noted— we take this opportunity to— for your information—	(These are all time killers and space fillers. Let's omit them and get on with the message)
under separate cover	(Say how sent—by parcel post, by messenger)
according to our records	(But naturally; why say it?)
above (as, 'the above') subject (as, 'subject order') same (as, 'thank you for same')	(Name what you are talking about or just say 'your order', or 'it')
at this writing	now
even date	(Name the date)
our Mr. Jones	Mr. Jones, our representative (our engineer, etc.)
forward	send
the delivery will go forward	we shall deliver
favour us with your favour	send us *or* give us your letter, order, request
we trust	we hope, believe, think
by return mail at an early date at your earliest convenience	(Omit unless special attention is necessary. Then say, 'Please answer promptly' or 'Please send us your reply by April 15')
in due course	soon, promptly, at once

Be Courteous and Personal

Offensive: We will send you the copy of Whitman's *Leaves of Grass* when you tell us which edition you want. Until such time as you send us this information, we will hold your order in abeyance.

This letter makes the customer feel that he has been stupid, or committed an unpardonable sin. A wiser procedure involves considering the point of view of the customer and putting him at his ease.

Courteous: We have in stock the third, fifth, and seventh editions of Whitman's *Leaves of Grass*. The price is the same for each of these editions, and all are in excellent condition. Please let us know which edition you prefer, and we shall fill your order at once.

TYPES OF BUSINESS LETTERS

LETTERS ABOUT EMPLOYMENT

Applying for a job

WANTED: Sales manager, extensive experience with manufactured products, some knowledge of French preferred. Write, stating full details. Box C123, *The Times*.

> 45 North Avenue,
> London, N24 7LT.
> June 24, 1976.

Dear Sir,

In response to your ad in Saturday's *Times*, I believe that I am the man for the job.

I am 33 and finished school in 1961. Since then, I have held several jobs dealing with sales and succeeded at all of them. I am sure I could do the same for your organization.

You can reach me for an interview by calling between seven and nine at 937 6876.

> Very truly yours,
> Edward Rack

Would you appoint this man?
You ought not, for his letter indicates (perhaps erroneously) that he is tactless, inaccurate, and vague:

1 He has omitted the *inside address.*

2 Paragraph 1:
   He fails to state what job he is applying for. The firm may have inserted several advertisements. (Incidentally, in letters of application, use *advertisement*, not *ad.*)
   His tone is obnoxiously immodest.

3 Paragraph 2:
   He fails to name his school or to give details of his record there.
   He fails to give his marital status.
   He fails to make *specific* references either to the firms he worked for or to the duties he performed.
   He ignores the reference to knowledge of French.
   His tone is again unjustifiably self-confident.

4 Paragraph 3:
   His tone challenges the employer: 'Here I am; come and get me'.
Thus, the letter of application must, like all business letters, be:

Clear and Correct.
Direct and Natural.
Courteous and Personal.

Specifically, the letter of application must:

1 Establish a point of contact with the employer
    How I know about the vacancy (advertisement, agency, third person, or
    an unsolicited letter of application)
    What job I am applying for

2 Arouse the interest of the employer
    My general qualifications: age, marital status, etc.
    My education, training, and experience

3 Convince the employer
    Why I think I can do the job
    Others who will vouch for my ability

4 Gain an interview with the employer
    Request for an interview
    Arrangements necessary for an interview

Both these letters illustrate the principles of effective applications for jobs.

A
                                                    1 Oakley Avenue,
                                                    London, W11 2BH.
                                                    24th June, 1976.

Telephone:
    Office: 583 8234
    Home: 788 6111

Box C 123,
The Times,
London, WC1X 8EZ.

Dear Sir,
    I am writing in answer to your advertisement in Saturday's *Times* for a sales
manager.
    I am twenty-nine years old, married and have had nine years' experience in
the sales departments of two large organizations.
    I was educated at Croydon Grammar School where I obtained O level
passes in seven subjects and A level passes in French and German. After
leaving school in 1965, I went to the sales department of the Wiltshire Domestic Appliances Company, 135 Millbank, London, SW1 5HP under their three-
year training scheme. When I had finished my training, I was offered a position as salesman with the same firm and stayed with them for a further two
years. I then went to my present position of assistant sales manager with the
Universal Plastics Company, 285 Regent Street, London, W1D 7HL. My
special duties here include training new sales personnel, writing all correspondence in French and German; and organizing market research and programmes for the promotion of our products. I am very happy with this firm
but believe that my experience has now prepared me to assume the responsibilities of complete sales management.
    I have permission to refer you to my Managing Director, Mr. Philip

Everest, and to the sales manager of the Wiltshire Domestic Appliances Company, Mr. Andrew McPherson, who supervised my training.

I should be pleased to give you any further information you request. May I have an interview at a time convenient to you?

Yours faithfully,

B

Note: Another way to answer an advertisement and get results is to write a brief letter and to enclose, on a separate page, a personal data sheet:

1 Oakley Avenue,
London, W11 2BH.
24th June, 1976.

Box C 123,
The Times,
London, WC1X 8EZ.

Dear Sir,

I am writing in answer to your advertisement in Saturday's *Times* for a sales manager.

I have had nine years' experience in the sales departments of two large organizations, beginning as a trainee and progressing to my present position of assistant sales manager. In the last four years I have had the opportunity of carrying out independent experimental work in market research as well as helping with the development of successful techniques for selling plastics abroad. I believe that I am now ready to assume the responsibilities of complete sales management.

I have enclosed a list of personal details. If my qualifications interest you, I should be happy to come for an interview at any time convenient to you.

Yours faithfully,

Enc.

Personal Details

Name: John Thompson

Address: 1 Oakley Avenue,
London, W11 2BH

Telephone: Office—583 8234
Home—788 6111

Age: 29 years. Married.

Education: Croydon Grammar School
O level passes in seven subjects
A level passes in French and German
(I attended four advanced translation courses in French at the Holborn College of Languages, 1966–69, and now write and speak fluently.)

Experience: 1965–1968—Completed training scheme for salesmen with the Wiltshire Domestic Appliances Company.
1968–1970—Salesman with the same company.
1970–1976—The Universal Plastics Company,
Assistant Sales Manager
In charge of: training new sales personnel, writing all correspondence in French or German and organizing market research.

References: Philip Everest, Esq.,
Managing Director,
Universal Plastics Company Limited,
285 Regent Street,
London, W1D 7HL.

Andrew McPherson, Esq.,
Sales Manager,
Wiltshire Domestic Appliances Company Limited,
135 Millbank,
London, SW1 5HP.
(Mr. McPherson supervised my training under the Wiltshire Company's three-year scheme.)

Asking for a personal reference

In an application for a job, evidence of a candidate's personal qualities is often required. The best referee is a person of acknowledged responsibility in the community who has known the candidate well for a number of years. *Never* give the name of a referee without asking his permission first. Once he has agreed to act, his name is given to the prospective employer who writes direct to him seeking a confidential reference. The candidate can make it easier for his referee by supplying him with a reminder of his past experience relevant to the post which is advertised.

Example

Dear Mr. Hobbs,

As you knew me well during most of my time at Brightbury School, especially in the final year when you were in charge of the Sixth Form and very kindly gave me a great deal of personal advice, I am writing to ask whether you would be willing to act as a referee for an application I am making to enter the trainee-management division of Bounty Bank Limited.

I now regret very much that I missed the 'A' level examinations in my last year at school. It was a time when I saw no point in gaining qualifications to get on in a world whose values I did not share. My first two years after leaving school I still felt the same way and got by on casual work and social security. The next year, however, I went to Brightbury Technical College, revived my 'A's and ended up with 2 B's and a C. The United Bank took me on and I have had good reports from my manager during the four years I have been with them. I would now like to move into another bank, the Bounty, which is well known for its excellent in-service training and open access to higher management.

I hope that all goes well with you and the School. Do let me know if you would rather not act as my referee. I realise that you are very busy, particularly at this time of the year.

Yours sincerely,
Gilbert Havering

Dear Gilbert,

I was so pleased to hear from you again and delighted to know that you have been doing so well. I am very willing to act as your referee in your application to the Bounty Bank and shall wait to hear from them. I wish you the best of luck and shall be interested to hear the outcome of the application.

Yours sincerely,
Graham Hobbs

Giving a reference

Give a brief indication of how long the candidate has been known to the referee and in what capacity, and follow with as warm an account of the candidate's good qualities (relevant to the post) as can honestly be given; plus any notes of reservation.

The Personnel Manager,
Trainee-Management Division,
Bounty Bank Limited,
181 Chapel Street,
Wilchester, W2D 7UT.

Dear Sir,

Gilbert Havering

In answer to your enquiry of the 15th June I am delighted to support fully Mr. Havering's application to enter your trainee-management division. I have known Mr. Havering for some twelve years, having taught him English language and literature for five years at Brightbury School, and was responsible for him pastorally as Sixth Form Master in his final year when I came to appreciate the qualities of his character.

From his academic record you will see that he failed to take 'A' levels with us but secured good results three years after leaving school when he studied at Brightbury Technical College. Havering was always quick-thinking and thorough in everything he did in and out of class at Brightbury and we had expected outstanding 'A' level results. His refusal to sit the examinations at that time did not surprise us, however, as his youthful idealism and high level of integrity resulted in a phase of disillusionment with society that halted him in his academic progress. His later 'A' level results have made up for this pause, however, and his academic side is now matched by a very mature outlook on life.

Havering can be awarded high scores in all the personal categories listed in your enquiry. What should be stressed most (as was shown, for example, in his work as school representative of Task Force in his last two years) is his combination of intelligent initiative and sympathetic understanding of other people's problems, qualities that suggest considerable potential in the field of management.

I have no reservations whatever in recommending Mr. Havering's application to you for your most careful consideration.

Yours faithfully,
Graham Hobbs

After the appointment has been made it is courteous to write and thank the referee and tell him what has happened, whether the application has been successful or not.

Dear Mr. Hobbs,

Thank you very much for acting as my referee in my recent application to the Bounty Bank. I know how many demands there are on your time and I do appreciate the trouble you have taken. Unfortunately, I did not succeed in gaining a place in the trainee-management division on this occasion but the head of the department has written to me saying that there was a particularly large and well-qualified entry this year and that I should try again next year. Actually, the discussions I have had in the course of this application have made me even more interested than before in taking up banking as a career and I can see now how ill-prepared I was for the interviews this time. I shall devote this year to working hard on the theoretical aspects of banking and make a more determined attempt to get in next year.

Thank you again for your help and interest. I will keep you informed of my progress.

Yours sincerely,
Gilbert Havering

Asking for a Rise

Always base the request on fair return for quality of work rather than the personal needs or difficulties of the employee.

Examples

Dear Mr. Hardcastle,

I hoped to have a word with you when you called in on Wednesday but, in the event, we had a sudden rush of customers and I was not able to take my attention off the shop.

I have been wondering whether you would give your consideration to the possibility of an increase in my salary in the new financial year. I have been managing the shop for two years now during which time the profits have almost doubled and we have built up a reputation for personal service to customers that is likely to lead to an even greater increase. As you know, I started on a modest salary because we did not know at that time how successful I would be at this sort of work and it was understood that I would have to gain experience in the job. However, I have worked hard during these two years at building up my knowledge of the trade and now feel qualified to develop the full potential of the shop.

I have hesitated to approach you earlier as I knew that you had financial anxieties about the venture and were also uncertain of my abilities. But now that we are doing so well and I am experienced enough to be of real use in the next phase of growth I would greatly appreciate it if you could see your way clear to make a reasonable increase in my salary.

Yours sincerely,

Dear Colonel Bingham,

I am writing to ask whether you would be willing to increase my pay. I have had it in mind for some time to speak to you about it but did not like to worry you. It is now five years since I first came to help you in the garden and during that time my pay has remained the same although wages generally have increased considerably. I like working for you and have no wish to leave but I am sure that you will realise, if you make enquiries around the district, that I could be getting a much larger wage. I know that it is difficult to keep up with the changes in rates of pay these days but I would appreciate it if you were able to bring my wages up to the standard level for the area.

Yours sincerely,

Clarifying Salary Details

The Treasurer,
Bilbury County Council,
County Hall,
High Street,
Bilbury, BL9 6VO.

Dear Sir,

Salary code number: 05798428.

I am writing to ask for a definitive statement of my current annual salary. Ever since salary payments started to be made through the Council's computer I have suffered from the embarrassment of not knowing exactly what salary I was receiving until after the end of the financial year.

I am sure, Sir, that you know the figure of your current salary and I would be grateful to have my own personal assessment, in the light of the new national scales agreed six weeks ago, sent to my home address shown above.

Yours faithfully,

Giving Notice

Be simple and direct. Give the reason for leaving but there is no point in going over past wrongs.

Dear Mr. Williams,

I wish to give notice that I shall be leaving your employment on the 31st August. It has been interesting working for you and I have learned a lot from your organisation but I have now found a post where I shall have more opportunity to act on my own initiative and have greater chances of promotion.

Yours sincerely,

Dear Mrs. Wilberforce,

I regret that I must give notice that I shall be leaving at the end of the month. I shall be sorry to leave the children, of whom I am very fond, but I have been offered a job with shorter hours where the work is more clearly defined and I feel that this will suit me better.

Yours sincerely,

BUSINESS ENQUIRIES AND REPLIES—vary considerably. Correspondents may either enquire about the adaptability of a product to their specific needs or request information having little or nothing to do with a purchase. Likewise, a reply may give details about a product or simply offer a special service unrelated to sales. Certain conventions, however, distinguish both the enquiry and the reply:

The Enquiry: State specifically the kind of information you need, and why you are asking the person to provide it.

Explain clearly how and when you intend to use this information.

Express your appreciation. Avoid 'Thank you in advance' and like expressions which seem to prevent the other fellow from refusing or to indicate your unwillingness to write again.

The Reply: Answer the questions asked.

When necessary, give detailed explanations.

Offer additional service.

Example of an Exchange of Enquiry and Reply

Dear Sir,

I have recently seen a sample of your cork tile flooring laid in the Building Centre and I think it would be suitable for the ground floor of my house. I have not been able to find anyone locally who represents you and I wondered whether you would give me some information.

1 What preparation is necessary for the sub-floor?
2 Is it affected at all by rising damp?
3 Is it necessary for the floor to be laid by a specialist and, if so, are you able to recommend one?
4 May I see samples of the colour range?

I should appreciate your answering these questions.

Yours faithfully,

Dear Sir,

Thank you for your enquiry about our cork flooring. We are pleased to send you samples of our colour range and our informative booklet, 'Cork Tiling for Every Room'.

Smith and Catchpole do all our work in your district and are very reliable flooring specialists. I have asked Mr. Catchpole to telephone you for an appointment so that he can come and inspect your floors. He will advise you about the amount of preparation necessary for the sub-floor and whether there is sufficient dampness to create a problem.

I am sure that our flooring will give you many years of great satisfaction and it is well worth having the job done professionally in the beginning.

Yours faithfully,

ORDER AND REMITTANCE. Most business organizations provide printed forms to make the task of ordering simple and efficient. When no form is available, the correspondent should observe the following conventions:

Tabulate the items to be ordered.

Specify the quantity, quality, shape, style, colour, price. If the material is listed in a catalogue, give the catalogue number.

List substitutes, or state that no substitutes will be accepted.

Specify the method of delivery.

From where will the order be sent?

How will the order be delivered: air mail, special delivery, parcel post, by air or mail?

When will the order be delivered? If a time limit is important, state the deadline.

Specify the method of payment: by national giro, by cheque, by postal order, C.O.D.?

Example:

Dear Sir,

I enclose a cheque for £43.95 for the following items:

1 Croton stainless steel aquarium, five-gallon size, No. X27	£12·40
1 Croton fluorescent light fixture for use with five-gallon aquarium	£3·25
1 Three-pound bag of washed sand	0·55
1 Argus thermostat, No. M4	£3·80
1 X-Cel Tank thermometer, No. 2	£1·45
1 Superba Air Pump, No. 522	£22·50
	£43·95

Please deliver these items by parcel post. If there are any shortages or changes in price, please let me know before delivering the order.

Yours faithfully,

ACKNOWLEDGEMENT. Most acknowledgements are sent out on the day an order is received and take the form of printed post cards or brief form letters. On occasion, a letter acknowledging an order from a new customer or an old one warrants a special letter. In all letters of acknowledgement, the following conventions prevail:

Statement of appreciation for the orders.

Reference to the date of receipt of the order.

Statement of when the order will be filled and when it will be delivered.

Statement of desire to be of further service to the customer.

Example:

Dear Sir,

Thank you for your order of June 12.

Deliveries have been slightly delayed, but your order will be sent to you as soon as possible. If you have not received it within two weeks, please notify us.

We appreciate your co-operation.

Yours faithfully,

COMPLAINTS

Be reasonable but firm and present the relevant details clearly and logically. Always complain to the highest possible level in any organization.

Example of a letter to a builder who has not got on with the job

Thomas Middleton and Son,
12 Margate Road,
Barton, CE5 2NO.

Dear Mr. Middleton,

Despite many telephone calls it is now two months since any work was done on the conversion of my loft by your men. I see that about one quarter of the job estimated for has been completed and this represents roughly the proportion of the total bill that I have already paid.

My mother-in-law is due to move in on 7th October following your earlier promises that all would be finished by the end of September. Unless you keep to your bargain and work recommences forthwith I must at once engage another contractor (from those who have been seeking work from me recently) and will feel it necessary to retain all materials and equipment on site pending a final settlement with you after paying the second contractor for his section of the work.

I look forward to hearing what you propose to do. I hope you will be able to honour your contract and finish the job yourself within the agreed time.

Yours faithfully,

Example of a letter to a shop about the unsatisfactory qualities of a purchase

The Managing Director,
Billion Brothers,
High Street,
Hornton, 9BN PU4.

Dear Sir,

Eight months ago I purchased from your electrical department an Electron washing machine with a twelve-month warranty by the manufacturers. I regret to say that, after five breakdowns attended to with increasing delays by the manufacturer's service department, I am still waiting (now in the fourth week) for an engineer to come and rectify the latest fault.

As I no longer have confidence in this machine and little in the manufacturer's guarantee of service I must now hold you liable as the retailer who sold it to me. I therefore request you either to supply me with another machine that works efficiently or to send your own engineer to restore my faulty machine to perfectly reliable working order.

Yours faithfully,

THE METHOD OF WRITING PERSONAL LETTERS

Whereas business letters may be considered a success as long as their contents are completely clear, personal letters need to do more than this for they must carry the individual mark of the writer. Many people find it difficult to expose themselves in this way and to show the same vitality and intimacy in writing as they would in conversation, but unless they can achieve some sort of spark of direct contact the letters will fail in their purpose. Coming across warm and lifelike is simply a matter of thinking about the recipient while the letter is being written. This state of mind can be encouraged by taking the trouble to re-read the last letter, by sparing a moment to think about what is to be said (preferably jotting down a few headings) and by not writing it with half a mind on other things. The letter really cannot go wrong if the writer's attention is properly focused.

The telephone has taken over many of the functions of personal letter-writing but there are still occasions when it is pleasant to be able to show that more trouble has been taken than is involved in picking up a telephone. The telephone also cannot compete with a letter for dealing with any special problem, complication or difficulty in a relationship as it is usually much easier to control the emotional tone of what is said and to make sure that it is clearly understood when it is put in writing. The personal letter is, at its best, a creative bridge between the individual and society; it can develop and strengthen relationships and ease social communication in a wider field and it is worth taking the trouble to do it well.

TYPES OF PERSONAL LETTERS

FRIENDS AND RELATIONS

The conversational letter: The purpose of this sort of letter is to keep friendship in good repair. It is the best way of communicating intimately and informally with absent friends and relations and should read as though the writer is, in fact, in the room and having a conversation. Although it is vital to keep the tone natural, the material does need to be thoughtfully selected so that the letter does not become too boring and too self-centred. There should be a feeling of give and take and the recipient should never be given cause to suspect that he is being fobbed off with recent pages of diary or a stock letter that has been run off to numerous other friends at the same time.

Dear Keith and Margery,

We have been thinking of you so much since you left and are most anxious to hear all about the journey back and how Sydney looks to you now that you are home again. I am sure that it must be quite difficult to settle in to normal life after a whole year away and the children must find it a very different sort of existence too. Do please write to us soon and tell us all about the arrival and who was at the airport to meet you, how you found the house and what has happened since Richard and Michael went back to school. I hope that they won't feel too much out of step with school life because of their year away. We are missing them very much here and William is constantly wishing that they were still with us, especially since the holidays started and he is at home by himself remembering all the things they were doing together at this time last year. We are also interested to know about Keith's work and whether the university zoology department was able to survive his absence. I am sure that everyone must be very glad to have him back and I can imagine that he is busy putting things in order for the new year. Of course, I know that you are all very busy but I hope that at least one member of the family will find time to write to us, giving a full report on everyone's health and spirits and an account of all that has happened since you returned.

Everything is going very well with us and we are now looking forward to Christmas. David has had an exceptionally busy but very interesting term as he has been setting up the new courses that he discussed with Keith earlier and has had the consequent large influx of new students to assimilate. It has all gone very well, though, and he feels that it is taking shape in the way that he envisaged. He says, Keith, that he will be writing to you separately about all this as he has quite a lot of information that he thought might interest you. We went to the conference in York in November but it was largely repeating what was said at Sussex in June so you didn't miss much. At home, we have been working on changing round the girls' rooms now that Helen is away during term time and Mary is approaching more serious exams and will be spending on increased amount of her time sitting at her desk. We have made a new bed-sitting room for Helen in the attic which forms a nice retreat for her. It was exhausting while the builders were here doing the basic work but we are enjoying it now that we have got to the finishing touches. The next stage is to make over the room they have been sharing into one for Mary alone and, as you can imagine, she has lots of ideas about how it should be done. We will gather strength to face that after the holidays. Do you remember when David and William filled in that competition on the side of the breakfast cereal packet? Well, a few weeks ago they got a letter to say that they had won one of the toy racing-car track assemblies. It has now arrived and they have set it up on William's floor and both spend hours racing the cars against each other and sadistically enjoying the appalling crashes and pile-ups that seem to happen all the time. It is the first time we have won anything but I can see that there will be constant filling in of forms from now on. The Mitchells came to lunch last Sunday and were asking most warmly after you. They are still talking about that weekend you all had together in Paris and obviously nothing has come up to it since.

We have decided not to go away during the holidays as we thought that we would enjoy an opportunity to do the things that we don't usually have time for at home. We shall have our usual party on Christmas Day and that is when you will be most sadly missed. We shall have to make do with thinking of you lying on your beach in the sun and try not to feel too remote. Everyone sends love and best wishes for an especially happy Christmas. We look forward to hearing all about it and I shall write to you again after the holidays are over.

> With love to all,

Thank-you letters: Warm and whole-hearted.

Dear Mrs. Warren,

Thank you very much for having me for Easter and giving me one of the best holidays I have had. I loved the country and the climbing and I greatly enjoyed the company of the family and all the visitors. Thank you also for looking after us so well and cooking us all those enormous and delicious meals. I look forward to seeing Julia next term and I hope that I shall meet you again when you come up to visit her later on.

Yours sincerely,

Dear Mrs. Ponsonby,

Thank you very much for letting me stay the night on Tuesday. I felt that it was not very easy for you when you had so many in the house but it was a tremendous help to me to be able to stay on after the party when I had missed the last train home. I greatly appreciated your kindness in taking me in and do hope that it has not made it more difficult to get back to normal this week.

Yours sincerely,

Dear Dorothy,

Thank you for a delightful evening. We enjoyed very much seeing you again and also meeting the others. Your cooking goes from strength to strength and we are still talking about that marvellous pie. We want you to come and meet the Nicholsons when they are in London next month and I will get in touch with you again as soon as I know their dates.

Yours as ever,

Dear Mr. and Mrs. Stewart,

Thank you very much indeed for the beautiful wine-glasses. Both John and I like them very much. They are such an elegant shape and go particularly well with other things we have chosen. We shall enjoy and treasure them for many years and both thank you for such a thoughtful and generous present.

We look forward to seeing you at the wedding and afterwards I hope that you will come to visit us and see the glasses in use.

Yours sincerely,

Dear Alison,

Thank you for the extremely interesting book on antiques. It was most thoughtful of you to find me something that would give me so much pleasure now and, in addition, provide such a splendid future source of interest. I shall have endless enjoyment pottering round the shops and museums trying to recognise things that are illustrated in the book.

I had a very pleasant birthday as my niece came for the day and two of my neighbours remembered and called in so that we were able to have a tea party. I am coming to town on the 26th and shall telephone you the week before in the hope that we can meet.

With love from

Dear Dr. Foster,

Now that my husband is completely well again I would like to thank you very much indeed for being so helpful and kind to us both over the worrying period of his operation. It was naturally a time of great stress and your informed interest and positive attitude were a great comfort throughout.

Yours sincerely,

Letters of congratulations: Generous and informed

Dear Michael,

We were very happy to hear the news of your scholarship and all join in sending warmest congratulations. I know how strong the competition always is for this award and think it is a great credit to you that you have been one of the few to bring it off.

We shall follow the course of your future career with interest.

Yours,

Dear Ian and Elizabeth,

Congratulations on the birth of your son. I was delighted when I heard and have been thinking of how much the whole family must be enjoying him. I do hope that the actual birth went well and that Elizabeth is quite recovered and the baby thriving.

I look forward to coming to see you all as soon as you feel up to coping with visitors.

With love from,

Letters of apology: Genuine and humble.

Dear Miss Barratt,

I am extremely sorry that I forgot our arrangement to meet last Thursday. I had been looking forward to it very much but somehow became confused between that and another appointment on the following day. I do apologise for the trouble that you were caused and hope that you will suggest another time next week so that I have a chance to show that I can be more reliable.

Yours sincerely,

Dear Jane,

I have been feeling very upset about breaking your beautiful dish last night and have been reviling myself ever since for being so careless. I thought that it was best not to carry on too much about it at the party but I do want you to know now how very sorry I am.

I went into Melville's China Shop this morning and have asked them to send you a dish that is similar in design to yours. I know that it does not really replace the one that you have lost but I would be most grateful if you would accept it with my sincere apologies.

Yours,

Letters of condolence: Think of what the bereaved person must be feeling and be warm and direct. Speak openly about the death and do not use euphemisms such as 'the departed' or 'passed away'.

Dear Margaret,

I was very shocked to hear of Roger's death and can imagine so well what a terrible blow this must be for you. I wish that I could be with you and of some comfort. He was such a vital and gifted person and such an exceptional friend that it is difficult for many of us to believe that he is gone. I am glad that we were able to have some time together only two weeks ago and it seems extraordinary that then he was so well and that there was no indication of what was to follow. I am thinking of you constantly and am most anxious to do anything possible that might help now or in the future.

With my deepest affection,
Yours,

Letter of complaint to a neighbour: Friendly but firm.

Dear Ted,

We have always valued our friendship with you as a neighbour, and I hesitate to write to you now, but we have a problem that I thought it better to bring up openly. By an accident of building, our bedroom abuts upon your sitting-room and the sound-proofing between the two is very inadequate. I notice it particularly when you have your stereo playing, and at those times, I might just as well be in the same room. As you know we lead a much quieter life than you do and, I am afraid, we keep very dull hours. Because I have to leave for work early in the morning I need to get off to bed early at night but I am having great difficulty in actually going to sleep with the music playing. Perhaps we could meet some time soon to discuss the possibility of lining the wall with some sort of acoustic material? But until that time, I would really appreciate it if you would keep it a little quieter, especially after 10 o'clock at night. I do not want to limit your playing in a general way as I know how important music is to you.

I hope that you will not be annoyed that I have mentioned this and that we will be able to have a talk about it as I am sure that you will have ideas on how to solve the problem.

Yours,

PARENTS AND CHILDREN

Letter to the headmaster of a private preparatory school: A degree of diffidence and evidence of being a congenial and undemanding parent are usually desirable.

The Headmaster,
Swanage School,
Upshot,
Surrey, GL1 2BT.

Dear Mr. Arnold,

I am writing to ask whether you would have a vacancy for my son, Nicholas, during the coming year. It would mean a great deal to us if he could come under your influence at this early point in his school career and benefit from the communal life at Swanage. He is seven years old (eight on the 6th August) and is at present at Dale House. I would like him to go to you in September if that were possible, but if you have no place then, he could stay on at Dale House until you were ready for him.

If there is any possibility that you may take him, my wife and I would very much like to come and see you at a time convenient to you.

Yours sincerely,

Letter to the headmaster of a state comprehensive school: The tone can be much more direct.

The Headmaster,
Campden Park School,
Northfield Road,
London, N10 9LB.

Dear Dr. Payne,

I am writing to ask whether you would have a vacancy in September for my twelve-year-old daughter, Francesca. We have been living abroad for two years but have now returned to London and will be living at 72 St. Mark's Square, N.11. Before we left London, Francesca was at the Rosefield Primary School and the headmistress, Miss Hill, would give you any details of her record that you require.

I do hope that you will have a place for her.

Yours sincerely,

Letter of complaint to a school: Co-operative but caring.

Dear Miss Peck,

I have had some trouble in the last few weeks in persuading Andrew to go to school each day and, although I have insisted that he should go, I have become increasingly conscious that there must be something that does frighten him about going to school. He has become very withdrawn and tearful and frequently comes home with bruises and other minor injuries. It is difficult to find out from him exactly what is happening but I feel that there must be some sort of bullying going on in the playground. I understand that there is sometimes no supervision during the lunch-hour or after school and, although I know that you are very short-staffed, I wonder whether it would be possible to make sure that there is always a member of staff on duty when the children are playing outside.

I would not like you to take any action that would draw attention to Andrew, himself, as it might make things worse for him but a closer supervision of play might be helpful to him and to other children as well.

Yours sincerely,

Letters to form teachers on minor matters: Brief and to the point.

Dear Mr. Evans,

I kept William at home from school on Monday and Tuesday because of a sore throat.

Yours sincerely,

Dear Miss Brown,

Rosemary has her period today and I would be grateful if you would excuse her from swimming.

Yours sincerely,

Dear Mrs. Mason,

Would you excuse Stephen from school on Thursday afternoon, please, as he has a dentist's appointment. I am very sorry that I was not able to make this at another time.

Yours sincerely,

Dear Miss Rogers,

Miranda is allergic to fish and I would be grateful if you would excuse her from eating it whenever it is served for luncheon at school.

Yours sincerely,

Letter to a residential riding school: Business-like and brief.

The Manager,
The Downs Riding School,
Northcliffe,
Sussex, BN1 9RL.

Dear Mrs. Startup,

Thank you for your brochure about your residential riding courses. My daughter, Penelope, would very much like to join the two-week course which begins on the 1st July. She is fourteen and very keen although she needs much more experience and tuition.

I enclose the completed form and my cheque for the course and will arrange for her to be there by midday on the 1st July.

Yours sincerely,

Letter to a hospital consultant about a sick child: Vigilant but controlled and co-operative.

The Consultant,
Paediatric Department,
St. Matthew's Hospital,
Sharp Street,
Woolstone, ND8 1MX.

Dear Mr. Warwick,

I am the father of a two-year-old boy, James Morris, who has been attending your paediatric clinic at St. Matthew's Hospital since the 26th April. My wife has been taking him to your Tuesday afternoon clinic and has been seen by your registrar, Mr. Ford, on four different occasions. He has had a number of tests made and last Tuesday Mr. Ford explained to my wife what was wrong and said that an operation would be necessary. However, my wife came home in great distress because, owing to her general anxiety (and probably her fatigue after the journey to the hospital with James who was not at all well that day), she was not able to concentrate on what Mr. Ford was saying and does not feel that she understands about the operation and has been quite unable to explain it to me.

I wonder whether it would be possible for us to come in together to see you or Mr. Ford to discuss the matter and to make sure that we do understand exactly what is wrong with James and what his treatment will be.

Yours sincerely,

CLUBS AND SOCIETIES

Letters to a prospective speaker and replies: Be precise about what the speaker is being asked to do and under what conditions.

Dear Mr. Bradbury,

I am writing on behalf of the Central London Gardeners' Society to ask whether there would be any possibility of your coming to speak to us during the next few months. We have all been helped by your outstanding book on window boxes and I am sure that 'Window Boxes' would be an ideal subject for your talk if that suited you. My members would also appreciate an opportunity for discussion and questions after the lecture. Our meetings are on the first Tuesday of every month at 7.30 p.m. in the upstairs lecture room of the Covent Garden Library and we have kept both the 6th October and the 2nd November clear in case you could come to one of them.

If convenient to you an hour's lecture would be best for us, followed by a short period of discussion, and then coffee will be served before we close the meeting at 10 p.m. We expect usually an audience of between forty and fifty and I enclose our programme for last year to give you an idea of the scope of our interests.

As we are a voluntary society with a low subscription, our funds are modest and we regret that we are not in a position to offer you a fee but we would, of course, wish to cover any expenses that you might incur.

Yours sincerely,
Enid Russell

Mr. Bradbury knows where he stands and he may reply either:

Dear Mrs. Russell,

Thank you for your letter on behalf of the Central London Gardeners' Society. I should be very pleased to speak to your members on the 2nd November and shall prepare my talk on the subject of 'Window Boxes' as you suggest.

I have some slides which I would like to use for illustration and perhaps you would let me know whether there are facilities in the lecture room for showing these.

Yours sincerely,
Giles Bradbury

or:

Dear Mrs. Russell,

Thank you for your letter on behalf of the Central London Gardeners' Society. I am very interested in the splendid work done by your members in central London but I regret that, since I have become a full-time consultant and writer on this subject, I have had to make it a rule that I cannot lecture to voluntary societies without a fee. I now have a fixed scale of fees for this sort of instruction and can send you details of this at any time. Perhaps it may be possible at some later date for you to join together with another similar organization to make a larger audience and to charge a small amount to cover the expenses. I should very much like to meet your members in this way if it could be arranged.

Yours sincerely,
Giles Bradbury

Mrs. Russell may answer the first thus:

Dear Mr. Bradbury,

Thank you very much indeed for being so kind as to agree to speak to the Central London Gardeners' Society. We have set aside the evening of the 2nd November for this purpose and are all looking forward to it very much.

There is a 2 × 2 projector for showing your slides and an assistant who will help with this. If it is convenient for you, I shall meet you in the lecture room at 7 p.m. so that you have time to make any preparations.

Yours sincerely,
Enid Russell

or, the second as follows:

Dear Mr. Bradbury,

Thank you for your letter about a possible talk to the Central London Gardeners' Society. We understand completely about your fee and only regret that we are unable to manage this alone. However, I have already spoken to the secretary of the City Gardeners' Guild and we are hoping that it will be possible for us to have a combined evening some time next year and then, perhaps, we may approach you again. Meanwhile, we are continuing to get great pleasure and instruction from your book and will make do with that until we can meet you in person.

Yours sincerely,
Enid Russell

Letter asking for money:

The Chairman,
Bolsover Charitable Trust,
59 Sussex Square,
London, E1B 2LJ.

Dear Sir,

I am secretary of the Vespan Sports Association, a voluntary organization with modest grants from the local borough and the county education authority existing to provide sporting facilities and fixtures for young people in this area of social multi-deprivation.

Although the local grants are most welcome, the sums, as shown in the accompanying account, are purely to meet administrative and letting charges and scarcely achieve this in these inflationary days. I understand that your Trust is willing to consider making capital grants for recreational facilities for young people and I am writing to seek advice on how to proceed with an application.

Details of our scheme will follow later if you are able to encourage us to make an application. Briefly, we have been working towards setting up a properly based sports centre in the area and now have the opportunity of taking over an old cinema in a key position that could be converted very satisfactorily into the core of the enterprise. We already have architect's plans for the project and a great deal of local interest but, despite tremendous efforts at fund-raising, the amount we have been able to subscribe is still far below the estimated cost and it seems unlikely that we will be able to draw further substantial sums from this impoverished area. A contribution from your Trust to expedite the work at this stage would mean a great deal to our young people and I wait anxiously for your reply.

Yours faithfully,

Letters of resignation:

The Chairman,
The Walden Housing Association,
28 Selwood Street,
Walden, NJ7 6HA.

Dear Tom,

I wish to resign from the committee of the Housing Association in protest against the unfair allocation of housing that has been going on over the last six months. When I joined the Association, and later agreed to go on the committee, I understood that allocations of what housing we had would be made in strict rotation from our waiting list of people who had already been selected as in particularly desperate need of accommodation from our very much longer list of homeless. In the last six months, however, on several occasions I have seen hard-won accommodation going to families quite low on the list and, in the case of Mr. and Mrs. Dunbar, to a family not on the priority list at all.

I no longer wish to be associated with an organization that is not scrupulously fair and open in its dealings and I am sure that many of the people who have helped us generously in the past will feel the same once they realise what is happening.

Yours faithfully,

The Chairman,
Association of Hospital Patients,
Birch Street,
Buxton, 6UB 9FJ.

Dear Mr. Parsons,

I would like to give notice that I am not able to offer myself for re-election to the committee at the annual general meeting. I have enjoyed working with you and the committee and shall continue to take an interest in the Association but pressure of work in my business has made it necessary to reduce my outside commitments in this coming year.

I wish the Association very well and will follow its progress with interest.

Yours sincerely,

FORMAL AND OFFICIAL

Letter to a Member of Parliament: Put the case clearly and briefly as he will have many letters to read and is likely to favour the well-organized ones. He will have all the details checked so make sure that the information is accurate.

Dear Mr. Johnson,

My name is Ralph Williams and I live in your constituency, at the above address, with my wife and two children. I am a television engineer employed by Weston Television and Radio Centre, 38 High Street, Littlethorpe. I am writing on behalf of my mother, Mrs. Mabel Williams, who is also one of your constituents and who has been the victim of an over-zealous exercise of justice. She is a widow with no means other than her pension and lives at 23 Donnington House, which is the large block of Council flats at the corner of Sefton and Essex Streets. She is 78, has not been in good health for some years and at times becomes rather confused.

On the 3rd April of this year she was shopping at the Green Star Supermarket in the High Street and had placed three items (valued at 87p in all) in her basket and was moving towards the cashier when she was distracted by the greeting of a friend. After the conversation, she absent-mindedly started to walk towards the door and, the moment she put her foot over the threshold, was seized by the supermarket's private detective and charged with shop-lifting. Last Friday she was brought before the Owen Street Magistrates' Court and fined £100 (plus £20 costs) by the Magistrate, who is reported as saying that he intends to deal severely with anyone brought before him for shop-lifting.

As you can imagine, the suffering caused to my mother and to our whole family has been quite out of proportion to her mistake and I understand that there have been a number of such cases in recent months involving elderly people. I beg you to take up the whole matter of shop-lifting in supermarkets and bring before Parliament's notice the common use of sales techniques that have this sort of human error and its subsequent brutal punishment built into their system. I did not realise the full misery and helplessness of being in this situation until I was involved myself and there must be a number of other innocent people in the country at present suffering in the same way.

Yours sincerely,

Letter to a local-government committee: Be factual and relevant and show responsible understanding of the problems involved.

The Chairman,
Public Cleansing Committee,
Borough Council,
Town Hall, High Street,
Waddington, 6HA 4UT.

Dear Sir,

I am very concerned about the state of the refuse-collection service in the Borough and, especially, in my own area of it. Although at the last election we were promised a twice-weekly collection, we have had only one in each week and sometimes none at all for most of this year. In Crawford, Willis and Park Streets, the containers are always overflowing and there are large dumps of rubbish on the pavements. The smell of rotting food-stuffs is very noticeable and it is dangerously slippery under-foot. When the men do collect, they are so hard-pressed that they leave a trail of refuse behind them on the road and pavement that remains there until the following week unless householders, themselves, go out and clear it up. There seems to be no co-ordination between the refuse-collection and street-sweeping services so that the streets are very often swept **before** the collection of refuse instead of afterwards.

I am sure that you have had many letters on this subject and I know the financial difficulties that the Council is facing at present but I think that this health hazard in the Borough should now receive urgent attention. I would be most grateful if you would raise the issue as a matter of priority at the next Council meeting.

Yours faithfully,

Letter to a university: Students proceeding direct from school will find full instructions on how to write to universities in the UCCA (Universities Central Council of Admissions) Handbook. Mature students (25 years and over) may write as follows:

The Registrar,
Wessex University,
Westchester, 8SN 4FX.

Dear Sir,

I would be very grateful if you would send me a copy of the Prospectus of Studies for the Arts Faculty for the coming year.

I understand that you make special admission arrangements for mature students. My age is twenty-five and I secured a grade B pass in the recent English Literature 'A' level examinations (University of London). My secondary schooling ended at sixteen with six C.S.E. subjects including three Grade Is and it was not until I was twenty that I realised that my keen interest in drama and literature could be furthered by academic study. It was largely as the result of attending W.E.A. classes in which the tutor was encouraging about my written work that I decided to test myself by enrolling for the two-year 'A' level English Literature course at Sewell Technical College.

I look forward to receiving the prospectus and details of admission for mature students.

Yours faithfully,

Letter asking a building society for a mortgage:

The Manager,
Redbourne Building Society,
98 Sutton Street,
Redbourne, 7NA ST2.

Dear Sir,

I would be very grateful if you would make a time to discuss with me how I may set about applying for a mortgage from your society. I have just received a substantial rise and feel that it is a good time to leave the furnished flat occupied by my wife and myself for five years and buy one of the houses in the new Riverview Estate one mile away.

I have been a member of your society for eight years and have always kept a good credit balance. For ten years I have been a milk roundsman with the Liquid Resource Company but have now been appointed local manager. I shall be happy to supply further details and references when required.

I look forward to hearing from you.

Yours faithfully,

Letter reserving hotel rooms:

The Manager,
Halton Hotel,
Winston, TU7 3PX.

Dear Sir,

I wish to book a double bedroom with bathroom (if possible, in your middle price-range) from Friday to Sunday evenings, 5–7th March, 1976. We hope to arrive for dinner on the Friday evening and will leave after breakfast on Monday 8th March.

Kindly let me know if a reservation can be made and indicate the cost.

Yours faithfully,

Letters to newspapers: A letter will only be published if the subject is likely to interest enough readers and if it is kept as relevant, compact and pithy as possible.

The Editor,
The Sentinel,
Gray Square,
London, N1X 9PB.

Dear Sir,

Your leading article on the correct fuel policy for the nation deserves whole-hearted support. It is clear that global oil reserves will not see us far into the twenty-first century unless their use is radically curtailed. On the other hand, more careful use of coal resources for electricity generation would get us well into the twenty-second century.

However, Sir, you fail to recognise the important implications of this appraisal for research on transport and on electricity generation. It amazes me that no government has yet seen fit to give the highest priority to research on electrical traction for individual users even if our cars in the near future require a little petrol as well as a great deal of stored electricity for their driving power. Experimental development of light car bodies and the smallest possible batteries should now be awarded the maximum resources in national research. At the same time it is surely pure folly to ignore the large contribution that atomic and solar power can make to electricity generation. Proper attention now to these important factors would help us to prepare a more healthy and useful environment for future generations in which to practise the art of living peacefully together.

Yours very truly,

The Editor,
The Times,
New Printing House Square,
London, WC1X 8EZ.

Dear Sir,

I spotted two full-grown white-backed bikinis on the Yucca lawn at Holland Park on the 23rd February. Is this a record?

I am, Sir, Your obedient Servant,

Figure 6. THE FORMAL INVITATION AND REPLY

Formal invitations and replies are best handwritten on white cards or paper and worded and posted punctiliously. Invitations should be sent out at least two weeks before the event and replies should be prompt and precise.

Mrs. David Copperfield requests the pleasure of Mr. Clive Newcome's company on Saturday, 9th July at 8 p.m. at 10 Kenilworth Square, SW1 8EB.
R.S.V.P.
3 Mansfield Park   Buffet.

Mr. Clive Newcome accepts with pleasure the kind invitation of Mrs. David Copperfield for Saturday, 9th July at 8 p.m. at 10 Kenilworth Square, SW1 8EB.

Mr. Clive Newcome very much regrets that a previous engagement prevents his accepting the kind invitation of Mrs. David Copperfield for Saturday, 9th July at 8 p.m. at 10 Kenilworth Square, SW1 8EB.

No salutation, no complimentary close, no signature, no abbreviations.

TEST NO. 2
Final Test

GRAMMAR

Identify the part of speech of each of the italicized words.

1 With *how* sad steps, O Moon, thou climbest the skies.
2 I bring fresh showers for the *thirsting* flowers.
3 You shall *not* crucify man upon a cross of gold.
4 My children do *whatever* they wish to do.
5 I will go; *however*, you are free to go if you wish.

USAGE

Part I: Choose the correct form for each of the following:

1 Neither of his friends (*is, are*) more literate than he.
2 Randolph is the man (*who, whom*) I believe is best suited for the promotion.
3 There is so much talking (*at the back of, behind*) me that I cannot hear the *speaker*.
4 I am so tired that I (*can scarcely, can't scarcely*) stand.
5 My tastes in women are different (*from, than*) his.
6 Had you been there, you (*heard, have heard, would have heard*) him.
7 I don't know (*if, whether*) I should tell you about my decision.
8 The mink coat (*lay, laid*) where the politician's wife left it.
9 I (*shall, will*) arrive tomorrow, and thereafter I am determined that all (*shall, will*) obey my commands.
10 She disliked liquor that tasted (*bitter, bitterly*).
11 Everyone expects (*his, their*) candidate to win.
12 June is one of those women that (*collect, collects*) husbands.
13 In the cold weather I feel (*brisk, briskly*).
14 I am willing to (*accept, except*) any excuse (*accept, except*) those which are manifest lies.
15 Florence has (*swam, swum*) in many oceans.

Part II: Rewrite the following sentences to assure **clarity** and **correctness**.

1 When driving through the tunnel, the air pressure affected his ears.
2 A love like ours only comes once in a decade.
3 Pat's charm was not only her physical beauty but she was also gracious and intelligent.
4 Being that he is that kind of a person, he cannot be expected to in any circumstance be popular.
5 Ought we watch television or to have an evening of discussing politics.

SPELLING

Correct any misspelt word. If the word is correct, let it remain as it is.

allies	irrefuteable	procede
consumate	benefited	lieutenant
aclimate	foundrys	innoculate
freind	supercede	rarify
decieve	preceed	innuendo

PUNCTUATION

Insert punctuation wherever it is necessary.

1 He gave the order however only a few obeyed it.
2 If it is essential that we work then work we must.
3 My friend who loves the name Jojo despises the name Archibald.
4 Onwards and upwards said his father but Tommy answered what if I want to go backwards and downwards.
5 With men of a speculative turn writes Teufelsdrockh there come seasons when in fear you ask that unanswerable question Who am I.

VOCABULARY

Part I: Add suffixes needed to change the following words to adjectives.

EXAMPLE: America—Americ*an*

1 deride
2 maniac
3 admonish
4 secret (*noun*)
5 exhort

Part II: Give at least one word derived from each of the following roots.

1 nostos (*return home*)
2 thermē (*heat*)
3 derma (*skin*)
4 cognoscere (*know*)
5 genus (*kind, class*)
6 tangere (*touch*)
7 gamos (*marriage*)
8 pathos (*suffering, disease*)
9 skopein (*see*)
10 ferre (*carry, bring*)

ANSWERS

TEST NO. 1
SENTENCE ERRORS

PART I

1 are (see Agreement)
2 go (see Agreement)
3 has (see Agreement)
4 was (see Agreement)
5 who (see Case)
6 me (see Case)
7 her, me (see Case)
8 him (see Case)
9 he (see Reference)
10 its (see Reference)
11 sweet (see Adjectives)
12 sought (see Verbs)
13 saw (see Verbs)
14 would have seen (see Verbs)

PART II

1 If we all strive towards peace, *we* may hope. . . . (see Shifts)
2 Wash your hair with *Squeaky Lotion* and then massage it with *Eeky Hair Tonic.* (see Parallelism)
3 I expect Bill to arrive early and to bring his cousin Ann. (see Parallelism)
4 Put the warm lemonade in the refrigerator. (see Modifiers)
5 His ankle broken, the racing colt had to be destroyed by his owner. (see Modifiers)

SPELLING

Listed below are correct spellings for the misspelt words.

embarrassed	marriage	receipt
forcible	height	picnicking
boundaries	dynamos	benefited

PUNCTUATION

1 Jane, answer the telephone. (see Direct Address)
2 correct (see Restrictive Clauses)
3 If I draw . . . bank, I shall be . . . (see Subordinate Clauses)
4 Millie, who has several suitors, loves none of them. (see Non-Restrictive Clauses)
5 'Gretchen', he begged, 'won't you, for goodness' sake, share a sandwich with me?' (see Quotation Marks)

VOCABULARY

PART I:

1 asymmetrical
2 benevolent
3 monogamy
4 malignant
5 taciturn

PART II:

1 epicure
2 accidental
3 abundance
4 reward, recompense, pay
5 acting; affected, artificial

TEST NO. 2

GRAMMAR

1 adverb (modifying *sad*)
2 adjective (modifying *flowers*)
3 not (adverb of negation) modifies verb *shall crucify*
4 whatever (indefinite pronoun)
5 however (conjunctive adverb)

USAGE

PART I:

1 is	6 would have heard	11 his
2 who (subject of *is*)	7 whether	12 collect
3 behind	8 lay	13 brisk
4 can scarcely	9 shall, shall	14 accept, except
5 different from	10 bitter	15 swum

PART II:

1 When driving through the tunnel, he felt the air pressure.
2 A love like ours comes only once in a decade.
3 Pat's charm was not only her physical beauty but also her grace and intelligence.
4 Since he is that kind of person, he cannot be expected in any circumstances to be popular.
5 Ought we watch television or discuss politics.

SPELLING

Listed below are the correct spellings for the misspelt words.

consummate	irrefutable	proceed
acclimate	foundries	inoculate
friend	supersede	rarefy
deceive	precede	

PUNCTUATION

1 He gave the order; however, only a few obeyed it.
2 If it is essential that we work, then work we must.
3 My friend, who loves the name Jojo, despises the name Archibald.
4 'Onwards and upwards,' said his father, but Tommy answered, 'What if I want to go backwards and downwards?'
5 'With men of a speculative turn,' writes Teufelsdrockh, 'there come seasons when in fear you ask that unanswerable question, "Who am I?" '

VOCABULARY

PART I:

1 derisive	4 secretive
2 maniacal	5 exhortatory
3 admonitory	

PART II:

1 nostalgia, nostalgic	6 intangible, tangent
2 thermostat, thermal, thermometer	7 monogamy, polygamy, amalgam
3 epidermis, dermatologist	8 sympathy, pathetic
4 cognition, recognize, reconnaissance	9 periscope, scope, telescope
5 generic, general	10 transfer, ferry, refer

Exercise No. 1

1 <u>Death</u> spares none.
2 Not a sentence.
3 Not a sentence.
4 [You] let no man be called fortunate until he is dead. (Subject understood.)
5 Not a sentence.
6 Not a sentence.
7 <u>Life</u> is made up of marble and mud.
8 <u>It</u> is life near the bone where it is sweetest.
9 <u>Variety</u> [i]'s the very spice of life.
10 <u>Life</u> is just one darned thing after another.

Exercise No. 2

1 *Mary*—noun
  had—verb
  little—adjective
  lamb—noun
  Its—pronoun
  fleece—noun
  was—verb
  white—adjective
  snow—noun
  And—conjunction
  everywhere—adverb
  went—verb
  He—pronoun
  followed—verb
  her—pronoun
  to—preposition
  school—noun
  one—adjective
  day—noun
  was—verb
  against—preposition
  rule—noun
  It—pronoun
  made—verb
  children—noun
  in—preposition
2 adjective; adverb
3 verb; adjective
4 adjective; noun

5 verb; noun
6 verb; noun
7 *quick*—adjective
  brown—adjective
  fox—noun
  jumps—verb
  over—preposition
  lazy—adjective
  dog—noun
8 *He*—pronoun
  stood—verb
  hesitantly—adverb
  on—preposition
  board—noun
  gazed—verb
  longingly—adverb
  at—preposition
  water—noun
  but—conjunction
  never—adverb
  dived—verb
  into—preposition
  it—pronoun
9 interjection
10 *But*—verb
  me—pronoun
  no—adjective
  buts—noun

Exercise No. 3

1 The Hudson, a river 306 miles long, flows south to New York Bay. It was discovered by a Dutch explorer named Henry Hudson.
2 The students—who came from China and Japan—preferred science to history, Esperanto to English, mechanics to music. All, however, were required to take a course entitled ['] Introduction to British Institutions['].
3 Both Mammon and Mercury were gods once. Today, *mammon* means 'riches' and *mercury* signifies 'a heavy silver-white metallic element'.

Exercise No. 4

1 Abstract: proportion, manners, customs, amusements, nation, regulations, penal code.
2 Concrete: men, battles, bull-fights, combats, gladiators, hanging, burning, rack.

Exercise No. 5

Collective nouns: board (when employed to signify 'group': e.g., *board of directors*), class, ministry, nation, people, group, assembly.

Exercise No. 6

duties	swine	appendix
fly	spoonfuls	series
monkeys	louse	p's and q's
brother	court-martial	stratum
geese	passers-by	oases
mongooses	hangers-on	mesdames
sheep	die	beau
Negroes	gin-and-tonics	seraph
dominoes	geniuses, genii	mathematics
halves	apparatus, apparatuses	dilettante

Exercise No. 7

1 spinster
2 bitch
3 filly
4 baroness
5 wardress
6 tomcat
7 landlord
8 shepherd
9 Miss, Mrs., Mme
10 widower

Exercise No. 8

1 *Cleo*, nominative case, subject of verb *refused*.
Tony, objective case, object of verb *refused*.
2 *David*, nominative case, predicate nominative after linking verb *was*.
king, priest, prophet, nominative case, appositives of *David*.
people, objective case, object of preposition *of*.
3 *Man*, nominative case, subject of linking verb *is*.
architect, nominative case, predicate nominative after linking verb *is*.
character, objective case, object of preposition *of*.
4 *Judgement*, nominative case, word in direct address.
beasts, objective case, object of preposition *to*.
5 *Brutus*, objective case, object of verb *have played*.
Brutus, nominative case, subject of verb *has lost*.
6 *Queen of England's*, possessive case, indicates possession (or habitual residence).
palace, nominative case, subject of linking verb *is*.
hour's, possessive case, idiomatically indicates duration.
drive, nominative case, predicate nominative after linking verb *is*.
centre, objective case, object of preposition *from*.
London, objective case, object of preposition *of*.
7 *plural*, nominative case, subject of verb *baffled*.
forms, objective case, object of preposition *of*.
ingenuity, objective case, object of verb *baffled*.
grammarians, objective case, object of preposition *of*.
time, objective case, object of preposition *for*.

8 *Guiness'*, possessive case, indicates manufacturer.
  Stout, objective case, object of verb *try*.
  goodness', possessive case, idiomatically indicates attribute.
  sake, objective case, object of preposition *for*.
9 *Shelley*, objective case, object of verb *did see*.
10 *man's*, nominative case, subject of verb [*i*]*'s*.
  shirt, objective case, object of preposition *without*.

Exercise No. 9

1 *He*, personal pronoun.
  whoever, compound relative pronoun, nominative case, subject of verb *trusted*.
  him, personal pronoun.
2 *whomever*, objective case, object of preposition *by*.
3 *myself*, reflexive pronoun, objective case, object of verb *bit*.
4 *we*, personal pronoun, nominative case, subject of verb *despise*.
  ourselves, reflexive pronoun, objective case, object of verb *despise*.
5 *all*, indefinite pronoun, nominative case, appositive of nominative *we*.
  I, nominative case, appositive (with *Einstein* and *Fermi*) of *we*.
6 *each other*, reciprocal pronoun (denoting interaction involving two people).
7 *who*, relative pronoun, nominative case, subject of verb *knew*.
  whom, relative pronoun, object of preposition *to*.
8 *whose*, relative pronoun, possessive case, indicates possession. (Preferred because *hill* seems personified, and *whose* refers to people.)
  everything, indefinite pronoun, objective case, object of preposition *at*.
9 *the use of which*. (Preferred because *which* refers to things; but *whose* is also acceptable.)
  nobody, indefinite pronoun, nominative case, subject of verb *knows*.
10 [*u*]*'s*, personal pronoun, objective case, object of verb *let*.
  me, personal pronoun, objective case, appositive of [*u*]*'s*.

Exercise No. 10

1 Everybody has a right to *his* own opinion, right or wrong. (*Everybody*, antecedent of *his* is singular.)
2 Either the marines or their gallant commander, Captain Jinks, may be relied upon for *his* customary rescue, to occur just before the final curtain. (When *either . . . or* connects nouns of differing number, the pronoun agrees with the noun closer to it.)
3 'In Britain,' he said, 'we know that we are free; but sometimes we become a little afraid that we might not put our freedom to the best use.'
4 What a sweet child it [he] is; it [he] seems the image of your friend Jack. (A baby may be referred to as *it*; but then *it* must be consistently employed.)
5 If the pig or the fool is of a different opinion, it is because he knows only his side of the question.

Exercise No. 11

1 *me*, object of the preposition *between*.
  he, subject of the verb *knows*.
  she, subject of the verb *knows*.
2 *them*, object of the preposition *like*.
3 *we*, predicate nominative after linking verb *was*.
4 *them*, subject of the infinitive to be.
5 *me*, appositive of person (in objective case).
6 *he*, subject of (understood) verb *is*. (You are, very obviously, as ugly as he [is].)
7 *whom*, object of verb *love*.
  who, subject of verb *are*.

8 *who*, subject of verb *envies*.
9 *him*, object of preposition *but* (here signifying 'except').
10 *who*, subject of (understood) verb *is*. (He is more audible than who [is audible], would you say?)

Exercise No. 12

1 *sit:* I	2 *may:* A	3 *let:* T
pity: T	*have:* T	*make:* T [that or which (understood)
had: T	*be:* L	is object of *make*]
landed: I	*can:* A	*does:* A
was: L	*are:* L	*mean:* T
should be: A	*had:* T	
had: T		

Exercise No. 13

1 I saw him when he burst my balloon.
2 He swam out beyond the breakers.
3 He has got gold, but the process has frozen the gentle current of his soul.
4 I have lain awake on rainy mornings, wondering why I had laid away money for them.
5 When the warden rang the bell, the prisoner was hanged.
6 I bore the burden that I was born to bear.
7 Because he had drunk so much, his wife wrung his neck.
8 The sun shone over Ruth as she bound the sheaves.
9 The Romans lent Antony their ears.
10 When the bee stung him, he sprang to his feet.

Exercise No. 14

1 Neither John nor I am utterly senseless.
2 The herd of cattle which is [are] grazing on the field has [have] been sold down the river. (Singular verbs are to be preferred because the herd was apparently sold as a unit; however, plural verbs are also defensible—if consistently employed.)
3 He is one of those men who need to be seen doing good.
4 There are a table, a chair, and a tape recorder: now talk!
5 The wages of sin is death.
6 He is one of those pedagogues who have given *pedantry* its meaning.
7 It is I, not he, who am at fault.
8 There are ['re] gold pieces in plenty here.
9 Seven days without water makes one week.
10 The general, together with five thousand picked troops, storms the tavern.

Exercise No. 15

1 *had reached:* past perfect
2 *will have collected:* future perfect
3 *have had:* present perfect
4 *insists:* present
  shall be: future
5 *had risen:* past perfect
  had been: past perfect
  had decreased: past perfect
  lost: past
  had lingered: past perfect
6 *believe:* present
  was: past

split: past
believe: present
had [n't] been: past perfect
would have been: past perfect [verb-phrase made with auxiliary]
7 *made:* past
had distinguished: past perfect
8 *can be found:* present [verb-phrase made with auxiliary; passive voice]
will deny: future
can exist: present
has reached: present perfect
is turning: present [continuous form]
9 *is:* present
has set: present perfect
will soften: future
10 *will have been decimated:* future perfect [passive voice]

Exercise No. 16

1 were	6 is
2 is	7 consider
3 were	8 suspect
4 are	9 were
5 be	10 be

Exercise No. 17

1 Everybody had a most enjoyable time.
2 Most teachers believe that people write passive sentences when they have not thought out the communication they intend before they set pen to paper.
3 Correct, since *head*, not *phrenologist*, should be emphasized.
4 He saw that she wanted to be kissed, and he kissed her.
5 After Jonathan J. Logorrhea had spoken for an hour, nobody listened to what he was saying.
6 I admit that the bank notes which her father flashed before my eyes impressed me.
7 Correct.
8 Correct if Caesar is the centre of the communication. If Cleopatra is, rewrite: Cleopatra first conquered, then cuckolded Caesar.
9 Soldiers read books—comic books, chiefly.
10 Correct, since who read the books does not matter.

Exercise No. 18

Progressive	*Emphatic*
1 I am playing	I do play
2 you were fiddling	you did fiddle
3 it will be fizzing	
4 she has been constituting	
5 they had been asseverating	
6 he will have been explaining	
7 (if) he be laughing	
8 he is being slugged	

Exercise No. 19

1 [*the:* limiting (definite article)]
full: descriptive
African: descriptive (proper)
wide: descriptive
lovely: descriptive

2 *invisible:* descriptive
  those: limiting
  immortal: descriptive
  their: limiting (pronominal, possessive)
3 *which:* limiting (pronominal, relative)
4 *which:* limiting (pronominal, interrogative)
5 *inebriated:* descriptive
  any: limiting (pronominal, indefinite)
6 *black:* descriptive
  hot: descriptive
  sweet: descriptive
7 *subtle:* descriptive
  specious: descriptive
8 *other:* limiting (pronominal, indefinite)
  Holmesean: descriptive (proper)
  worst: descriptive
  best: descriptive
9 *brilliant:* descriptive
  corrupt: descriptive
10 none

Exercise No. 20

1 a, a
2 a, a, the
3 the, the
4 a, a, a; the, the, the
5 the
6 An, a, a
7 a;
  a;
  the;
  the, the, the, the
8 the, the, the
9 The
10 the

Exercise No. 21

1 lesser
2 eldest
3 most kind
4 first, most, fundamental
5 cleaner, more intelligent
6 best known, most bloodthirsty
7 better (idiomatically, *best*)
8 more absurd, happier (less happy)
9 bigger, redder, hotter
10 inner (inmost)

Exercise No. 22

1 *almost:* degree
2 *therefore:* conjunctive
3 *formerly:* time
4 *south:* place
  consequently: conjunctive
5 *There:* place
6 *badly:* manner
7 *badly:* manner
8 *Yes:* conjunctive
  no: degree
9 *seldom:* degree
  sensibly: manner
  never: degree
10 *Well:* conjunctive
  now: time

Exercise No. 23

1 best
2 farther (further), worse
3 sooner, sooner
4 most (least) distinctly
5 highest, most highly

Exercise No. 24

1 *neither . . . nor:* co-ordinating (correlatives)
2 *than:* subordinating
3 *as:* subordinating
4 *when:* subordinating
5 *though:* subordinating
6 *because:* subordinating
7 *so that:* subordinating
8 *lest:* subordinating
9 *for:* subordinating
10 *not only . . . but also:* co-ordinating (correlatives)

Exercise No. 25

Preposition	Words related
1 in	heraldic—heat
on	scorpion—stone
2 into	nose—porridge
of	bread and butter—mine
for	man—himself
for	God—us
3 in	what is bred—bone
out of	will . . . come—flesh
4 from	came—Switzerland
through	came—France
over to	came—England
among	stayed—us
5 to	speak—whom

Exercise No. 26

1 *biting:* takes *dogs* for its object, is itself object of the preposition *to*.
2 *reading:* subject of verb *has served*, modified by the phrase *in abnormal psychology* and by the adjective *avid*, takes *Jojo's* for its subject.
making: takes *him* for its object, is itself object of the preposition *of*.
3 *spurning:* subject of the verb *demonstrates*, it takes *her* for its object and *his* for its subject (not *he spurning*, since the subject of a gerund is in the possessive case).
4 *gilding:* subject of verb *was*, takes *his* (not *him gilding*) for its subject.
5 *having read:* subject of verb *has . . . raised*, it takes *their* for its subject, *the entire contents of the public library* for its object.

Exercise No. 27

1 *Desperate:* modifies *reporter*, is modified by the phrase *for news*.
2 *Having read:* modifies *normality* (dangling), and should modify *Jojo*. Revised: *Having avidly read books on abnormal psychology, Jojo was oppressed by his normality.* In the revised sentence, *books* is object of the participle *having read*, which is modified by *avidly*.
3 *Having been spurned:* modifies *lady*, is modified by the phrase *by Jojo*.
4 *Having gilded:* modifies *he*, takes *lilies* for its object, is modified by *with loving devotion*.
5 *Having read:* modifies *intelligence quotients* (dangling) and should modify *they*. Revised: *Though they read the entire contents of the public library, their intelligence quotients remained static.* The revised sentence has a clause doing the work of the participle.

252

English Made Simple

Exercise No. 28

1 He wanted to see the headless horseman.
2 I think the criminal to be him.
3 To write with precision it is necessary to have thought logically first. (Split infinitive in original sentence.)
4 I know him to be a sheep in wolf's clothing. (Subject of the infinitive *to be* should be in the objective case.)
5 Invariably to be kind to children, one requires angelic qualities. (Split infinitive and dangling modification in original sentence.)

Exercise No. 29

1 *in the hand:* prepositional phrase, used as an adjective to modify *bird*.
  in the bush: prepositional phrase, used as an adjective to modify *two* [*birds*].
2 *Having seen three birds:* participial phrase, modifying *he*.
  in the bush: prepositional phrase, used as an adjective to modify *birds*.
  in his hand: prepositional phrase, used as an adjective to modify *one* [*bird*].
3 *in the bush:* prepositional phrase, used as an adjective to modify *birds*.
  having been captured: participial phrase, modifying *birds*.
4 *to snare birds:* infinitive phrase, used as an adverb to modify *lived*.
  [*to*] *burn bushes:* infinitive phrase, used as an adverb to modify *lived*.
5 *To part from friends:* infinitive phrase, used as a noun (subject of verb *is*).
  to die a little: infinitive phrase used as a predicate nominative (after linking verb *is*).

Exercise No. 30

1 *where she was going:* noun clause, object of verb *knew*.
  how she would get there: noun clause, object of verb *knew*.
2 *when he was hungry:* adverbial clause, modifies *ate*.
  whenever he could: adverbial clause, modifies *drank*.
3 *which he concealed:* adjective clause, modifies *purpose*.
4 *who have status:* adjective clause, modifies *criminals*.
5 *While making hay:* adverbial clause, modifies *ought*.
  whether the sun is shining: noun clause, object of *to see*.

Exercise No. 31

1 *Compound:* Jack loves Jill, but Jill loves herself.
  Complex: Although Jack loves Jill, Jill loves herself.
2 *Compound:* The pound has a diminished value; for example, it no longer buys a good seat at the opera.
  Complex: The pound, which has a diminished value, no longer buys a good seat at the opera.
3 *Compound:* Ideas have consequences; moreover, the consequences are sometimes far-reaching.
  Complex: Ideas have consequences which are sometimes far-reaching.
4 *Compound:* He reached for the moon and he stubbed his toe.
  Complex: While reaching for the moon, he stubbed his toe.
5 *Compound:* The American way of speaking and writing differs from the English way, but it is not therefore inferior.
  Complex: Although the American way of speaking and writing differs from the English way, it is not therefore inferior.

Exercise No. 32

1 scratches ('One . . . scratches')
2 is ('Cause . . . is')
3 were ('months . . . were')
4 are
5 is

Exercise No. 33

1 confront ('ordeals that confront'. Verb here agrees with the antecedent of the pronoun.)
2 fail
3 have
4 confuse
5 need

Exercise No. 34

1 irritate (Compound subject 'Laughing and giggling' requires a plural verb.)
2 go (Reverse the word order: 'There I go, but for the grace of God.')
3 were
4 were
5 add

Exercise No. 35

1 has (Either one or the other *has* played the trick.)
2 dominates
3 understand (When compound subjects joined by correlatives do not agree in number, the verb agrees in number with the nearer subject, in this case, the plural *teachers*.)
4 were
5 is

Exercise No. 36

1 enters (*along with* does not affect the number of the verb whose subject remains the singular *soldier*.)
2 dislikes
3 was
4 searches
5 leads

Exercise No. 37

Correct Form	*Antecedent*
1 their	all
2 his	each
3 their	lass and lad
4 their	authors
5 him	anyone
6 it	none
7 his	whoever
8 its *or* their	team (the antecedent may be taken collectively as a singular noun, or separately, as 'members of the team', to make the pronoun plural.)
9 they	some
10 they	groups

Exercise No. 38

Hesitantly, feeling the gloom enclose me, I approached the darkened stairwell. Although I was trembling, I began to mount the worn old steps I had trodden so often in the happier times of my youth. I sensed that at the summit of those steps my whole life would change, but I had to go on.

Exercise No. 39

1 I (*I* is part of the compound subject *David and I.*)
2 who (*who* is subject of the verb *may make*).
3 his (Before a gerund, the pronoun is usually in the possessive case. If you intend to stress the person, *accepting* must be considered as a participle and the objective case, *him*, should be used.)
4 her (part of compound object of preposition *about*).
5 him
6 us (object of preposition *against*. *Boys* is the objective complement of *us* and is also in the objective case.)
7 they (predicate nominative after linking verb *is*).
8 his (see 3 above).
9 Whom (reverse the word order: you wish to send this letter to whom? *Whom* is object of the preposition *to*.)
10 him, me
11 him (*but* acts here as a preposition).
12 they (complete the ellipsis: 'as intelligent as they are').
13 himself (reflexive pronoun is justified when the action reflects upon the subject).
14 him, me (apposition with *people*, object of preposition *of*).
15 Whoever (subject of verb *assumes*).
16 who (subject of verb *asked*. *I believe* is merely parenthetic.)
17 me (complete the ellipsis: 'better than *it fitted* me').
18 us (see 6 above).
19 we (predicate nominative after linking verb).
20 him (objective case after infinitive *to be*).

Exercise No. 40

1 The Clean-Up T.V. Association sent to its readers a magazine which had many wholesome suggestions.
2 Have your hat made smaller if it does not fit your head.
3 Edward's father is happy to be returning from abroad.
4 The financial experts say that everything will get better next year.
5 Commuters will suffer hardship when the Railway Board carries out its plan to increase the fare in order to reduce the annual deficit.
6 In *The Canterbury Tales* Chaucer writes entertainingly about the Middle Ages, those years in which feudalism and religion exercised profound influence on noble and serf alike.
7 Although I found the party dull, many, amazingly enough, enjoyed it.
8 If you borrow from another writer's work, acknowledge your source.
9 Franklin's *Autobiography* gives precepts on thrift.
10 Beethoven's later works are remarkable, more so when one considers that he was deaf when he wrote them.

Exercise No. 41

1 had laboured over	6 having been born
2 had once seen	7 to be
3 wore	8 to have read
4 visited	9 Having been taught
5 had neglected	10 Reaching

Exercise No. 42

1 shall	5 will	8 will
2 shall	6 shall	9 shall
3 shall, shall	7 will	10 shall
4 will		

Exercise No. 43

1 can
2 may (might. Both are defensible.)

3 could
4 would
5 should
6 ought

7 can, should
8 would
9 can
10 would

Exercise No. 44

1 well (modifies the verb *hear*)
2 easily (modifies the verb *lost*)
3 properly
4 fresh (modifies *marlin*)
5 profoundly (modifies adjective *serious*)
6 well
7 sweet (modifies *violets*)
8 certainly, good (*certainly* modifies *feels*; *good* modifies *air*)
9 wretched
10 tightly

11 well
12 firm
13 helplessly
14 loudly
15 softly, clearly
16 cacophonous
17 gently
18 angry (modifies *prisoner*)
19 wrongly
20 quickly, definitely, noisy

Exercise No. 45

1 Most students believe that their writing is better than *that of* their fellow students. (Or 'than their fellow students' writing')
2 Correct.
3 We think that our cat is unique.
4 Keeping tropical fish is almost as time-consuming as growing cactus, if not more so.
5 Lydia has more trouble taking care of Philip than other parents encounter with their children.
6 Correct.
7 Correct.
8 Correct.
9 Many soldiers have found that being in politics is not so simple as being in the army.
10 I have heard both his speeches, and I think yesterday's clearly the better.

Exercise No. 46

Following are suggested answers. Others (using subordinate clauses) are possible.

1 Hanging from the bell tower, the fanatic prepared to leap as crowds watched.
2 Having entered his car, he immediately opened the windows.
3 Gingerly walking barefooted on the cobblestones, he saw a mangled hand.
4 Listening to the concert with rapt attention, he felt more than ever that Beethoven was a magnificent composer.
5 Working too hard and earning too little, I feel my ulcer starting to bother me again.
6 Tired and indisposed, I shall not work tonight.
7 Leaving his flat in a violent temper, she became increasingly furious as she thought of his insolence.
8 He saw her diamond necklace hanging round her neck.
9 Because he had spilled gravy on her dress, Dante had ruined his evening with Beatrice.
10 Entering the doss-house, he let his cigarette dangle limply between his lips.

English Made Simple

Exercise No. 47

Following are suggested answers. Others are possible.

1 To travel in comfort, one must have money.
2 To smoke safely, use filters.
3 Wearing gloves permits one to row all afternoon without getting blisters.
4 One should maintain moderate speed if one is to get thirty miles to the gallon.
5 To work as a pianist, one must practise constantly.

Exercise No. 48

Following are suggested answers. Others are possible.

1 One must make reservations before leaving for Rome.
2 After he had attacked me for lateness, my employer dismissed me.
3 On his first attempt at riding, he was thrown heavily by the horse.
4 When entering the theatre, I was surprised at the clothes worn by the audience.
5 While turning the page, he spilt the ashtray on to his book.

Exercise No. 49

Following are suggested answers. Others are possible.

1 When he was three years old, John's mother taught him archery.
2 While I was visiting Wales, the weather was excellent.
3 Once she had allowed it to relax, Hilda's back felt better.
4 Stephen kept watching the light until it turned green.
5 Although famished, he refused to eat caviar.

Exercise No. 50

Following are suggested answers. Others are possible.

1 Even the most intellectual of his listeners will be confused by Dr. Timothy's lectures.
2 Vivien reads only the best in Irish literature.
3 The baby walked nearly across his playpen.
4 Teeth may be ruined if sweets are eaten frequently.
5 Scarcely had I opened the door when the dog leaped at me.

Exercise No. 51

Following are suggested answers. Others are possible.

1 The girl woke with a cry as a scream tore through the house.
2 Indians inhabit a village in eastern Mexico called Patzcuaro.
3 Columbus vowed that he would claim the New World for Ferdinand and Isabella as soon as he landed.
4 In all my travels I have never seen a cathedral like that one.
5 In the laboratory I located the trouble with my television set.

Exercise No. 52

Following are suggested answers. Others are possible.

1 We set out towards the end of the rainbow for the city in which we lived.
2 When we visited foreign lands, we spoke with the natives and tried to learn their folk-lore.
3 He examined in the microscope the specimen that was in a glass slide.
4 As we were leaving he promised to visit us.
5 Letters that show personality and spirit can win friends.

Exercise No. 53

Following are suggested answers. Others are possible.

1 Dr. Johnson despised the Scots, although he befriended Boswell and spent many pleasant hours with his Scottish biographer.

2 I warned him that I would take no more of his nonsense, even though we had spent many years together and had shared experiences neither of us would ever forget.

3 Correct.

4 He tried suddenly and violently to swerve his car away from the oncoming lorry.

5 The traffic in London is as fast-moving as that in other cities, if not more so.

Exercise No. 54

Following are suggested answers. Others are possible.

1 One should listen carefully to his employer if *he* wants promotion.

2 Lorelei was a cold-hearted girl whose best friends were diamonds.

3 Beethoven's *Fifth Symphony is* a famous musical achievement. (Although created in the past, works of art remain permanently great, and thus take the present tense.)

4 If he were to take an old friend's advice, he *would* leave his job.

5 I know that I wouldn't go out with that group unless *I* wanted to get into trouble.

6 A true democrat accepts the opinion of the majority even if *he* disagrees with it.

7 When Job heard the Voice from the Whirlwind, he *knew* that his moment of reckoning *had* come.

8 Everyone has some favourite recipe that *he concocts* for *his* friends.

9 Tom and Huck shared the universal fright that afflicts those who enter cemeteries at night.

10 Experienced wrestlers know how to feign agony, and *one can* always tell that they *are* not really hurt.

11 Whatever the temptation to let a stranger get a little lost and so see more of the town, it is only courteous to try to give simple and specific directions in order to guide him as well as possible.

12 The Roundheads defeated the King and hunted down his troops.

13 If I allow him enough rope, *he'll* hang *himself*.

14 Correct.

15 One must practice if *he* wishes to succeed.

Exercise No. 55

Following are suggested answers. Others are possible.

1 Some public officials, better called 'publicity hounds', always investigate dead scandals.

2 He believes that courage is better than *fear* and that faith is truer than doubt. (All nouns; *fearing* is a gerund.)

3 I want stout-hearted men who will fight when necessary.

4 The Indian Summer of life should be sunny and sad, like the season, and possess infinite wealth and depth of tone.

5 The local education authority voted to improve building facilities and to enlarge the teaching staff. (All infinitives instead of mixed phrase and infinitive.)

6 Find time to learn goodness and *to give* up laziness.

7 The child eagerly awaited the hour of his birthday, knowing that soon he would have all his new presents.

8 Saying is one thing; *doing* is another.

9 What Charles needs is a doctor and *a* rest cure.

10 We studied the life of the ant and its method of operating a social community.

Exercise No. 56

Following are suggested answers. Others are possible.

1 They couldn't decide whether *to leave* the theatre or *to hiss* the performance.
2 Either Bill stops mimicking me or I will bang his head. (Each correlative must be followed by corresponding part of speech: here noun or pronoun; in the original *Either* is followed by the verb *stops, or* by the pronoun *I*.)
3 Churchill was not only a skilful politician but also an able artist.
4 Neither can he do as he is told, nor can his parents hope to change him.
5 Billy wants to be either a business tycoon or an actor when he grows up.

Exercise No. 57

Following are suggested answers. Others are possible.

1 Henry Adams wrote history, fiction and an essay on architecture inspired by the cathedrals at Chartres and Mt. St. Michel.
2 Dumas has always excited readers young and old and will continue to do so.
3 The yokels were attentive *to* and then swindled by the confidence man.
4 The artist decided to exhibit his paintings, which hardly deserved public attention, and *to give* lectures.
5 The doctors warned Jones that to work would prove fatal, *that* to travel might prove helpful, but *that* to rest would effect complete recovery.

Exercise No. 58

Following are suggested answers. Others are possible.

1 Conscious of the Martian invasion of East Anglia, the Prime Minister warned against relaxing vigilance.
2 Extremely hungry, he opened the refrigerator and grabbed the chicken leg.
3 He promised them that the two large specimens of walrus in the city zoo would be delightful to watch.
4 If he takes the time to study French—and he must work hard—he will surely succeed. (The original is parallel in form, but not in thought.)
5 Infuriated by his attacks on her intelligence, the timid girl fled from the room. (*Timid* is a general state; *infuriated by attacks* . . . is a specific. Thus, the original sentence is not parallel and must be recast.)

Exercise No. 59

Following are suggested answers. Others are possible.

1 The house was burned, but the children *were* saved.
2 I remember Noel Coward better than *I remember* Ivor Novello.
3 I have six Jaguars, but he *has only* two.
4 The teacher *whom I offered as a reference* would not write a letter for me.
5 My dog and *my* girl friend are going with me on my holiday.
6 He has bought as many books as any man has *bought* or can buy.
7 Our only chance was *that* Johnson might send out an alarm.
8 The patient moaned, sweated, and *displayed* other symptoms of delirium.
9 The major problem is *that* she is not at all interested.
10 We were more familiar with the Smiths than *with* the Joneses.
11 His highly effective recitation was admired by all.
12 Possibly because rainmakers are 'seeding' too many clouds, tornadoes and typhoons are becoming more frequent.
13 So far as his writing is concerned, *it is* sometimes pointless in its thinking.
14 His vision at night was almost as good as *that* of a cat.
15 Harold read about and collected relics from Norman England.

Exercise No. 60

1 (*c*), (*f*) (topic sentence), (*e*), (*b*), (*a*), (*d*)
2 (*b*) (topic sentence), (*a*), (*d*), (*c*)
3 (*b*) (topic sentence), (*d*), (*c*), (*e*), (*a*)
4 (*b*) (topic sentence), (*c*), (*a*), (*d*)
5 (*c*) (topic sentence), (*a*), (*b*), (*d*), (*g*), (*e*), (*f*)

Exercise No. 61

1 Never! I would rather die!
2 Die you shall!
3 Jason asked why Luster had turned left.
4 He exclaimed angrily that he welcomed opposition.
5 'Never!' did you say?
6 Well played!
7 May I suggest that you let us have a cheque not later than the end of the month.
8 O Scotland! my dear, my native soil!
9 'Heigh-ho!' he exclaimed.
10 Bah! He's (he's) never met his deadline.

Exercise No. 62

Note: The brackets indicate options.

1 Just as the procedure of a Charity Appeal must be clear-cut and definite, the steps being taken with the sureness of a skilled chess player, so the various paragraphs of a begging letter must show clear organization, giving evidence of a mind that [,] from the beginning [,] has had a specific end in view.
2 In some jobs [,] it is necessary to understand, interpret [,] and apply rules and principles. In others, it is necessary also to discover principles from available data or information. These types of reasoning ability can be tested by different kinds of tests—for example, questions on the relationship of words, understanding of paragraphs [,] or solving of numerical problems.
3 A plane figure consists of a square, ten inches on a side, and an isosceles triangle whose base is the left edge of the square and whose altitude, dropped from the vertex opposite the ten-inch base of the triangle common to the square, is six inches.
4 Few people take the trouble of finding out what democracy really is. Yet this would be a great help, for it is our lawless and uncertain thoughts, it is the indefiniteness of our impressions, that fill darkness, whether mental or physical, with spectres and hobgoblins. Democracy is nothing more than an experiment in government, more likely to succeed in a new soil, but likely to be tried in all soils, which must stand or fall on its own merits as others have done before it. For there is no trick of perpetual motion in politics, any more than in mechanics. President Lincoln defined democracy to be 'the government of the people by the people for the people'.
5 I went to the woods because I wished to live deliberately, to front only the essential facts of life, and to see if I could not learn what it had to teach [,] and not, when I came to die, discover that I had not lived.
6 In all my lectures [,] I have taught one doctrine, namely, the infinitude of the private man. This the people accept readily enough, and even with loud acclamation, as long as I call the lecture Art [,] or Politics [,] or Literature [,] or the Household; but the moment I call it Religion [,] they are shocked, though it be only the application of the same truth which they receive everywhere else to a new class of facts. (R. W. Emerson)
7 When Melville died on September 28, 1891, he left in manuscript a novelette, *Billy Budd*, which was not published until 1924, though written about 1888–1891.

8 Man was not made for any useful purpose, for the reason that he hasn't served any; he was [,] most likely [,] not even made intentionally, and his working himself up out of the oyster bed to his present position was probably a matter of surprise and regret to the Creator.　　　　　　　　　　　　(Mark Twain)

9 Fitzgerald said, 'The very rich are different from you and me.' 'Yes,' Hemingway replied, 'they have more money.'

10 To see how this was so, let us ask ourselves why the spheres were ever supposed to exist. They were not seen or directly observed in any way; why, then, were they believed to be there?　　　　　　　　　　　　　　　　　　　　(H. Dingle)

11 We keep one eye open, however safe we feel. Indeed, some of us keep both eyes open; others of us, moreover, wish for a third eye.

12 For him, to think meant to act.

13 To die bravely fighting, at first seemed good; later, retreat seemed better.

14 Dear Jojo,

　　　I received your last letter. At least [,] I hope it was your last letter.

　　　　　　　　　　　　　　　　　Yours sincerely,

　　　　　　　　　　　　　　　　　Butch Butcher

15 The title role of *Elmer Gantry* (which Rebecca West has termed 'a sequence of sermons and seductions') is played by a profligate clergyman, a ponderous monster, bleater of platitudes, ankle-snatcher [,] and arch hypocrite, whom we meet first as an 'eloquently drunk' student at Terwillinger College [,] in Cato, Missouri.

　　　　　　　　　　　　　　　　　　　　　　　　　(H. Hartwick)

16 He had forgotten his wallet, which reposed in his green trousers; the silver which he had in the purple pair that he was wearing didn't equal the amount of the bill.

Exercise No. 63

1 Courtship in animals is the outcome of four major steps in evolution: first, the development of sexuality; secondly, the separation of the sexes; thirdly, internal fertilization, or at least the approximation of males and females; and finally, the development of efficient sense-organs and brains.　　　　　　　　(J. Huxley)

2 They wanted to know 'how modern man got this way': why some people are ruled by a king, some by old men, others by warriors, and none by women; why some peoples pass on property in the male line, others in the female, still others equally to heirs of both sexes; why some people fall sick and die when they think they are bewitched, and others laugh at the idea.

3 He is a man; hence [,] he is fallible. She is a woman; therefore [,] she will fool him.

4 It is hard to form just ideas; wayward notions, however, come without being called.

5 A small group of people arrive: I recognize Jean Negulesco, the director; Wolfgang Reinhardt, the supervising producer; and George Amy, the cutter.

　　　　　　　　　　　　　　　　　　　　　　　(Adolph Deutsch)

Exercise No. 64

1 'Will you walk into my parlour?' said the spider to the fly:
　'Tis the prettiest little parlour that ever you did spy.'

2 There are two methods of curing the mischiefs of faction: the one, by removing its causes; the other, by controlling its effects.

3 Dr. Jucovy, a noted psychiatrist, writes: 'The statement: "People are stout because they eat more and consume more calories" no longer suffices. Now we ask: "*Why* do some individuals eat more?" '

4 All will be well: God is silent; he is not indifferent.

5 In *The Short Bible: An American Translation*, Professor Smith translated Psalms 19.1 thus: 'The heavens are telling the glory of God, And the sky shows forth the work of his hands.'

Exercise No. 65

1 Persuasiveness of argument, apt examples from history and experience, inner logic, and perhaps our simple need to have a part of our experience given satisfactory meaning—these have played a far greater role in the history of theories in the social sciences than strict canons of evidence and proof. (Nathan Glazer)

2 Why haven't I a butler named Fish, who makes a cocktail of three parts gin to one part lime juice, honey, vermouth, and apricot brandy in equal portions—a cocktail so delicious that people like Mrs. Harrison Williams and Mrs. Goodhue Livingston seek him out to get the formula? (E. B. White)

3 More than forty of the teachers—about half of the staff of the school—are married women.

4 My expectations were not high—no deathless prose, merely a sturdy, no-nonsense report of explorers into the wilderness of statistics and half-known fact.

5 Henry's genius—if that's the word—was sometimes indistinguishable from another man's pigheadedness.

6 To be a scientist—it is not just a different job, so that a man should choose between being a scientist and being an explorer or a bond-salesman or a physician or a king or a farmer. (S. Lewis)

7 In the country there are a few chances of sudden rejuvenation—a shift in the weather, perhaps, or something arriving in the mail. (E. B. White)

8 Why they are called comics, when people who read them—both young and old—almost always look like undertakers, eludes me.

9 Restraint, Repression, Respectability—those are the three R's that make him [Sinclair Lewis] see Red. (W. L. Phelps)

10 And we—well, we shut our eyes, then say, 'We can't see a thing wrong.'

Exercise No. 66

1 In the days that followed (happy days of renewed vigour and re-awakened interest), I studied the magazines and lived, in their pages, the gracious life of the characters in the ever-moving drama of society and fashion.

2 As the Hebrews saw their history (Genesis to Judges), it fell into several discrete sections, writes H. H. Watts; and the author (authors?) of only the first section (Genesis 1–11) made no distinction between Hebrew and non-Hebrew fate.

3 Winchell, according to H. L. Mencken, invented *pash* (for passion), *lohengrined* (for married) and *Reno-vated* (for divorced).

4 If the rise over the continent of North America should amount to a hundred feet (and there is more than enough water now frozen in land ice to provide such a rise) most of the Atlantic seaboard, with its cities and towns, would be submerged. (M. K. Bennett)

5 Mr. W. M. Thackeray has published (under the Cockney name of 'Michael Angelo Titmarsh') various graphic and entertaining works: *The Paris Sketch-Book* (London, 1840), *Comic Tales and Sketches* (London, 1841), and *The Irish Sketch-Book* (London, 1842).

Exercise No. 67

1 Correct.
2 Correct.
3 Enclose *generally speaking* in commas or brackets.
4 Correct.
5 First pair of square brackets correctly placed; replace second with ordinary brackets.

Exercise No. 68

1 Bentley, the publisher of *Bentley's Miscellany*, said to Jerrold, 'I had some doubts about the name I should give the magazine; I thought at one time of calling it

Wits' Miscellany.' 'Well,' was the rejoinder, 'you needn't have gone to the opposite extreme.'

2 'One of the old philosophers,' Lord Bacon tells us, 'used to say that life and death were just the same to him.' 'Why, then,' said an objector, 'do you not kill yourself?' 'Because it is just the same.'

3   'Dear Pig, are you willing to sell for one shilling
        Your ring?' Said the Piggy, 'I will.'

4 'The so-called race between population and food supply has again come forward as an absorbing topic of conversation,' M. K. Bennett notes.

5 William Keddie, in his *Anecdotes Literary and Scientific*, tells this anecdote: 'A friend of the poet Campbell once remarked: "It is well known that Campbell's own favourite poem was his 'Gertrude'." I once heard him say, "I never like to see my name before the 'Pleasures of Hope'; why, I cannot tell you, unless it was that, when young, I was always greeted among my friends as 'Mr. Campbell, author of the "Pleasures of Hope".' 'Good morning to you, Mr. Campbell, author of the "Pleasures of Hope".' " '

Exercise No. 69

1 science-fiction
  space-travel
  time-travel
2 all-night
  thrice-escaped
  twenty-two-year-old
3 all-cargo
  on-time
  eighty-three
  trans-shipment

4 fly-over
  London–Birmingham
  non-stop
  up-to-date
5 anti-vivisectionism
  single-minded
6 land-rich
  money-poor
  knee-high

Exercise No. 70

1 Smith Brothers' Cough Drops
2 Newton's Law
3 earth's surface
4 geese's cackling
5 hero's welcome
6 Prince of Wales' horse [Wales's would cause too many *s*-sounds.]
7 James's novels
8 Queen Elizabeth II's coronation
9 Achilles' heel [Achilles's would cause an awkward combination of *s*-sounds.]

10 anybody else's word
11 princess' gown
12 princesses' gowns
13 Xerxes' triumph
14 here's how
15 at 6's and 7's
16 *Mississippi* has four *s*'s
17 six o'clock
18 you'll
19 they'd
20 who's

Exercise No. 71

1 A.D. preceding the date: e.g., A.D. 1776
2 B.A.
3 p.m.
4 Dr.
5 log (no full stop)
6 Luke 4.3
7 radar (no full stops)
8 t.b.
9 U.S.A.

10 viz. (full stop and italics optional)
11 sq. in.
12 gill (not abbreviated)
13 8.7 a.m.
14 Efta
15 cwt.
16 ton (not abbreviated)
17 Jan.
18 Mon.
19 NW.
20 (c)

Exercise No. 72

1 Every Sunday morning Julia goes to bed with *The People, The Sunday Times*, and even an *Observer*.
2 He sailed to America on the *Europa* last week.
3 'Sally Bowles', perhaps the best story in Christopher Isherwood's *Goodbye to Berlin*, was adapted into a mediocre play, *I Am a Camera*, by John van Druten.
4 Enthusiastic Anglo-Saxonists may write obstinately about *starcraft* or *leech*, instead of *astronomy* and *doctor*, but the language feels that it is already adequately supplied, though it may regret that young people are no longer *betrothed, plighted* or *affianced*, and that these beautiful words are replaced by *engaged*, with its automatic suggestion of a public lavatory.   (Ernest Weekley)
5 I saw the motion picture *Come Back, Little Sheba* in France, with French voices dubbed in. It seemed odd to hear Shirley Booth refer to '*la petite Sheba*'.

Exercise No. 73

1 The Anglo-Saxon language was the language of our Saxon forefathers though they never gave it that name. They called it English. Thus King Alfred speaks of translating 'from book-Latin into English'; Abbot Aelfric was requested by Aethelward 'to translate the book of Genesis from Latin into English'; and Bishop Leofric, speaking of the manuscript (the 'Exeter Manuscript') he gave to Exeter Cathedral, calls it a 'great English book'.

2
>   Upon Saint Crispin's Day
>   Fought was this noble fray,
>   Which fame did not delay
>   To England to carry.
>   O when shall English men
>   With such acts fill a pen,
>   Or England breed again
>   Such a King Harry?
>   (Michael Drayton)

3 *Stories in the Modern Manner*, edited by Philip Rahv and William Phillips, was published by Avon Books. Perhaps the best story in it is Gide's 'Theseus'.
4 The lion is a kingly beast.
  He likes a Hindu for a feast.
5 It is the grace of God that urges missionaries to suffer the most disheartening privations for their faith. This grace moved Saint Isaac Jogues to say (when he came to Canada), 'I felt as if it were a Christmas day for me, and that I was to be born again to a new life, to a life in Him.'   (Adapted from *Time*)

Exercise No. 74

1 weird	6 financier	11 cashier
2 glacier	7 feint	12 pierce
3 friend	8 ancient	13 wield
4 siege	9 conceive	14 deity
5 lieutenant	10 foreign	15 hygiene

Exercise No. 75

1 judging	5 courageous	8 changeable
2 eyeing	6 managing	9 sensible
3 peaceable	7 lovely	10 hoeing
4 dining		

Exercise No. 76

1 occupying	5 turkeys	8 business
2 loneliness	6 tries	9 reliance
3 trolleys	7 keys	10 occupied
4 dryness		

Exercise No. 77

1 ceiling	10 referring	18 siege
2 worries	11 unbelievable	19 alleys
3 field, daisies	12 seized	20 studious
4 monkeys	13 preference	21 studying
5 hoping	14 occurred	22 benefited
6 argument	15 thieves	23 relief
7 shining	16 noticeable	24 perceive
8 ninety	17 merciless	25 truly
9 received		

Exercise No. 78

1 frolicked	6 supersede	11 secede
2 addenda	7 succeed	12 Negroes
3 pimientos	8 mosquitoes	13 exceed
4 synopsis	9 intercede	14 enemies
5 innuendo	10 mimicked	15 dynamos

Exercise No. 79

1 advice	6 dessert, dining	11 led
2 effect	7 consul	12 past
3 all together	8 cited, site	13 fowl
4 beside	9 devise	14 persecute
5 coarse	10 its	15 quite

Exercise No. 80

1 clothes	8 supersedes	15 parliament
2 benefited	9 procedure	16 loneliness
3 sergeant	10 dictionary	17 pronunciation
4 effects	11 affected	18 conscience
5 recommend	12 principal	19 Arctic
6 superintendent	13 prophecy	20 weird,
7 omitted	14 interesting	cemetery

Exercise No. 81

embarrassed	morganatic	tranquillity
innuendo	cemetery	aggrandize
desiccate	hypocrisy	repellent
mimicking	questionnaire	scurrilous
mnemonic	manoeuvre	

Exercise No. 82

(*a*) opaque, inchoate

(*b*) satiated, abrasive

(*c*) cacophonic, calumnious, condign

(*d*) acerbating, anomalous, assiduous

(*e*) contiguous, contumacious, garrulous

(*f*) misogynous, poignant

(*g*) recalcitrant, viscous

(*h*) viscid, salubrious, peccant

(*i*) onerous, parabolic, plethoric

Exercise No. 83

invulnerable
aberrant
irrefragable
collapsible
confectionery
invidious

concomitant
coherence
feasible
forcible
portentous
dominance

enforcible
adaptable
adjustable
admissible
duties
instantaneously

Exercise No. 84—Part 2

(*a*) peccadillo
(*b*) chauvinist
(*c*) bas-relief
(*d*) cajole

(*e*) vendetta
(*f*) nadir
(*g*) filibuster

(*h*) sloop
(*i*) zenith
(*j*) incognito

Exercise No. 85—Part 2

(*a*) centennial
(*b*) incite
(*c*) pusillanimous, cognizant, belligerently
(*d*) incredibly, amorous, magnanimous, incognito, animated
(*e*) cursory, animadversion, succeed, recede

Exercise No. 86—Part 2

(*a*) fallacy, obdurate, ambidextrous
(*b*) ductile, conduits
(*c*) factotum, duress, perjured, factitious
(*d*) fervid, aggrandize
(*e*) abjure, transgresses

Exercise No. 87—Part 2

(*a*) colloquial, loquacious, mortify, admonition, omniscience, imponderable
(*b*) rapacious, renascence, ignominious, mediaeval

Exercise No. 88—Part 2

(*a*) introspection, perspicacity
(*b*) malevolent, virago
(*c*) tenets, stringent, tenaciously, adversary
(*d*) tangible, vociferously, aversion

Exercise No. 89—Part 2

(*a*) aesthete, sedentary
(*b*) homogeneity, amalgam, demagogue
(*c*) protagonist, misanthrope, archetype

Exercise No. 90—Part 2

(*a*) neophyte, etymology, cosmic
(*b*) idiosyncrasies, monomanias, neurotic
(*c*) philologists, neologisms, cosmopolitan
(*d*) apathetic, euphony, cacophonic

Exercise No. 91—Part 2

(*a*) psychoanalyst, zodiac
(*b*) archbishop, typical, telepathy, theosophy

Exercise No. 92—Part 2

incongruous	abnormal	improper
ignoble	counterplot	disinter
disingenuous	disquiet	disengage

Exercise No. 93

constitution	avarice	tillage
frequency	masculinity	spoilage
delicacy	denunciation	lucidity
eloquence	convocation	inversion
terrorism	supplication	superficiality
freedom	laggard	clothing
unity	devotion	

Exercise No. 94—Part 1

satirical	admonitory	derisive
maniacal	workable	accessible
virulent	continuous	fallacious
planetary	inventive	exhortatory
avaricious	British	wondrous

Part 2

liquefy	classify	regularize
integrate	hearten	itemize
exemplify	symbolize	personalize

Exercise No. 95

flurry = flutter and hurry
riffle = ripple and ruffle
smog = smoke and fog
squelch = quell and crush

Exercise No. 96

1 postpone
2 changeable
3 calumniate
4 inordinate
5 reward
6 mercenary
7 disuse
8 unremitting
9 cavilling
10 mirthful
11 lucid
12 closed. *clandestine* means 'secret' and is therefore nearer in meaning to *closed* than to any of the other words.
13 irregularity
14 many-languaged
15 conspiracy

Exercise No. 97

1 corpulent. (*Plethoric* is used generally to imply stuffy or bombastic writing. Since, however, the implication is 'overstuffed', *corpulent*, meaning 'fat', is the most likely choice.)
2 omnipresent
3 inflexible
4 resentment
5 communal
6 slander

 7 self-governing
 8 insensibility
 9 deserved
10 catastrophe
11 friendly
12 outcome
13 ready to believe
14 disparaging
15 transparent

Exercise No. 98

INFORMAL	FORMAL
grand	aristocratic
street-walker	prostitute
hard-up	impoverished
died	deceased
club	bludgeon
old-fashioned	conservative
having a baby	pregnant
lavatory	water closet
wife	spouse

Exercise No. 99

1 Informal   4 Informal
2 Formal   5 Informal
3 Formal

Exercise No. 100

1 Archaic   5 Illiterate   8 Colloquial
2 Colloquial   6 Colloquial   9 Colloquial
3 Dialectal   7 U.S.   10 Colloquial
4 Slang

Exercise No. 101

1 today
2 I believe
3 about
4 about
5 money
6 about
7 about
8 I am a lawyer
9 decide
10 I approve
11 when
12 (we, he, they) believe
13 touch (or, if the context demands it, *met*)
14 about
15 (we, he, they) direct
16 because

Exercise No. 102

1 His workmanship in jewellery is unique. (*Unique* means 'beyond compare'. He works as 'a jeweller' or 'at jewellery', not 'in the field of'.
2 The consensus favours his retirement from office. (*Consensus* means 'general agreement among many'.)
3 Her complexion is pink. (*Pink* is a colour: it is redundant to reidentify it as such.)
4 The modern woman makes up her mind without assistance. (*Modern* means 'of today'.)
5 Every genius needs a millionaire to further his career.
6 Few attended Simon's lecture. (*Few* suggests number.)

7 The vase I bought was elliptical. (*Elliptical* is a 'shape'.)
8 Combined, these fundamentals will teach any student to write well. (*Basic* and *fundamental* are synonymous as are *combined* and *together*.)
9 William's clothes are invariably too large.
10 Brett and Maria . . . are diametrical types of women.

Exercise No. 103

Bill Wilson, *intelligent* and *ambitious*, not only wants to improve his *economic* and *cultural* stature, but consciously works towards his goal. As a *lawyer*, he reads *law text books*, but he widens his knowledge of men and affairs by conversing with *artists*, *engineers*, and *doctors*. He knows that a *broad range of information* will *enhance his effectiveness* as a lawyer. For these *reasons*, I believe that Bill will make *significant contributions* to the community and become an important member of it.

Exercise No. 104

All truly responsible and Christian men, triumphant advance, intrepid custodian, our island heritage, staunch defender, hard-won liberties, creed, teachings of Jesus. No honest Christian who studies his Bible can ignore—suggests that only a dishonest Christian, to whom his Bible is a closed book, could ignore. *The parable of the talents*—the writer has combined patriotism with religious orthodoxy to confuse his reader. He does nothing to prove the connexion between the parable of the talents and the Conservative Party.
loyal, freedom-loving, agitators, would-be oppressors.

Exercise No. 105

1 notorious
2 embezzled; absconded
3 concisely
4 vivid
5 wit; intelligence

6 liable
7 modest
8 colossal
9 wholesome
10 cynic; misogynist

Exercise No. 106

Following are some among many possibilities:

1 slithered
2 calculated, estimated
3 roaring; ploughed

4 perched; sweeping
5 leaned; wafted

Exercise No. 107

1 The Member of Parliament spoke about eliminating the housing shortage. (Note that eliminating the linking verb helps to reduce the number of nouns.)
2 Words taken out of context do not always mean what they do in context.
3 He evaded the question put to him.
4 Shortages of raw materials cause increases in price.
5 His philosophy sought universal truths applicable only to him.

Exercise No. 108

Following are some among many possibilities:

1 warm; inept; witty
2 bitter; rancid
3 intense
4 dull, drab; fresh, gay
5 immense, huge, vast

6 consummate; insipid
7 superb; inane
8 eternal; divinely
9 wail; huge
10 enormous; broad; melon

Exercise No. 109

1 I intend to crusade for peace and freedom. (Mixed metaphors: *borrow a leaf* and *don shining armour;* clichés: *struggle onwards, enduring peace.*)
2 Terrified, the shivering . . . (Cliché: *sadder but wiser.*)
3 Luke entertained his friends by singing their favourite old songs. (The original is overwrought and pompous.)
4 Hay fever, epidemic during the summer, poses a constant challenge to the scientist. (Mixed metaphors: *spreads like wildfire* and *methods to iron out.*)
5 Jones alone is sufficiently forthright to battle political corruption. (Mixed metaphor: *lead us out of morass* and *beating about the bush;* cliché: *one man in a hundred.*)
6 Fish possess an instinctive wariness that protects them against fishermen. (Mixed metaphor: *fish are not uprooted;* clichés: *Mother Nature, watery home*; overwrought: *denizens of the deep, devotees of the hook and rod.*)
7 Excitedly, we watched the bride during the wedding ceremony. (The original is overwrought and trite. Note too its clumsy alliteration: *blushing bride, bated breath.*)
8 Hector's lively wit makes other comedians envious. (Clichés: *too funny for words, green with envy.*)
9 His career is finished now that his acceptance of bribes has been exposed. (Clichés: *dead duck, put on the record.*)
10 A fool and his money are soon parted. (The original is overwrought and pompous.)

Exercise No. 110

1 I am fond of ice-cream, a high-caloric food. (Ice-cream is one of the few high-caloric foods of which I am fond.)
2 Emma Lazarus was born in 1848, a year of revolutions. (Emma Lazarus was born in a year of revolutions—1848.)
3 Though I like all shellfish, I rarely eat oysters.
4 A habit is a fixed response to a stimulus, acquired by repeatedly performing an action.
5 Put your trust in God, my boys, and keep your powder dry.
   (Oliver Cromwell's advice)

Exercise No. 111

1 Writers often get into difficulty by not defining technical terms precisely; in order to avert the difficulty I [*or* the present writer] shall [will] begin by defining as precisely as I [he] can all the technical terms employed in the ensuing pages.
2 Readers seldom care about the history contained in a historical novel. Nevertheless, I have been careful to include no incidents which do not have a sound basis in fact. If any of them appear dubious, I suggest that the reader refer to the notes at the end of each chapter.
3 The reader will think me conceited, perhaps; but I ask him to consider my great and enduring achievements.
4 The mountaineer climbs mountains because they are there.
5 Men who live in our industrial society are different in some ways from men who live in other industrial societies [*or* from men who life in agricultural societies].

Exercise No. 112

1 Referring to authorities: Smith might be a great thinker: he has no special competence as a political analyst.
2 Misuse of statistics: A small and possibly prejudicially selected group may have been queried.

3 Non sequitur.
4 Equivocation.
5 Circular reasoning.
6 Facile assumption.
7 False cause.
8 Jack Spratt could eat no fat, whereas his wife could eat no lean.
9 Although he came of a long line of bachelors, he married.
10 Look before you leap.

Exercise No. 113

1 One cannot always guard against imposters, however irritating such people may be.
2 An extremely attractive young lady, she unfortunately possessed several grave intellectual deficiencies.
3 When the auditor asked for the telephone number of the Fraud Squad, Mr. Dobben seemed to be in a serious plight.
4 Madge has to work hard looking after five children.
5 I shall, as you suggest, tell you the plain truth.

Exercise No. 114

If we endeavour to form our conceptions upon history and life, we remark three classes of men. The first consists of those for whom the chief thing is the qualities of feelings. These men create art. The second consists of the practical men, who carry on the business of the world. They respect nothing but power, and respect power only so far as it is exercised. The third class consists of men to whom nothing seems great but reason. If force interests them, it is not in its exertion, but in that it has a reason and a law. For men of the first class, nature is a picture; for men of the second class, it is an opportunity; for men of the third class, it is a cosmos, so admirable that to penetrate to its ways seems to them the only thing that makes life worth living. These are the men whom we see possessed by a passion to learn, just as other men have a passion to teach and to disseminate their influence. If they do not give themselves over completely to their passion to learn, it is because they exercise self-control. Those are the natural scientific men; and they are the only men that have any real success in scientific research.   (C. S. Pierce)

Exercise No. 115

Almost every child, as soon as he is old enough, wants to kill flies and other insects; this leads on to the killing of larger animals, and ultimately of men. In the ordinary English upper-class family, the killing of birds is considered highly creditable, and the killing of men in war is regarded as the noblest of professions. This attitude is in accordance with untrained instinct: it is that of men who possess no form of constructive skill, and are therefore unable to find any innocent embodiment of their will to power. They can make pheasants die and tenants suffer; when occasion arises, they can shoot a rhinoceros or a German. But in more useful arts they are entirely deficient, as their parents and teachers thought it sufficient to make them into English gentlemen.   (Bertrand Russell)

Exercise No. 116

1 After ten rounds, during which he lost precisely four teeth and about two quarts of blood, the boxer acknowledged defeat.
2 We struck hard, having penetrated the enemy's flank and reassembled our forces.
3 Men are enslaved not by force only but by fraud also.
4 Although he liked dogs and tolerated cats, he despised children.
5 When he saw, a bit foggily, the vague luminous form approach with slow deliberate steps, he faltered.

Exercise No. 117

1 Out of his surname [people] have coined an epithet for a knave, and out of his Christian name a synonym for the Devil.
2 Boswell was regarded in his own age as a classic, and in ours is regarded as a companion.
3 I come to bury Caesar, not to praise him.
4 The evil that men do lives after them, the good is oft interred with their bones.
5 The Puritan hated bear-baiting not because it gave pain to the bear, but because it gave pleasure to the spectators.

Exercise No. 118

1 Science answers many questions, but never the ultimate question: 'Why?'
2 'Why?' the ultimate question, science never pretends to answer.
3 Dictatorship, as every intelligent observer knows, means not the triumph of the superior man but rather the triumph of the inferior one.
4 The Psalms, to be sure, are a passionate criticism of life.
5 Though I speak with the tongues of men and of angels, and have not charity, I am become as sounding brass, or a tinkling cymbal. And though I have the gift of prophecy, and understand all mysteries, and all knowledge; and though I have all faith, so that I could remove mountains, and have not charity, I am nothing. And though I bestow all my goods to feed the poor, and though I give my body to be burned, and have not charity, it profiteth me nothing. (I Corinthians)

Exercise No. 119

1 The art of conversation is the art of hearing as well as of being heard. Authors in general are not good listeners. Some of the best talkers are, on this account, the worst company; and some who are very indifferent, but very great talkers, are as bad. It is sometimes wonderful to see how a person, who has been entertaining or tiring a company by the hour together, drops his countenance as if he had been shot, or had been seized with a sudden lockjaw, the moment anyone interposes a single observation. The best converser I know is, however, the best listener.
(Hazlitt)

2 It is profoundly characteristic of the art of Virginia Woolf that when I decided to write about it and had planned a suitable opening paragraph, my fountain pen should disappear. Tiresome creature! It slipped through a pocket into a seam. I could pinch it, chivy it about, make holes in the coat lining, but a layer of tailor's stuffing prevented recovery. So near, and yet so far! Which is what one feels about her art. The pen is extricated in time, but during the struggle the opening paragraph has escaped; the words are here but the birds have flown; 'opals and emeralds, they lie about the roots of turnips.' It is far more difficult to catch her than it is for her to catch what she calls life—'life; London; this moment in June.'
(E. M. Forster)

3 We live in a most dangerous age—an age of supersonic airspeeds, of biological warfare, of atomic and hydrogen bombs, and who knows what next. In no exaggerated sense, we all today exist on borrowed time. If we of this generation deserve no better fate, surely our children do. (Ralph Bunche)

Exercise No. 120

1 The three conspirators drew lots to determine who would undertake the assassination.
2 The crucified shirt hung from the drying line.
(adapted from J. Joyce)
3 With bent, humped back, Pope looked like a question mark.

4 Julia's dainty leg is white and hairless as an egg.

(adapted from R. Herrick)

5 No man knows what awaits him when he opens a door; Even the most familiar room may harbour surprises.

Exercise No. 121

1 What was your purpose in bringing me these two books to read from.
2 Often the man who attempts to live and die in peace is grieved.
3 The boys make a racket with their playthings.
4 Being trustful by nature, she seldom goes through her husband's pockets.
5 His mother thought his adolescent ambition to fly was capricious.

Exercise No. 122

HEADING: (see Figure 3 in text)
      15 York Street,
      London, W2B 4JP.
      5th September, 1976.

INSIDE ADDRESS:
      George Smith, Esq.,
      Venus Foundation Garments Company Limited,
      29 St. John's Square,
      London, WC2B 5LJ.

SALUTATION:
      Dear Mr. Smith,

BODY OF THE LETTER:
      The margins are not consistent at either the right or left of the page.

COMPLIMENTARY CLOSE:
      Yours sincerely,

Exercise No. 123

ADDRESS:
      Centre the address on the envelope.
      Double space and indent each line of the address:
            P. Edwards, Esq., Ph.D., Headmaster,
                  Success Coaching Academy,
                        Dead Man's Lane,
                              Camberley,
                                    Surrey, GU1 2TB.

Index